Detlef Skrobanek was born, educated and trained as a chef in Germany. He then extended his culinary skills by working for six years in hotels and restaurants across Switzerland. In 1976 he moved to Canada and worked for the Four Seasons chain of hotels in major Canadian cities. In 1983 he became executive chef at the Jakarta Hilton International Hotel where he created and developed the concept of modern Indonesian cuisine.

Suzanne Charlé is an American writer and editor who has worked for the *New York Times* and *New York* magazines, contributed many articles about travel in Asia to these and other publications. She has lived in Bali for the last three years and has travelled extensively throughout Indonesia studying its history, culture and food.

Gerald Gay was born in Singapore but studied photography in Melbourne, Australia. He now has his own successful studio in Singapore. He enjoys food and fashion photography as well as product still-life work for advertising, and recently he contributed to *Thailand, Seven Days in the Kingdom* and *Singapore: Island.City.State*, both published by Times Editions.

THE NEW ART OF INDONESIAN COOKING
Times Editions Pte Ltd
Times Centre, 1 New Industrial Road
Singapore 1953

© 1988 Detlef Skrobanek, Jakarta Hilton International Hotel
Suzanne Charlé, Gerald Gay, Times Editions

Enquiries re copyright
Times Editions Pte Ltd
Reprinted 1988, 1991, 1992, 1995

Colour separation by Far East Offset, Malaysia
Typesetting by Superskill Graphics, Singapore
Printed by Welpac Printing and Packaging Pte Ltd

ISBN 981 204 579 1

THE · NEW · ART · OF

INDONESIAN COOKING

THE · NEW · ART · OF

INDONESIAN COOKING

RECIPES BY
DETLEF SKROBANEK

INTRODUCED BY
SUZANNE CHARLÉ

PHOTOGRAPHED BY
GERALD GAY

EDITED BY
JULIA ROLES

FOREWORD

I am happy to write this foreword to *The New Art of Indonesian Cooking*, the first book to be written on modern Indonesian cuisine.

I was glad to encourage the experiment undertaken by the Jakarta Hilton to launch a novel presentation of the richly varied food eaten by Indonesians, in a manner acceptable to a non-Indonesian audience in a modern setting. It would solve a problem I had been confronted with as Indonesian foreign minister hosting foreign dignitaries at official functions. At the same time, I saw it as an excellent opportunity to raise Indonesian food to the level of a cuisine comparable with that of China and France. I remember the numerous trial lunches and dinners the experiment went through before the new cuisine was formally launched by the Jarkarta Hilton. I consider myself fortunate to have been part of the process of developing this new Indonesian cuisine.

I am a believer in the universal community transcending national boundaries and I believe that beautiful things like music, art and dance, know no boundaries. Food is another area in which nations can learn from each other, and those involved in the culinary arts will readily adopt the best techniques available to achieve the optimum results. I view this as indicative of a wider movement, which I think is inevitable in this modern world with increased communication and people adventuring more and more across boundaries in a spirit of discovery, education and cultural exchange.

Dr. Mochtar Kusuma-Atmadja

PREFACE

When I first came to Indonesia in 1983 to work at the International Hilton Hotel in Jakarta, I expected Indonesian cuisine to be rich in flavours and spices but I did not anticipate the tremendous variety of fish and other seafood, poultry, vegetables and fruit. I was also intrigued by the uses and combinations of various aromatic grasses, leaves, roots and rhizomes.

The hotel already served the traditional *rijstaafel*, or rice table, an almost overwhelming array of dozens of dishes from all over the archipelago. But such a buffet-style feast does not lend itself to formal occasions. Why not take a new approach, using the same ingredients, but cooking the food in a lighter, healthier manner, and serving the meal course-by-course, with particular emphasis on a presentation which would appeal to more cosmopolitan tastes? A core group of twelve Indonesian chefs and I started work on dishes which would be Indonesian in character but which would also reflect the refinements in cooking techniques and artistic presentation developed in the finest European and American kitchens.

We spent months gathering as much information as possible. We visited fish, vegetable and spice markets in and out of Jakarta. Here we found long, slender bundles of lemon grass, elegant in appearance and fragrance; and dark brown pods of tamarind piled high next to blocks of its sour, sticky pulp. Makeshift tables buckled under the weight of huge jars of strongly aromatic *terasi*, *tempe* and *tauco*, the fermented pastes of shrimps and soya beans. Beyond were mounds of turmeric, galangal and ginger. Women in brightly coloured sarongs sang out the prices of fruits — some, such as papaya and mango, already familiar items in the West; others virtual strangers.

Then the real work began — applying modern cooking methods to what is essentially a village cuisine. We started to create our own recipes, and as our repertoire grew, so did the level of enthusiasm both in the kitchen and in the dining room. We created over 500 recipes, a selection of which is included in this book. Some are essentially variations of traditional village dishes, others take an old recipe and combine it with something new to Indonesia, while many are entirely new creations.

This is not a separate cuisine; we are not reinventing the wheel. It is simply our belief that Indonesian cuisine, as one of the great cuisines in the world, should have its epicurean dishes as well as its everyday fare. Cooks who are looking for traditional Indonesian recipes will not find them here, but should instead refer to some of the cookbooks already available. Nor is this a definitive work. This book represents only the start of a modern Indonesian cuisine that will evolve side-by-side with the traditional.

To all our readers, we wish *selamat makan* — good eating.

Detlef Skrobanek

CONTENTS

In this book we present a new approach to Indonesian cuisine, uniting traditional Indonesian ingredients and flavours with modern Western cooking and presentation techniques.

Indonesian cooking has been affected by many different influences — Chinese, Indian, Arab, Dutch, Portuguese — and the spices and herbs upon which these countries made, and lost, vast fortunes still grow here in abundance: nutmeg, cloves, pepper, cinnamon, cumin and more. The ethnic diversity of the nation's population, the fifth largest in the world, is almost inconceivable; there are 25 different languages and literally hundreds of dialects. More than 13,000 islands stretch, east to west, over 4,800 kilometres of sea, some little more than shifting sandbars, others the sites of ancient kingdoms. Here is Sumatra, where men still hunt wild boar in the jungles; and Java, where others risk their lives scaling high cliffs above the Indian Ocean in search of nests for bird's nest soup. Here, too, the lush island of Bali, where rice terraces wreathe mountains and people make offerings to Dewi Sri, the goddess of rice and fertility; and Sulawesi, famed for its fishermen and sailors who were once the fierce pirates of these waters.

Despite all this diversity and the abundance of local ingredients, Indonesian cooking has remained essentially a village cuisine. For the most part, it is done over open fires with lots of oil and little attention to presentation. This book presents a more elegant, refined version of this cuisine, one that appeals to Western tastes and that can be served at the most formal occasions; a happy meeting of East and West.

Indonesian Cuisine, Old and New

Although the presentation of the dishes in this book bears little resemblance to the Dutch *rijstaafel* or the Indonesian feast called the *selamatan*, the basic principles of cooking are the same as they have been for centuries. Both old and new cuisines use the same excellent and diverse ingredients, and create the same complex combinations of flavours. The philosophy of balance so important in a traditional Indonesian meal is equally important in this new cuisine. For every sweet taste there is something sour or salty; for every hot spice there is something cool and refreshing. Marinades pervade both the old and new cuisines, some brushed on just before cooking, others used for hours. No dairy products are used in traditional Indonesian cooking and very few in the new. Coconut milk, peanuts, candlenuts and mixtures of leaves and spices have always been used as binding agents instead of butter and flour.

There are, of course, differences: the principles of *nouvelle cuisine* have been applied to this traditional fare and affect mainly the presentation and cooking

Left: Rice terraces in Bali.
Right: An Indonesian sailing boat or *prahu*.

The only differences in ingredients are the omission of coconut oil for cooking as it burns quickly and tends to turn rancid, the use of dairy products in a very few instances, and the occasional decrease in the amount of hot spices. Over the centuries, spices — particularly ginger, pepper and chilies — have been used in large quantities, in part for taste and in part because they were believed to act as preservatives. To this day, chilies are often measured not by the piece, but by the handful. Such generous use of hot spices tends to alter or overpower the natural flavours of meat, fish and poultry. In some of the recipes in this book, the hot spiciness is reduced to let the flavours of the basic ingredients come through; in other instances, particularly in the sauces, the original fire of the chilies and other hot spices has been retained. In all cases, the cook should try the recipe and, if desired, gradually increase the number of chilies. For those who wish to make the dishes hotter at the table in the traditional Indonesian manner, we have included some *sambal* recipes in the Basics, Sambals and Sauces chapter.

Rice recipes are not included in this book, but it is assumed that plain rice will be served as an accompaniment to most of the hot dishes.

Connoisseurs of traditional Indonesian food may also note the absence here of *krupuk* (the rice wafer described by writer Aldous Huxley as "a queer kind of unleavened bread") and of *emping* (a cracker made from melinjo nuts). They are essential to traditional Indonesian meals, but not to the new — serve them only if you wish.

techniques. The Indonesian cook usually prepares meals in advance, leaving food out on the table under protective baskets for members of the family to eat as and when they are ready. In village life, families rarely sit down and eat together. Even at feasts, food is served in bowls or on large platters placed on a table. Celebrants help themselves, heaping plates with food — rice, chicken, meat, fish and poultry, vegetables, salads, pickles, spicy *sambals* and prawn-flavoured wafers called *krupuk*. Such banquets are grand, festive occasions, sometimes bewildering in their array of tastes, textures, and colours.

This book suggests a more Western approach to serving. One course is presented after another, dishes meant to be hot are served hot, cold dishes are served cold (another departure from traditional cuisine, which developed before refrigeration and gas and electric ovens were available).

The range of cooking methods has also been expanded to make the food lighter and healthier. Traditionally, Indonesian food is *goreng, goreng, goreng* — fried, fried and fried again. The *nouvelle* approach employs other techniques, including poaching, grilling, roasting, baking and sautéing.

Left: Traditional Indonesian cooking is essentially a village cuisine.
Right: A colourful *krupuk* stall.

9

The Search for the Spice Islands

Indonesia was home to some of the earth's earliest men. The remains of "Java man", found in the valley of Solo, indicate that the area was already inhabited by a primitive form of man by about 300,000 B.C. Much later, perhaps around 10,000 B.C., bands of hunters arrived from other parts of Asia. Some tribes simply hunted for their food and gathered fruits and vegetables, a way of life that is still practised by the hunter-gatherers living in the forests and jungles of Kalimantan, Irian Jaya and other remote parts of Indonesia. Other groups established highly complex rice cultures, evident to this day in the elaborate rice terraces of Java and Bali.

Life, however, was destined to change, for these tropical islands lay at the strategic crossroads of two great civilizations — China and India. The Chinese were early traders here. They brought with them porcelain dishes and huge ceramic jars, some of which can still be found throughout the islands. They carried back cloves and other produce of the islands. Some traders never returned home but instead established their own communities throughout the archipelago.

Today, Chinese influence is readily apparent in the cuisine of the islands; almost every village of any size has a Chinese restaurant, and every household kitchen has its *wajan*, or *wok*. The use of beansprouts, soya sauce and other soya-based products is widespread, not only in Chinese dishes, but traditional Indonesian recipes as well.

Perhaps the single largest early external influence, however, came from across the Indian Ocean. Indian traders and priests sailed to the islands, bringing two great religions — Hinduism and Buddhism. For more than 700 years, mighty Hindu and Buddhist empires ruled much of the archipelago until the Majapahit Empire collapsed in the fifteenth century under the onslaught of a new and powerful Islamic state in Java. Only in Bali did the Hindu gods find a safe and enduring home.

Arab traders had roamed these islands for many centuries before the fall of the Hindu empire and it was through these traders that Islam was first introduced to the islands. It is no coincidence that the sites established by Arab spice traders as major trading ports are, to this day, areas in which Orthodox Islam thrives. For generations, these Arab merchants managed to keep secret their trade

Hindu (left) and Buddhist (right) images bear witness to the powerful influences from India.

routes and sources of supply, duping European trading partners with fantastic fictions of winged monsters guarding remote forests of cinnamon, and false accounts of the spices' origins.

The Arabs' hold on the spice trade was finally broken, not by any great war but, in large measure, by the publication at the turn of the fourteenth century of a single book — Marco Polo's account of his 26-year journey through China and Asia. His tales of gold, jewels and spices sparked the imaginations and appetites of European kings, merchants and navigators. Christopher Columbus' copy of Polo's book was dog-eared and filled with marginalia. In fact, the explorer was searching for the Indies, indeed believed that he had found them, when he discovered the New World.

The Portuguese were the first among the European powers to arrive in the "Eastern Islands" in 1498. The British sailed these waters as well. But it was the Dutch who colonized the islands, slowly gaining control until, by the turn of the twentieth century, virtually the entire archipelago was under their flag. In 1945, Indonesia declared its independence, though Dutch influence still lingers in the nation's cuisine and in other aspects of life. Many of the Dutch settlers had tried to recreate the Netherlands in these tropical islands: they constructed canals, built homes with white stucco walls and red-tiled roofs, and planted familiar crops in their gardens: tomatoes, potatoes, stringbeans, carrots, cauliflowers, cabbages — produce which modern Indonesia now exports to other Southeast Asian nations.

A Tropical Treasurehouse

Certainly the most important aspect of Indonesian cuisine, whether traditional or modern, is the use of a vast and exotic array of spices, herbs, fruits, vegetables, grasses, roots, fish and seafood. These tropical islands, straddling the equator, have been generously endowed by nature. "No region on earth can boast an equal abundance and variety of indigenous fruits," wrote an early nineteenth century naturalist, who went on to give equal praise to the rest of the region's plant and sea life. Since the first traders set foot on these islands, the history of the archipelago and the lives of its people have been integrally linked with the production of these raw materials.

Nutmeg ○ Looking at a map, it's hard to imagine that islands so tiny could once have had world powers fighting over them. Six coral and volcanic islands of the Banda Archipelago, a stretch of the Moluccas lying in the Banda Sea southwest of Irian Jaya, were the original Nutmeg Islands where the sweet spice was harvested in the well-tended gardens, and traded to Chinese, Javanese, Bugis and Arabs.

In the early seventeenth century the Portuguese began making annual voyages from Malacca to fetch cargoes of nutmeg and mace. The Dutch arrived soon after and claimed Banda as their own — their first acquisition in the East Indies. By 1650, the Dutch had banished the Portuguese and had raised the price of nutmeg by reducing supply. The lovely islands became tropical gold mines — in Amsterdam the nutmeg was worth hundreds of times the amount paid in Banda Neira.

Like other Dutch spice monopolies, the nutmeg monopoly collapsed in the early nineteenth century and Banda was soon all but forgotten. Now, most of Banda's gardens, highly praised for their beauty by the original Portuguese explorers, are in disrepair. The old mansions of the Dutch merchants and officials are decaying and tumbling down. The huge trees that shaded the main street were cut down years ago for firewood. The main industry of the island, it would seem, is catering to the few tourists who come to explore other gardens — those of coral in the clear sea.

But if Banda's nutmeg gardens are not faring so well, other areas growing *buah pala* — specifically Ambon and north Sulawesi — seem to be thriving. In these areas, just about everyone grows some

The waters surrounding the Indonesian archipelago provide plentiful supplies of varied fish and seafood.

pala, and visitors soon become accustomed to seeing nutmeg and mace drying in the sun and to smelling the hot perfume of the spice.

On the tree, the nutmeg looks something like a peach. As it ripens, it opens to show a woody pit inside, swathed with a coral-red net. The net is mace and inside the dark, purple-brown shell is the nutmeg kernel. The tree fruits continuously throughout the year, and the farmer usually harvests about four times, either knocking the fruits down with a stick, or climbing up the tree and pulling them off. In a good year, a twenty-year-old tree will produce about 2,000 fruits. Before being packed for export, the nutmegs are graded by colour (the paler seeds are immature and undesirable), size and sound. With unconscious grace the women sorters take the nutmegs between their fingers and clack them together. A high-grade nutmeg sings with a high pitch, a lesser quality is flat and the lowest grade has no resonance at all.

Cloves ◦ The search for the source of cloves, along with nutmeg and mace, the other spices indigenous to the Moluccas, was at the very heart of the Age of Exploration. It also occasioned battles, bloodshed and treachery.

Chinese traders had been sailing to these eastern islands since the third century B.C. — according to court documents, subjects were required to sweeten their breath with cloves before speaking to the Emperor. However, it was not until the Portuguese arrived in 1512 in Ternate and Tidore — two tiny volcanic islands that were then the primary source of the world's supply of cloves — that the Europeans actually traded directly with the "Spice Islands". Some explorers, including Ferdinand Magellan who crossed the Pacific in 1521 under the Spanish flag, died in the attempt. Others were successful and were rewarded with titles and riches when they returned to Europe.

The Portuguese were at first welcomed by the king of Ternate but they met his greetings with plunder and oppression. The Dutch, who managed to drive the Portuguese out in the early seventeenth century, destroyed the clove trees on all islands but Ambon in order to limit supply and thus raise prices in Europe. Eventually, they lost the monopoly, thanks in part to the wiles of the governor of Ile de France (now Mauritius) named, as fate would have it, Monsieur Poivre. In 1770 he arranged to have clove tree seedlings smuggled out of the Dutch East Indies and soon clove plantations were established in French possessions.

Indonesia remains one of the world's largest producers of cloves, or *cengkeh*. But the country is also the world's largest consumer. Every year, the nation uses over half the world's supply in the manufacture of *kreteks*, the distinctively-scented clove cigarettes.

Meeting this overwhelming demand has meant prosperity for the Minahasa district of north Sulawesi — now Indonesia's premier clove-producing area — and in particular for Sonder, a charming town of white and pastel houses lying in the shadow of the volcano *Gunung Lengkoan*, where gardens of *cengkeh* were planted in the 1800s after the Dutch abandoned their "Ambon-only" policy.

From June to September, the town's 15,000 residents, plus 10,000 workers from outside the area, harvest the cloves, which are the trees' young flower buds. The first of the elegant, conical

Top: A tile on an old Dutch house shows the nutmeg flower, and peach-like fruit, opening to reveal the red net of mace swathed around the pit. Bottom: Nutmegs being sorted and graded.

evergreens to be picked grow in rows near the shore; as the weeks progress, the rosy-hued buds etch the tree tops at successively higher altitudes, and the pickers climb the slopes of the volcano until, approaching the peak, they sleep overnight in the gardens, so no time is wasted. If they don't pick the *cengkeh* just at the right time, before the bud has opened, it is worthless.

Ambon, too, still produces cloves. The farmers treat their trees much like members of the family, knowing the age of each one and how much it will yield. "The tree is like a woman," says one farmer, "the better care you take of her, the more you appreciate her, the better she will produce." He explains, "Before the tree flowers, when it is 'pregnant', you can't disturb it; you must leave it alone, like a pregnant woman. You dare not make much noise or the buds will fall off. Just as when you expect a baby, you must watch and take care so the baby is healthy."

Cinnamon ○ The cinnamon trees with their sweet, near-magical bark, grew on the highest mountain peaks near Arabia. Giant birds used the twigs to build their nests, and the only way to get the twigs was to tempt the birds with huge chunks of meat that were so heavy that the nests would crumble when the birds settled down to feast. Herodotus the fifth century B.C. Greek historian had learnt this story from the Arab traders who told it to justify the high prices charged for cinnamon.

The story was, of course, a myth created by Arab traders to keep the true locations of the cinnamon trees a secret from their customers. For the trade was a valuable one, for which generations of men had risked their lives. According to one historian, J. I. Miller, as early as the second millenium B.C., traders may have sailed in primitive outrigger canoes from Indonesia to Madagascar, along what he calls the Cinnamon Route, so that the cinnamon could be transported along the east African coast to the Nile Valley where the ancient Egyptians paid high prices for the spice.

Eventually the sources of *Cinnamomum zeylanicum* (Sri Lanka) and its close relative *Cinnamomum cassia* (Indonesia), known as false or bastard cinnamon, were discovered, and European traders scurried to secure great quantities of them. Cinnamon and cassia were among the spices Vasco da Gama brought to the Portuguese king in 1501, after his successful voyage to India. And when the *Victoria*

arrived in Spain in 1522 — the only ship of five to complete Ferdinand Magellan's ill-fated but financially rewarding westward circumnavigation — her captain was presented with a coat of arms that included two cinnamon sticks, three nutmegs and twelve cloves.

Today Sri Lanka, the Seychelles and the Malagasy Republic produce most of the world's cinnamon, while Indonesia accounts for 90 per cent of the world's cassia. (Most of what is called cinnamon in the United States is actually cassia; in Europe, true cinnamon is preferred.)

Padang, on the west coast of Sumatra, exports most of Indonesia's cassia. It is a pleasant city, its port crowded with ships waiting for their cargoes of spices, its warehouses overflowing with piles of the sweet-smelling, red-brown bark of *kayu manis* — literally, sweet wood. In the Padang area alone there are probably about 8,000,000 cassia trees, though most are quite young. Many fine old trees were cut down when prices fell in the late 1960s and early '70s and were replaced by coffee and clove trees. Until the *kayu manis* tree is eight years old, it has little economic value since the bark has a low volatile oil content and no flavour, but by the

Detlef Skrobanek (left) peeling the sweet-smelling bark from the trunk of a *kayu manis* tree.

Pepper ○ Today, pepper is the world's most important and one of the most common of spices, and much of that pepper comes from Indonesia. But for many centuries, pepper was regarded as a rare and valuable commodity; in the thirteenth century, peppercorns were counted out one-by-one in Europe as payment for taxes, rents and other debts. The seas surrounding Java, Sumatra and Borneo were alive with adventurers from Portugal, England and the Netherlands, all in search of pepper. Wrote Joseph Conrad, "For a bag of pepper they would cut each other's throats without hesitation and would forswear their soul." After the collapse of the Dutch East India Company, the United States got into the world pepper trade. Schooners from Salem, Massachusetts, made the formidable round trip, braving pirates and storms at sea; their precious cargoes the foundations of the fortunes of the young nation's first millionaires.

Growing good pepper, though easier than growing cloves, is a relatively lengthy process. Shade trees must first be planted as supports for the pepper vines, and the earth must be weeded and turned with manure. For the first three to four years, the vine must be constantly pruned, and it is only in the fifth year that it will produce clusters of berries. If properly tended, a mature vine will produce for about twenty years, yielding about five kilograms a year. Unlike Indonesia's vast coconut plantations, most pepper fields are 200-square-metre plots with about 3,000 vines that are owned and tended by single families.

The colour of the pepper depends primarily on when the berries are harvested and how they are processed. In the south Sumatran province of Lampung, men climb narrow ladders to pick the berries while the skins are still green, just before turning red. After the berries have been picked, they are spread out on mats, with the skins intact, and laid in the sun for five to six days, until they dry to small black peppercorns. At harvest time, the narrow lanes of the villages look as if they are paved with pepper, and the air is tangy with the pungent smell.

For white pepper, the berries are fully mature when picked, then packed in burlap bags and soaked in water for about eight days, to loosen the outer skin. Workers trample the berries, until the skins fall off, and then lay them in the sun to dry until the berry turns white.

tenth year, a mild flavour exists and the tree will yield about eight kilograms of cassia, the highest grade coming from the trunk, the rest from the branches. The quality of the cassia improves as the amount of oil increases, until the tree is 30 years old, when it can yield as much as 100 kilograms. Unfortunately, there are virtually no such trees left around Padang, according to one young spice merchant. Nor are there likely to be any in future.

"Even today, when the price is high, you'll see farmers cutting the trees too early," says the spice merchant. "They should wait 20 to 25 years. But that's a long time. If they need money for their children to go to school, they cut the trees. If they need money for a wedding, they cut the trees. But the trees are too young, the quality is not high, so the price goes down."

Most of the old trees that do remain are found in an area called Kerinci, where the trees grow wild on rugged mountains shrouded in mists. Only the most determined men will attempt to harvest the wood, for they have to cut through dense forests and struggle up steep mountainsides not unlike those described by the Arab traders hundreds of years ago.

Sticks of the "near-magical" cassia or cinnamon bark for which generations of men risked their lives.

Coonuts ○ It is impossible to overrate the importance of the coconut to the lives of most Indonesians. The tall, graceful trees line the shores of virtually every island, houses are built with the wood of the palm and roofs are thatched with its leaves. Coconut meat is processed into oil, the husks used as kindling. The wealth of a village is, in part, measured by the number of coconut palms within its limits, and villagers often play down the size of their coconut groves to keep the taxman at bay. So precious are the coconut palms in the dry eastern islands of Nusa Tenggara that they are protected by law from being cut down as they provide the islanders with food and liquid during periods of drought.

Without the coconut, Indonesian cuisine, whether traditional or modern, would not exist. The coconut is an essential in all its many guises: the *kelapa muda*, or young coconut, with its translucent flesh and refreshing coconut water; the *kelapa setengah tua*, or ripe coconut, with its drier flesh which can be grated and roasted for use as a topping for main dishes and desserts; and most important of all, *santan* or coconut milk, made from water pressed through grated coconut flesh, and used in many dishes.

Chilies ○ Anyone who has tasted Indonesian cooking knows how vital chilies are to the cuisine, despite the fact that the capsicum family is not indigenous to the islands but transplanted from the New World centuries ago by the Portuguese. The chili, sometimes known in the West as the chili pepper or hot pepper, is omnipresent in sauces,

soups, main dishes and even salads, all over the archipelago. One island, just west of Bali, is actually called Lombok, which means chili or pepper. The burning sensation experienced when eating chilies is caused by capsaicin, a crystalline substance that is found in varying amounts in different varieties, ranging from the rather large and mild *cabe lombok*, to the searing *cabe rawit*, or tiny bird's eye chili. Indonesian housewives serve diced *cabe rawit* in sweet soya sauce at the table to be used as a seasoning, and many Indonesians enjoy dipping the explosively hot, tiny chilies in salt and simply eating them whole!

Not surprisingly, Indonesians have a number of legends and stories about the chili pepper. One, a sort of spicy Cinderella variation, concerns a selfish, vain girl by the name of Cabe Lombok, and her hardworking stepsister, Cabe Rawit. One day, when Cabe Rawit was washing clothes by the river, an old woman gave her a watermelon. Her greedy stepmother tried to snatch it from her but it fell to the ground, spilling out gold and jewels. Cabe Lombok was sent by her mother to get another watermelon from the old woman but when this split open, out slithered spiders and snakes.

Left: A heavy load of freshly harvested coconuts.
Right: The chili seller with her piles of chilies, shallots and garlic is a common sight in Indonesian markets.

Fish and Seafood ○ Literally hundreds of varieties of fish and crustaceans make their homes in the deep seas and shallow coral gardens of Indonesia. Such bounty attracts fishermen from all over the world, as it has for centuries. After the coastal waters of New England had been fished out, nineteenth century American whaling ships made their way to the eastern seas of Indonesia, and today huge Japanese trawlers ply the waters.

But there are also the traditional fishing boats. In Bali, brightly coloured *jukung* outrigger canoes line the beaches, the wildly painted "eyes" on the bows on constant lookout for dangers lurking in the deep (or perhaps for a stray tourist interested in being taken for a sail). Ujung Padang, the capital city of Sulawesi, is the centre for the archipelago's traditional sailing craft. Every day, hundreds of tiny outriggers set out from the harbour, their black sails dark triangles on the golden waters.

Further north, singing magic songs that they believe attract only the female fish, fishermen search for the flying fish with its precious roe. This musical persuasion works well for the fishermen. During the dry season, from May to August, nearly 150 boats sail the seas in search of the flying fish. The men of one small village have done this for many generations but it is only recently that the female fish have been sought for their roe. In the past the fish were sold and the roe was given away in the village, or thrown out. Now it is the roe which commands the high prices in fashionable gourmet emporiums and *sushi* bars in major cities world-wide, and the villagers eat only the fish.

Fruits ○ Visitors to Indonesia never fail to be impressed with the abundance of fruit on the islands. A respected nineteenth century English naturalist, Alfred Russel Wallace, wrote: "The banks of the Sarawak River are everywhere covered with fruit trees, which supply the Dyaks with a great deal of their food. The Mangosteen, Langsat, Rambutan, Jack, Jambou and Belimbing are all abundant; but the most abundant and most esteemed is the Durian." Despite its offensive smell, this was, he proclaimed, "the king of fruits ... In fact to eat Durians is a new sensation, worth a voyage to the East to experience."

Nowadays it is not uncommon to see "No smelly fruits in the rooms" included in the lists of rules on Indonesian hotel room doors. A strange restriction to Westerners, but not so in Indonesia, where the durian — that huge, high-smelling, highly praised fruit — is perhaps one of the favourite desserts.

Even less exotic fruits are surprising in their variations. There are some forty varieties of mangoes growing in these islands and over a hundred kinds of bananas. In fact, of the many plants growing in Indonesia, the banana is perhaps one of the most varied in its uses, and most households have some growing in the yard. They require little cultivation, bear fruit in eight to fifteen months, then die, but are soon followed by suckers growing from the rhizome. The leaves are used as wrapping for bundles of food, as colourful and easily replaced plates, and as baking dishes that impart a special flavour to food. The banana leaf often serves as a handy umbrella during unexpected downpours. In Bali, a banana plant in full bloom is tied to small shrines in preparation for cremations. In Java, the same inflorescence hung on an entrance gate signifies a wedding in the home.

Left: Strong-smelling but highly prized durians are often sold by the roadside to be taken by country people as gifts for city relatives.
Right: Fishing boats return at dawn to unload their catch.

Rice ◦ Indonesians can't live without rice or, if they do, they do so unhappily. The word *nasi*, or cooked rice, is also often used to mean "eating" and "food", the implication being that rice will form the central part of the meal. Three colours of rice are grown in Indonesia — white, red and black — as well as glutinous varieties. The Javanese are quick to claim that the finest rice in the world is grown in Cianjur, which is known as the rice bowl of Indonesia, while the Balinese are equally certain that their traditional rice, *beras Bali*, is the best.

Rice is, in fact, deified on many islands. The Bataks in northern Sumatra, near the volcanic Lake Toba, call the rice soul "tondi"; the Toradja of Sulawesi give the rice soul the same name as the human soul — "tawuna". The Minangkabau, according to one anthropologist, go as far as to have rules proscribing humans' conduct toward rice. It is forbidden to take off one's shirt in the ricefield or to swear, for fear the rice might become ashamed and lose its perfume and taste. In Bali, Dewi Sri, the rice mother, is worshipped regularly, and her image can be seen in the form of small doll-like figures of rice stalks that are taken to the fields at harvest, and decorate the handsome,

steep-roofed barns. (Rice barns have been the inspiration for the design of many of the island's thatch-roofed tourist bungalows — a source of many laughs for the Balinese, who find it humorous that tourists rather than grain are stored in the structures.)

In Bali the government has introduced new strains of rice which produce higher yields and also require shorter growing periods. But, in many cases, these shorter growing periods have meant a change in the times for planting and harvesting, and thus the ceremonies for the gods. Whether this has disturbed the deities, no one can tell, but residents still talk of a disaster some years ago when the old schedules were ignored, and the crops failed. Regardless of new systems, the Balinese calendar is still consulted for propitious times to plant, and offerings made on the appropriate days. Around Ubud, the artistic centre of Bali, the farmers plant in August, as they always have, so that the rice flowers during October, a very holy month. Gusti Pekak, a man who has spent his life studying rice and growing it, explains: "This way, when the gods come down from the mountains, they can enjoy the view of the rice."

Working in the rice fields (left) and storing the harvested rice in thatch-roofed barns (right)

The rice likes to be sung to, Gusti Pekak notes. One bamboo instrument, the *tluktak*, makes a sound much like its name. It is just a length of bamboo on a hinge that catches the running water, fills up, then drops the water to the next level. As it swings up to catch more water, the hollow end hits a stone and makes a lovely sound, *tluktak*. "You hear the sound and you know that the water is still flowing as it should," says Gusti Pekak, who likes the sound of the *tluktak* to lull him to sleep in his simple hut in the fields. "Away from the streets, high in the rice terraces, they are like a chorus. But only the bravest farmers will have them," he adds. "The witches of black magic also like the sound, and will come to dance in the fields."

Like many Balinese farmers, Gusti Pekak appreciates the increased yields, but he doesn't really like the new rice: "It has no grace, no beauty. It is nothing to me. It is what you call a cash crop; it is good only for paying for cigarettes and electricity. But *beras Bali* is the rice for gods and for men. When you see it in the field, it is lovely, the heavy heads bent, like men with much wisdom. The new rice stands up straight, empty headed. And its taste...."

Leaves, Grasses and Ferns ○ The islands of Indonesia are a botanical treasure-trove and the cooking reflects this bounty. First and foremost among the grasses used is *sereh*, or lemon grass, which imparts a beautiful, lemony fragrance to dishes. Dozens of leaves are used in cooking — long bean leaves, red pumpkin leaves, cassava leaves, and *pakis* (the delicate head of a wild fern) are some of the better known. Leaves and grasses are used as vegetables as well as spices, in main dishes, soups and salads. Most give flavour, some impart fragrance, others are used only to add colour and to dress up a dish.

This diverse and plentiful plant life is also a main theme in the islands' artistic life. The elaborately chiselled panels of the great temple of Borobodur and the carved wooden gates of traditional Javanese homes and palaces are alive with the flowers of the hills, the fruits of the markets. The many and varied weavings and *batiks* of the islands also feature patterns based on nature. Some are woven by hand from cotton dyed with roots and vegetables. Others, called *songket*, are made of silk or gold thread on silk or cotton grounds.

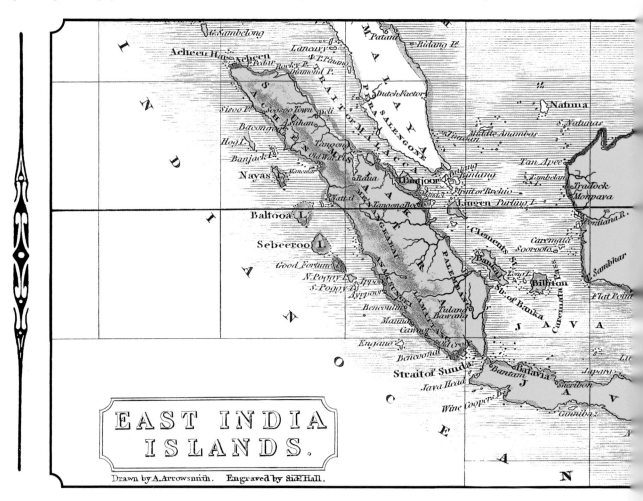

EAST INDIA ISLANDS.

Drawn by A. Arrowsmith.   Engraved by Sid. Hall.

Bird's Nest ○ Every May, on a date prescribed by the Javanese calendar, the villagers of Karangbolong hold a special ceremony to ask God for a bountiful harvest. For a day and a night, everyone joins in. Men dance in trance, families make special prayers, and a *wayang kulit*, or shadow puppet play, is performed.

When the signs are right, the men go to Karangbolong (which literally means "rock of holes"), a massive cliff jutting into the Indian Ocean. For this is not a harvest of rice or corn, but the harvest of the delicate white nests of the swiftlet. Like their fathers, and their fathers' fathers before them, the men carefully lower themselves down by ropes, dangling precariously over deep chasms, to the caves where the small swiftlets nest. There they gather the nests, gently scooping them off the walls, making sure not to disturb nests with eggs or young birds. Then comes the long, dangerous ascent to the top of the cliff while hundreds of metres below, huge waves pound against the dark rocks and — according to local legend — the goddess of the south seas, Nyai Roro Kidul, waits to claim another victim.

The tiny white nests are built by the birds at mating time by weaving long, glue-like strands of secretion from their salivary glands. The nests, shaped like teacups cut in half, are attached to the walls of the caves. Brittle as spun glass when dry, the nests become translucent when cooked and form a gelatinous, spaghetti-like mass, which is rather tasteless to the novice. But to Chinese aficionados, the bird's nest is an almost magical food, a source of longevity, wisdom and virility for men, or beauty for women, as well as a restorative of the body and mind.

With such a reputation, it is not surprising that the nests are in great demand. Indonesia reports exports of almost 60,000 kilograms, an arresting statistic considering that there are approximately 110 nests to each kilogram. In the nineteenth century, the value of these nests in China was estimated as being weight for weight equal with silver. Today, the prices are closer to those of gold, and middlemen are very secretive about their sources of supply, and their delivery dates. According to one dealer, 'Thieves know the value of the nests. It's as if they're spun from gold."

BASICS, SAMBALS AND SAUCES

BASICS, SAMBALS AND SAUCES

In this section, we have compiled useful kitchen notes as well as information about some of the ingredients central to Indonesian cuisine: coconut milk (*santan*), chili juice and tamarind water. Also included are recipes for beef, chicken, fish and lamb stocks, direndam (a marinade for beef, veal and poultry), sugar syrup, *sambals* that may be served as side dishes, and sauces which form a vital part of most dishes in this book. Descriptions of spices, herbs, fruits, vegetables, and flavourings which are purchased ready-prepared are given in the glossary.

BASICS

KITCHEN NOTES

On Substitutions ○ Thanks to good transportation, increased interest in Asian foods and growing Asian populations in Western countries, most "Indonesian" ingredients mentioned in the book are easily found, usually in Asian food stores. There are also mail-order catalogues specializing in Asian herbs, spices and other foodstuffs. These sources are often advertised in food magazines.

Changes in the leaves, spices and herbs will actually affect the taste of the dish, but in the glossary we have suggested possible substitutions whenever they exist. Unfortunately there are certain items for which there are no counterparts. If you are unable to obtain a certain leaf or herb and no alternative is given, it is best to drop it from the recipe. This will make a difference to the flavour, but the recipe will still work.

On the Complete Kitchen ○ Most of the utensils required for new Indonesian cooking are more than likely already present in a well-equipped kitchen: several different sizes of frying pans, a roasting pan, stockpots, a steamer, sieve, ladle, piping bag, blender or food processor and some good knives. If you plan to make fresh coconut milk, you will need a grater for the coconut meat. A stone pestle and mortar is useful for crushing spices and herbs but otherwise the ingredients can be finely chopped by hand or in a blender.

On Cooking ○ Ingredients have been listed in the metric system in order to provide the greatest accuracy. Cooks more comfortable with American or Imperial equivalents should refer to the conversion charts at the end of the book.

All of the recipes have been carefully measured and tested. However the recipes are not dicta, nor is cooking an exact science; food should please chef and guests alike and the measurements in the recipes may be changed to suit individual tastes.

Oven temperatures may vary from one oven to another; it is always best, when first cooking a new recipe, to monitor the progress.

On Shortcuts and Timesavers ○ Unless otherwise indicated, stay away from ready-prepared ingredients; the time saved is not worth the flavour lost.

Generally it is best to prepare sauces the day the meal is to be served, but if you simply must make some preparations a day in advance it is better to chop and prepare the ingredients — this step usually involves the most time and labour — rather than to make the entire sauce. These chopped ingredients may be refrigerated for a day or two. Any extra cooked sauce may be kept in the refrigerator for two days, or frozen.

On Serving ○ At the risk of stating the obvious, the dishes in this book should be served Western style: hot foods should be served hot and cold dishes, cold.

Indonesians do not traditionally drink wines with their meals. If you wish to serve them, you will need to experiment matching the wine to the dish. This can be tricky because of the complexity of the sauces and flavours. Generally speaking, white wines go well with Indonesian food. Beer may also be served — its bitterness always complements spicy foods.

Many excellent teas come from Indonesia and are well suited to the food, as long as the tea selected is not too fruity or scented. A simple black or green tea is best. Do not serve sugared drinks as their sweetness will overlay the taste of the dishes.

COCONUT MILK

Coconut milk, or *santan*, is indispensable to Indonesian cooking. Used as a flavouring and also as a thickening agent for sauces, it is produced by mixing grated coconut flesh with water and squeezing it until the thick oily sap has been dissolved. It should not be confused with — nor substituted by — the liquid that is found in the young green coconut, which is coconut water. There are three ways to make coconut milk.

Fresh Coconut Santan ○ Made fresh from coconuts, this is always the best coconut milk in terms of colour, taste and texture, but it is also the most time consuming to make.

To prepare, grate the flesh of a mature coconut (approximately 250-300 g of flesh) into a bowl. Add 300 ml warm water and squeeze well until the water has extracted the juice from the flesh and turned white. Strain the liquid through a sieve, then squeeze the flesh a bit more to extract the remaining juice. This yields about 375 ml *santan*. This is the first squeezing and produces the best coconut milk. The process can be repeated with the same coconut flesh once or twice more, but each squeezing will yield successively thinner *santan*.

Dried Coconut Santan ○ The second best coconut milk after fresh, its taste is sweeter than fresh coconut milk and the colour is whiter. In order to achieve a flavour similar to that produced by the use of fresh *santan*, increase the amount of spices called for in the relevant recipe.

To prepare, place 300 g dehydrated grated coconut in a bowl. Cover with 750 ml warm water and let it soak for 10 minutes. Squeeze the coconut flesh, then strain the liquid and squeeze the flesh a bit more. As with fresh grated coconut, the process can be repeated once or twice. This yields 375 ml.

Coconut Cream Santan ○ This coconut milk, produced from commercially packaged canned or frozen coconut cream, is recommended only if a *santan* cannot be made from fresh or dried grated coconut. It is a very fatty coconut milk, with a slightly coarse texture and very little natural sweetness. Its bright white colour will make sauces much lighter in colour than those based on the two other types of *santan*. If using coconut cream *santan* in a savoury dish, be sure to increase the quantity of spices used in the recipe. This type of *santan* should really only be used in desserts, and even then be sure to buy the unsweetened variety of coconut cream — the heavily sweetened kind will alter a recipe too much.

To make the *santan*, empty 125 g coconut cream, canned or frozen, into a bowl, add 500 ml warm water and stir with a whisk until smooth. Yields about 500 ml.

How to Store Coconut Milk ○ *Santan* does not keep well and should be used within 24-30 hours of being made. It must be stored in a refrigerator. It may thicken like cream, but when heated it returns to its original state. *Santan* can be frozen and, if properly sealed, will keep for several months. Before using refrigerated or freshly made *santan*, stir well, mixing the cream and the water. Unless otherwise stated in the recipe, add the *santan* just before completing the dish. If you intend to refrigerate or freeze food, it should not contain *santan* unless the dish has been cooked long enough for the *santan* to have been thoroughly absorbed.

CHILI JUICE

Chili juice, either red or green, is used in marinades and sauces to give them a hot spiciness. Red chili juice (made from red chilies) tends to be hotter in taste than green chili juice (made from green chilies), and both may be stored in a refrigerator for up to 10 days. Commercially pre-packaged chili sauce is totally different and cannot be used as a substitute.

1 kg red or green chilies
1 litre water
30 ml white vinegar
30 g salt

1   Wash and clean the chilies, being sure to discard the stems. Do not remove the seeds from the pods since they add the spiciness to the juice.
2   Combine the chilies with the water, white vinegar and salt in a saucepan. Bring to the boil, then reduce the heat and let it simmer for 20 minutes.
3   Drain off half of the liquid and pour the other half with the chilies into a blender and purée until smooth.
4   Remove from the blender and strain through a fine sieve before storing in a refrigerator. The juice should be thin like water. If it is thick, add a little more water until the desired consistency is achieved. Yields 1 litre.

TAMARIND WATER

Tamarind water is used in some sauces and soups, imparting a sour but pleasant taste. The basic ingredient is tamarind pulp, which is readily available in Asian or health food shops.

125 g tamarind pulp
1 litre water

1   Cut the tamarind pulp into pieces.
2   Place the pieces in a saucepan, together with the water.
3   Bring to the boil, stirring constantly with a wooden spoon. In 5 minutes, the tamarind pieces should have disintegrated.
4   Strain the liquid through a sieve into a bowl, making sure to squeeze the pulp in the liquid to extract all its essence.
5   Let the liquid cool before storing in a refrigerator, where it can be kept for a week. Yields 1 litre.

DIRENDAM

This is a marinade that can be used for beef, veal and poultry.

30 ml peanut oil
20 g shallots (bawang merah), peeled, finely diced
10 g garlic, peeled, finely diced
5 g greater galangal, peeled, finely diced
30 g candlenuts, ground
1 salam leaf
1 lemon grass stalk, finely diced
2 g turmeric powder
30 g sugar
salt

1   Combine all the ingredients in a bowl and mix vigorously with a whisk. Let the marinade sit for approximately 1 hour, then discard the salam leaf.
2   Brush the marinade on both sides of the meat and let it marinate in the refrigerator for 8-12 hours before cooking the meat.

SUGAR SYRUP

This is one of the basic requirements for some of the recipes in the Desserts chapter. It can be made in advance and it keeps well for several days in the refrigerator.

500 ml water
500 g white sugar

1   Combine the ingredients in a saucepan. Bring the mixture to the boil and let it simmer for 8-10 minutes.
2   Withdraw the pan from the heat and strain the liquid through cheesecloth. Let the syrup cool completely before using. Yields 900 ml.

BEEF STOCK

Although commercially prepared stocks are available, try not to use them as they tend to be overly seasoned, particularly with salt, and will obscure the flavours of the dishes in which they are used. It is better to take a little extra time and make your own stock. The excess can be stored in the refrigerator for up to 4 days, or they can be frozen.

4 litres water
1 kg beef bones, chopped into 2-cm pieces
30 ml vegetable oil
100 g leeks, peeled, chopped
100 g onions, peeled, chopped
50 g shallots (bawang merah), peeled, chopped
4 salam leaves
2 lemon grass stalks, crushed
2 garlic cloves, peeled
30 g salt

1 Place half of the water together with the chopped bones in a stockpot and bring to the boil. Use a perforated ladle to remove the scum floating on the surface. Drain off the water.
2 In another stockpot, heat the oil.
3 Sauté the leeks, onions, shallots, salam leaves, lemon grass and garlic for 2-3 minutes without browning.
4 Add the bones and the remaining water to the pot. Bring the water to simmering point and season with salt.
5 Let the stock simmer for approximately 2½-3 hours on a very low heat, constantly removing the scum which appears on the surface.
6 Strain the stock through a very fine sieve or cheesecloth into a bowl. Let it cool at room temperature before storing in a refrigerator.

CHICKEN STOCK

Follow the same procedure used for preparing beef stock, but replace the beef bones with chicken bones and let the stock simmer for only 45 minutes.

FISH STOCK

30 ml vegetable oil
100 g leeks, peeled, chopped
100 g onions, peeled, chopped
50 g shallots (bawang merah), peeled, chopped
2 salam leaves
2 lemon grass stalks, crushed
1 kg fish bones or fish meat trimmings
1.5 litres water
6 g coriander leaves with stems
15 g salt

1 Heat the oil in a stockpot. Sauté the leeks, onions, shallots, salam leaves and lemon grass for 2-3 minutes without letting them brown.
2 Add the fish bones and continue to sauté for 2 minutes more.
3 Add the water and the coriander leaves to the pot. Season with the salt and bring the water to the boil.
4 Reduce the heat and simmer at low heat for 45 minutes. Constantly scoop off the scum which forms on the surface.
5 Strain the stock through a fine sieve or cheesecloth and let it cool before storing it.

LAMB STOCK

30 ml peanut oil
400 g lamb bones, cut into 2-cm pieces
1 x 50-60 g onion, peeled, diced
5 x 2 g garlic cloves, crushed
20 g greater galangal, diced
10 g ginger, diced
3 lemon grass stalks, crushed
4 salam leaves
50 g leeks, diced (use only the bottom part)
100 g tomatoes, diced
30 ml white vinegar
1 tablespoon black peppercorns, crushed
2 litres water
salt

1 Heat the oil in a stockpot. Add the lamb bones and sauté, stirring constantly, until the bones are light brown.
2 Add in the onion, garlic, greater galangal, ginger, lemon grass, salam leaves and leeks and continue to sauté for 4-5 minutes.
3 Add in the tomatoes, vinegar, peppercorns and water. Bring the stock to the boil, then reduce the heat. Let it simmer for approximately 2 hours or until the liquid is reduced by half. While simmering, constantly skim off all surfacing scum in order to produce a clear stock.
4 Remove the pot from the heat. Strain the stock through a fine sieve or cheesecloth.
5 Let it cool at room temperature before storing in a refrigerator.

Some of the ingredients essential to these basic recipes are shown opposite. They are (from left to right, top to bottom): garlic, shallots (bawang merah), tamarind pods, lemon grass stalks, green chilies, red chilies, turmeric roots, leeks.

SAMBALS

At a typical Indonesian feast, many types of *sambals* are served as side dishes. In this book, *sambals* are used in sauces and as toppings for very hot dishes, but can also be accompaniments. Some *sambals* are cooked, others uncooked. All use ground or blended chilies as their base, with additions of shallots, garlic, gingers, tomatoes, sugar, spices, lime juice and salt.

SAMBAL BAWANG MERAH

Served uncooked, this sour, hot *sambal* makes a good relish to accompany grilled or roasted fish, poultry or beef dishes.

> 150 g red chilies, seeded, cut into half lengthwise, sliced finely
> 300 g shallots (bawang merah), peeled, sliced
> 50 g garlic, peeled, finely diced
> 60 ml freshly squeezed lime or lemon juice
> 5 g salt

1　Mix all the ingredients in a bowl, seasoning with the salt.
2　Let the mixture sit in the refrigerator for 2 hours before using it. If a hotter sambal is preferred, let it sit overnight in the refrigerator.

SAMBAL TERASI

Dried shrimps should really be used in this recipe, but if there are none available, then fresh, shelled shrimps or baby prawns may be substituted, resulting in a milder-tasting *sambal*.

> 45 ml vegetable oil
> 80 g shallots (bawang merah), peeled, finely diced
> 20 g garlic, peeled, finely diced
> 100 g red chilies, stems removed
> 30 g shrimp paste
> 15 g lemon grass stalk, finely sliced
> 5 g greater galangal, finely diced
> 30 g brown sugar (gula Jawa)
> 50 g dried shrimps
> salt

1　Heat the oil in a saucepan and sauté the shallots and garlic, stirring constantly, until the ingredients have browned.
2　Add in the chilies, shrimp paste, lemon grass, greater galangal and brown sugar, and continue sautéing for 2 minutes more.
3　Mix in the dried shrimps and season lightly with the salt.
4　Reduce the heat and let the mixture cook slowly for 10-15 minutes, stirring constantly. Remove from the heat, pour into a blender and purée until fine.
5　Let the sambal cool at room temperature before storing in a refrigerator.

SAMBAL TOMATO

Use ripe and full-flavoured tomatoes when preparing this *sambal* to ensure it is as tasty as possible.

> 30 ml vegetable oil
> 50 g shallots (bawang merah), peeled, finely diced
> 20 g garlic, peeled, finely diced
> 250 g tomatoes, chopped
> 60 ml red chili juice (see page 23)
> 10 g shrimp paste
> 1 tablespoon brown sugar (gula Jawa)
> salt

1　Heat the oil in a saucepan and sauté the shallots and garlic for 2 minutes until light brown.
2　Add the tomatoes, chili juice, shrimp paste and brown sugar. Season lightly with the salt.
3　Bring the mixture to the boil for 15 minutes, stirring frequently.
4　Pour the hot liquid into a blender and purée until smooth. Let the sambal cool at room temperature before storing in a refrigerator.

SAMBAL MAKASSAR

As with all other cooked *sambals*, this *sambal* should be a thick paste. To thicken a thin *sambal*, pour the mixture back into the saucepan and cook over low heat until it is thick.

> 125 ml water
> 150 g red chilies, stems removed
> 2 tomatoes, quartered
> 30 ml vegetable oil
> 40 g shallots (bawang merah), peeled — 20 g finely diced;
> 　　　20 g sliced, deep-fried until crisp
> 5 g garlic, peeled, finely sliced
> 2 g shrimp paste
> 30 ml freshly squeezed lime or lemon juice
> salt

1　Pour the water into a saucepan, then add in the chilies and tomatoes. Boil for 5 minutes and drain off the water.
2　Using a stone mortar and pestle, grind the chilies and tomatoes into a purée. Set the mixture aside.
3　Heat the oil in a frying pan. Sauté the diced shallots and the garlic for 1 minute.
4　Add in the shrimp paste and sauté for another minute, until the shrimp paste has been thoroughly mixed in.
5　Add in the tomato and chili purée and continue to sauté over low heat for 5 minutes more.
6　Drop the fried shallots into the mixture, pour in the lime or lemon juice and season lightly with salt. (Use salt sparingly as the shrimp paste is already salty.) Sauté for a further 3 minutes. Remove from the heat and purée the mixture in a blender.
7　Put the sambal in a bowl and let it cool at room temperature. When storing in a refrigerator, be sure to seal it properly.

SAUCES

As in most cuisines, sauces play an important role in Indonesian cooking. The sauces are as varied as the spices used in making them, and they are as pleasing to the eye as to the tastebuds. Feel free to experiment using the different sauces given in this chapter with a variety of the dishes in other chapters. Most may be used to accompany fish, poultry, lamb, beef or pork. They may also be served hot or cold since nearly all are prepared with a coconut-milk base. Sauces which should be served hot or cold only are noted in the specific recipe, and sauces which are normally served with a particular dish are given with that recipe and not in this general sauce chapter.

Tips for Successful Sauces

○ When using fresh chilies, be sure to seed them; the seeds release oils during the cooking process which cause the sauce to be fiery hot in taste. If you use bird's eye chilies (*cabe rawit*), start with only a small quantity and add 1 g more at a time if required, tasting and adjusting as you go along.

○ When using chili juice, increase the amount by 1 teaspoon at a time should you require the sauce to be more fiery and more spicy.

○ After coconut milk, candlenuts are the strongest binding agents used in preparing these sauces. Use only the amount indicated in the recipes; usually 20-30 g is sufficient to bind 500 ml of liquid. For a thinner sauce, decrease the amount of candlenuts.

○ In most of the sauce recipes, the amount of salt has not been specified. Since various herbs, spices, leaves and rhizomes are used, salt should be added only sparingly.

○ In the case of spices like nutmeg and coriander where the amount is not specified, a pinch is usually sufficient.

○ In some instances, there is no weight indication for leaves, but rather cup measures are used because leaves are very light in weight.

○ Coconut milk tempers the fire of the chilies. Therefore, in order to reduce the fieriness while maintaining the balance of the spiciness of the sauce, increase the amount of coconut milk 1 teaspoon at a time. You may also use stocks or simply use less than the amount of chilies or spices specified in the recipe, and then gradually add until the desired result is achieved.

Saus Bumbu Bajak

SPICY BAJAK SAUCE

This is a new Bajak Sauce for poultry and meats that is based on a traditional fiery *sambal*.

30 ml peanut oil
40 g shallots (bawang merah), peeled, finely diced
5 g garlic, peeled, finely diced
1 lemon grass stalk, crushed
2 salam leaves
10 g tamarind pulp
40 g candlenuts, ground
100 g tomatoes, peeled, seeded, diced
5 g white sugar
250 ml red chili juice (see page 23)
375 ml coconut milk (see page 22)
salt

1 Heat the oil in a saucepan and sauté the shallots, garlic, lemon grass and salam leaves for 3-4 minutes in the oil without letting them colour.

2 Stir in the tamarind pulp and candlenuts, and continue sautéing for another 4 minutes.

3 Add in the tomatoes, sugar, chili juice, coconut milk and salt. Bring the mixture to the boil, reduce the heat and simmer until the sauce starts to thicken, approximately 10 minutes.

4 Remove the pan from the heat; discard the lemon grass and salam leaves.

5 Pour the sauce into a blender and purée until smooth, approximately 3-4 minutes. Yields 500 ml.

Saus Bali

BALI SAUCE

This sauce should be served chilled.

20 ml peanut oil
80 g red chilies, seeded, finely diced
10 g green chilies, seeded, diced
20 g lemon grass stalk, diced
10 g garlic, peeled, diced
40 g tomatoes, peeled, seeded, diced
500 ml coconut milk (see page 22)
10 g coriander powder
10 g shrimp paste
10 g brown sugar (gula Jawa)

1 Heat the peanut oil in a pan and sauté the chilies, lemon grass, garlic and tomatoes in the oil until golden brown.

2 Add the coconut milk, coriander, shrimp paste and brown sugar, and boil for 8-10 minutes, stirring slowly, until the sauce has thickened slightly.

3 Remove the pan from the heat and pour the contents into a blender. Purée until smooth, then chill. Yields 625 ml.

CHILI BASIL SAUCE

Saus Kemangi
CHILI BASIL SAUCE

Kemangi, the local sweet basil, is perhaps one of the most widely used leaves in Indonesian cuisine. It is found raw and cooked in salads, stews and sauces.

    30 ml vegetable oil
    30 g shallots (bawang merah), peeled, finely diced
    10 g garlic, peeled, finely diced
    40 g sweet basil leaves (kemangi), chopped
    30 g candlenuts, ground
    30 ml green chili juice (see page 23)
    30 ml white vinegar
    375 ml coconut milk (see page 22)
    15 g turmeric root, finely diced
    salt
    10 g sweet basil leaves

1 Heat the vegetable oil in a saucepan and sauté the shallots and garlic for 2 minutes in the hot oil.
2 Add in the chopped basil leaves and sauté for another minute.
3 Add the candlenuts and continue to sauté for 2 minutes more.
4 Pour in the chili juice, vinegar and coconut milk. Sprinkle in the turmeric and season with salt. Bring to the boil.
5 Reduce the heat and simmer for approximately 8 minutes, stirring constantly.
6 Pour the mixture into a blender and process the sauce until it is smooth.
7 Pour the sauce back into a saucepan, add in the whole basil leaves and serve hot. Yields 375 ml.

Saus Ubi Jalar
SWEET POTATO SAUCE

Although sweet potatoes are not used in traditional sauces, they are favourite snacks — boiled, fried or served with brown sugar. This new sauce is particularly good with lamb, and can also be served with beef. The chili juice makes a good counterbalance to the sweetness of the potatoes.

    15 ml peanut oil
    30 g shallots (bawang merah), peeled, finely diced
    10 g garlic, peeled, finely diced
    5 g ginger, peeled, finely diced
    2 g coriander leaves, finely chopped
    5 g turmeric root, finely chopped
    1 lemon grass stalk, crushed
    30 g brown sugar (gula Jawa)
    100 g sweet potatoes, diced, blanched
    30 ml tamarind water (see page 23)
    60 ml red chili juice (see page 23)
    250 ml chicken stock (see page 24)
    90 ml coconut milk (see page 22)
    salt

1 Heat the oil in a pan and sauté the shallots and garlic in the hot oil for 1 minute until light brown.
2 Add the ginger, coriander, turmeric, lemon grass, brown sugar and sweet potatoes. Continue to sauté for 2 minutes.
3 Pour in the tamarind water, chili juice, chicken stock and coconut milk. Season with salt and bring to the boil. Reduce the heat and let the mixture simmer for approximately 10 minutes, stirring frequently.
4 Remove the pan from the heat and discard the lemon grass.
5 Pour the mixture into a blender and process until smooth, approximately 2-3 minutes. Serve hot. Yields 500 ml.

SWEET POTATO SAUCE

Saus Kacang

PEANUT SAUCE

Although peanut sauce can be found all over the archipelago, most people agree that the classic peanut sauces originate in Bali and central Java.

> 250 g raw peanuts, shelled, skinned
> 30 ml peanut oil
> 20 g shallots (bawang merah), peeled, finely diced
> 10 g garlic, peeled, finely diced
> 40 g red chilies, seeded, diced
> 15 g brown sugar (gula Jawa)
> 20 g tamarind pulp
> 2 kaffir lime leaves
> 1 lemon grass stalk, crushed
> 375 ml water
> salt

1 Deep-fry the peanuts at 375°C until they are light brown, approximately 5-8 minutes. Then grind the peanuts finely in a meat or coffee grinder. Set aside.
2 Heat the peanut oil in a saucepan and sauté the shallots, garlic and chilies for 2-3 minutes without colouring.
3 Stir in the brown sugar and tamarind pulp. Add in the lime leaves and lemon grass, and continue to sauté for 2 minutes more.
4 Mix in the ground peanuts and sauté an additional 2 minutes.
5 Pour in the water and season with salt. Bring the mixture to the boil, reduce the heat and simmer, stirring constantly, for approximately 10 minutes.
6 Remove the pan from the heat. Discard the lemon grass and lime leaves.
7 Pour the sauce into a blender and blend at medium speed for 2-4 minutes, until the sauce becomes a smooth, thick paste. Yields 625 ml.

Saus Labu Merah

PUMPKIN SAUCE

This hot sour sauce can be used to accompany veal, pork, beef, chicken and fish. It should be served hot.

> 30 ml peanut oil
> 40 g shallots (bawang merah), peeled, finely diced
> 20 g garlic, peeled, finely diced
> 5 g ginger, peeled, finely diced
> 1 lemon grass stalk, crushed
> 2 salam leaves
> 2 g anise seeds
> 30 ml tamarind water (see page 23)
> 45 ml red chili juice (see page 23)
> 250 ml coconut milk (see page 22)
> 125 ml chicken stock (see page 24)
> 150 g ripe pumpkin, boiled until soft — 8-12 minutes
> salt

1 Heat the peanut oil in a saucepan and sauté the shallots and garlic for 2-3 minutes in the hot oil until light brown.
2 Add the ginger, lemon grass and salam leaves. Continue to sauté for another 2 minutes.
3 Add the anise, tamarind water, chili juice and coconut milk. Pour in the chicken stock and bring to the boil. Reduce the heat and let the mixture simmer for 3-4 minutes. Stir it frequently.
4 Add in the pumpkin and season with salt. Continue to cook for approximately 8 minutes.
5 Remove the pan from the heat and discard the lemon grass and salam leaves.
6 Pour the mixture into a blender and process for 2-3 minutes until smooth. Yields 500 ml.

PEANUT SAUCE

Saus Tauge Pedas

SPICY BEANSPROUT SAUCE

The beansprout is usually associated with Chinese cooking. In Indonesia, however, after centuries of Chinese influence and trade, the beansprout is one of the most commonly used vegetables. Serve this sauce hot with fish and seafood.

30 ml peanut oil
30 g shallots (bawang merah), peeled, finely diced
10 g garlic, peeled, finely diced
50 g red chilies, seeded, finely diced
10 g greater galangal, peeled, finely diced
10 g lemon grass stalk, finely diced
375 ml coconut milk (see page 22)
100 g beansprouts, cleaned
salt

1　Heat the peanut oil in a saucepan. Add in the shallots, garlic and chilies and sauté until light brown.
2　Stir in the greater galangal and lemon grass, and continue to sauté for 2 minutes more.
3　Pour in the coconut milk and bring the mixture to the boil, then turn down the heat.
4　Add the beansprouts, season with salt and simmer for 10 minutes, stirring frequently.
5　Remove the pan from the heat and serve the sauce hot. Yields 500 ml.

Saus Cabe Hijau

GREEN CHILI SAUCE

This is a pleasantly mild chili sauce.

30 ml peanut oil
20 g shallots (bawang merah), peeled, finely diced
10 g garlic, peeled, finely diced
10 g greater galangal, peeled, finely diced
10 g ginger, peeled, finely diced
1 lemon grass stalk, crushed
3 salam leaves
10 g shrimp paste
2 tomatoes, chopped
250 g green chilies, seeded, diced
375 ml coconut milk (see page 22)

1　Heat the peanut oil in a saucepan. Add the shallots, garlic, greater galangal, ginger, lemon grass and salam leaves, and sauté until the ingredients are light brown.
2　Add in the shrimp paste, tomatoes and green chilies, and sauté for a further 2-3 minutes.
3　Pour in the coconut milk, bring the mixture to the boil and simmer for approximately 5 minutes, stirring gently until the sauce thickens.
4　Remove from the heat and discard the lemon grass and salam leaves.
5　Pour the sauce into a blender and blend for 2-4 minutes until smooth. Yields 625 ml.

Saus Rujak

RUJAK SAUCE

Central Java is the home of the *rujak*, a salad of assorted fresh fruits with a dressing made of *gula Jawa* and chili juice. This is our version of the *rujak* sauce — a syrupy delight for raw fruit and vegetable salads, or a mixture of the two.

200 g brown sugar (gula Jawa)
100 ml lukewarm water
40 g red chilies, finely diced
15 g tamarind pulp
125 ml red chili juice (see page 23)

1　In a saucepan, dissolve the brown sugar in the lukewarm water until the mixture is completely smooth.
2　Add in the remaining ingredients and mix well.
3　Bring the mixture to the boil, then reduce the heat and simmer for approximately 8 minutes.
4　Remove the pan from the heat and let the sauce cool completely before using. Yields 375 ml.

Saus Pesmol

PESMOL SAUCE

This is one of the most important sauces in Java, and virtually everyone has a different idea as to what constitutes the perfect pesmol. Coconut milk and turmeric, however, are always included, and the taste is always sweet and sour.

30 ml peanut oil
30 g shallots (bawang merah), peeled, finely chopped
10 g garlic, peeled, finely chopped
40 g tomatoes, chopped
20 g red chilies, cleaned, seeded, finely chopped
20 g ginger, peeled, chopped
20 g greater galangal, peeled, chopped
1 lemon grass stalk, crushed
1 g turmeric root, finely diced
500 ml coconut milk (see page 22)
10 g white sugar
10 ml white vinegar

1　Heat the oil in a saucepan and sauté the next 7 ingredients for 3-5 minutes until light brown.
2　Sprinkle in the turmeric root and continue to sauté for another 2 minutes.
3　Add in the coconut milk and sugar. Bring to the boil and let it simmer for about 8 minutes until the sauce begins to thicken. Stir occasionally.
4　Add in the vinegar and continue to simmer for an additional 3 minutes.
5　Remove the pan from the heat. Put the sauce in a blender and blend until smooth. Remove and keep warm. Yields 500 ml.

Saus Madu dan Cabe Merah

HONEY CHILI SAUCE

This is a spicy, sweet sauce for grilled or roast chicken and veal. It is served hot.

15 ml peanut oil
30 g shallots (bawang merah), peeled, finely diced
10 g garlic, peeled, finely diced
coriander powder
15 ml lemon juice
185 ml red chili juice (see page 23)
30 ml tamarind water (see page 23)
90 ml honey
165 ml water
salt

1 Heat the peanut oil in a saucepan. Add the shallots and garlic and sauté for 1 minute until light brown.
2 Add in the coriander powder and continue to sauté for an additional minute.
3 Pour in the remaining ingredients, seasoning with salt. Bring to the boil. Reduce the heat and simmer, stirring frequently, until the sauce thickens, approximately 10 minutes.
4 Remove from the heat and serve hot. Yields 500 ml.

Saus Pecel

SWEET SPICY PECEL SAUCE

Pecel — cooked vegetables served with a peanut sauce — originally came from east Java. *Kencur*, or lesser galangal, and the brown palm sugar, *gula Jawa*, give the sauce its distinctive flavour.

15 ml peanut oil
30 g shallots (bawang merah), peeled, finely diced
10 g garlic, peeled, finely diced
5 g lesser galangal, peeled, finely diced
50 g peanuts, deep-fried, chopped
30 g brown sugar (gula Jawa)
30 ml tamarind water (see page 23)
60 ml red chili juice (see page 23)
10 ml dark sweet soya sauce
375 ml water
salt

1 Heat the peanut oil in a saucepan and sauté the shallots, garlic, lesser galangal and peanuts for 2-3 minutes.
2 Add in the brown sugar, tamarind water and chili juice. Stir in the sweet soya sauce and then pour in the water. Season with the salt. Bring the mixture to the boil, reduce the heat and simmer for 8 minutes, stirring from time to time.
3 Remove the pan from the heat and pour the mixture into a blender. Run the machine for 2 minutes until the sauce is smooth.
4 Serve warm with meat, or cold with vegetables. Yields 500 ml.

Saus Setup Banyuwangi

BANYUWANGI SAUCE

This sauce takes its name from a city in east Java, where the recipes frequently call for the use of coconut milk. The light fieriness of this sauce harmonizes well with the sweet basil.

15 ml peanut oil
40 g shallots (bawang merah), finely diced
10 g garlic, finely diced
40 g red chilies, seeded, finely diced
40 g green chilies, seeded, finely diced
15 sweet basil leaves (kemangi), finely chopped
250 ml coconut milk (see page 22)
10 g sweet basil leaves

1 Heat the peanut oil in a frying pan. Sauté the shallots, garlic and chilies in the oil for 3-5 minutes without browning.
2 Add in the chopped basil leaves and coconut milk. Bring the mixture to the boil, reduce the heat and simmer for 10 minutes.
3 Pour the sauce into a blender and blend for 2-3 minutes at high speed until smooth.
4 Remove the sauce from the blender and pour it back into the saucepan. Stir in the whole basil leaves. Yields 250 ml.

Saus Pala

NUTMEG SAUCE

Despite the small amount of nutmeg used in the recipe, this sauce has a strong nutmeg flavour and should go well with poultry and gamebird dishes.

15 ml peanut oil
250 g chicken bones
10 g garlic, peeled, coarsely chopped
30 g shallots, peeled, coarsely chopped
10 g ginger, peeled, chopped
2 salam leaves
50 ml dark sweet soya sauce
3 g nutmeg powder
500 ml chicken stock (see page 24)
salt

1 Heat the peanut oil in a frying pan and sauté the chicken bones in the hot oil over high heat until they are light brown.
2 Add the garlic, shallots, ginger and salam leaves, and sauté until they are dark brown.
3 Pour in the sweet soya sauce, nutmeg and chicken stock, and season with salt. Turn down the heat and let the mixture simmer for 20 minutes.
4 Remove the pan from the heat and strain the sauce through a fine sieve. Yields 500 ml.

SPICY BEANSPROUT SAUCE

SWEET SPICY PECEL SAUCE

GREEN CHILI SAUCE

BANYUWANGI SAUCE

PESMOL SAUCE

NUTMEG SAUCE

OPOR SAUCE

RED KIDNEY BEAN SAUCE

PINEAPPLE COCONUT SAUCE

SOUR TURMERIC SAUCE

SPICED SOYA SAUCE

PAPAYA SAUCE

Saus Opor

OPOR SAUCE

This sweet sauce is found almost everywhere in Java and Sumatra, and no ceremony would be complete without a dish using it.

    30 ml peanut oil
    50 g shallots (bawang merah), peeled, finely diced
    5 g garlic, peeled, finely diced
    20 g candlenuts, ground
    5 g ginger, peeled, chopped
    5 g greater galangal, peeled, chopped
    1 salam leaf
    500 ml coconut milk (see page 22)
    250 ml chicken stock (see page 24)
    salt

1 Heat the peanut oil in a saucepan and sauté the shallots, garlic, candlenuts, ginger, greater galangal and salam leaf for 5 minutes without browning.
2 Add in the coconut milk and chicken stock and bring the mixture to the boil.
3 Reduce the heat and simmer until the sauce starts to thicken, approximately 8-10 minutes. Season with salt.
4 Remove the pan from the heat and discard the salam leaf.
5 Pour the sauce into a blender and process for 2-3 minutes until smooth. Serve hot. Yields 750 ml.

Saus Nanas Opor

PINEAPPLE COCONUT SAUCE

    30 ml coconut oil
    50 g shallots (bawang merah), peeled, finely diced
    10 g garlic, peeled, finely diced
    10 g greater galangal, peeled, finely diced
    10 g lemon grass stalk, finely diced
    1 salam leaf
    5 coriander leaves
    5 g anise seed
    20 g candlenuts, ground
    130 g pineapple, diced
    375 ml coconut milk (see page 22)
    salt

1 Heat the coconut oil in a saucepan and sauté the next 6 ingredients in the oil for 2 minutes without browning.
2 Add in the anise, candlenuts and pineapple. Continue to sauté for 2 minutes more.
3 Pour in the coconut milk. Season with salt and bring to the boil. Reduce the heat and simmer for approximately 10 minutes.
4 Remove the pan from the heat and discard the salam leaf.
5 Pour the sauce into a blender and process for 2 minutes until smooth. Yields 375 ml.

Saus Semur

SPICED SOYA SAUCE

    30 ml peanut oil
    20 g onions, peeled, finely diced
    10 g garlic, peeled, finely diced
    5 g ginger, peeled, finely diced
    5 g black peppercorns, crushed
    20 g brown sugar (gula Jawa)
    6 dried cloves
    2 g coriander seeds
    1 g nutmeg powder
    2 g cinnamon powder
    200 ml dark sweet soya sauce
    250 ml water
    salt

1 Heat the oil in a saucepan and sauté the onions, garlic and ginger for 2-3 minutes without browning. Stir frequently.
2 Add the peppercorns and brown sugar, and continue to sauté for 2 minutes more.
3 Mix in the cloves, coriander seeds, nutmeg and cinnamon powder. Pour in the sweet soya sauce and water. Season with salt. Bring the mixture to the boil, reduce the heat and simmer for 8-10 minutes. The sauce should have a syrupy consistency; if it does not, let it simmer some more until the desired consistency is achieved. Remove from the heat.
4 Pour the mixture through a sieve and discard all the solid ingredients. Yields 375 ml.

Saus Kacang Merah

RED KIDNEY BEAN SAUCE

    30 ml peanut oil
    20 g shallots (bawang merah), peeled, finely diced
    10 g garlic, peeled, finely diced
    5 g ginger, peeled, finely diced
    10 g brown sugar (gula Jawa)
    2 salam leaves
    150 g red kidney beans, soaked overnight, boiled 45-60
        minutes until soft
    90 ml red chili juice (see page 23)
    250 ml coconut milk (see page 22)
    salt

1 Heat the peanut oil in a saucepan and sauté the shallots, garlic and ginger in the oil until light brown, approximately 2-3 minutes.
2 Add the brown sugar, salam leaves and red kidney beans. Continue sautéing for 2 minutes more.
3 Pour in the chili juice and coconut milk, season with salt and bring to the boil. Reduce the heat and let the sauce simmer for 10 minutes, stirring frequently.
4 Remove the pan from the heat and discard the salam leaves.
5 Pour the sauce into a blender and purée for 2-3 minutes until smooth. Yields 500 ml.

Saus Acar Kuning

SOUR TURMERIC SAUCE

30 ml peanut oil
20 g ginger, peeled, finely chopped
20 g shallots (bawang merah), peeled, finely chopped
10 g garlic, peeled, finely chopped
1 bay leaf
1 lemon grass stalk, crushed
3 g turmeric powder
40 g candlenuts, ground
5 g white sugar
500 ml coconut milk (see page 22)
30 ml white vinegar
salt
pepper

1 Heat the oil in a pan and sauté the ginger, shallots, garlic, bay leaf and lemon grass for 2 minutes.
2 Add in the turmeric powder, candlenuts and sugar, and continue to sauté for 3-5 minutes.
3 Pour in the coconut milk and vinegar, and simmer for 10 minutes. Season with salt and pepper.
4 Remove from the heat and discard the bay leaf and lemon grass.
5 Pour the sauce into a blender and purée until smooth. Yields 500 ml.

Saus Pepaya

PAPAYA SAUCE

The fruitiness of the papaya makes this sauce a fine accompaniment to fowl and gamebirds. Only well-ripened, red-fleshed papayas should be used in order to acquire the right colour and flavour.

15 ml peanut oil
40 g shallots (bawang merah), peeled, finely diced
5 g garlic, peeled, finely diced
5 g ginger, peeled, finely diced
10 g lemon grass stalk, finely diced
200 g ripe papaya, peeled, diced
10 g white sugar
15 ml white vinegar
125 ml red chili juice (see page 23)
185 ml chicken stock (see page 24)
salt

1 Heat the peanut oil in a saucepan and sauté the shallots, garlic, ginger and lemon grass for 2 minutes in the hot oil until light brown.
2 Stir in the papaya, sugar and vinegar, and continue to sauté for 2 minutes more.
3 Pour in the chili juice and chicken stock, and season with salt. Reduce the heat and simmer for approximately 5-7 minutes, stirring from time to time. Remove the pan from the heat.
4 Pour the sauce into a blender and purée for 2 minutes until smooth. Remove from the blender and serve warm. Yields 500 ml.

Saus Bengkulu

BENGKULU SAUCE

Because of its relatively mild flavour, this sauce goes well with many dishes.

30 ml peanut oil
40 g shallots (bawang merah), peeled, finely diced
20 g garlic, peeled, finely diced
50 g red chilies, seeded, diced
10 g green chilies, seeded, diced
10 sweet basil leaves (kemangi)
100 g tomatoes, peeled, seeded, diced
150 ml lamb stock (see page 24)
2 g shrimp paste
salt

1 Heat the peanut oil in a saucepan and sauté the shallots, garlic and chilies for 2 minutes without browning.
2 Add in the basil leaves and tomatoes. Continue to sauté for 2 minutes more.
3 Add in the lamb stock and shrimp paste, bring to the boil and reduce the heat. Season the sauce lightly with salt and simmer at low heat for approximately 15 minutes.
4 Pour the sauce into a blender and process until smooth. Yields 400 ml.

Saus Tauco Sumatra

SUMATRAN BLACK BEAN SAUCE

45 ml peanut oil
40 g onions, peeled, finely diced
10 g garlic, peeled, finely diced
20 g red chilies, cut into strips
20 g green chilies, cut into strips
1 lemon grass stalk, finely diced
10 g greater galangal, peeled, finely diced
1 salam leaf
120 g sour finger carambolas, cut into strips
200 ml fermented black soya beans
125 ml water
60 ml dark sweet soya sauce
salt

1 Heat the oil in a pan and sauté the onions, garlic, chilies, lemon grass and greater galangal in the hot oil for 2-3 minutes, stirring constantly.
2 Add in the salam leaf, sour finger carambolas, fermented soya beans and water. Bring the mixture to the boil.
3 Add in the sweet soya sauce and simmer until the sauce starts to thicken, approximately 5-8 minutes.
4 Remove from the heat and discard the salam leaf.
5 Pour the sauce into a blender and process at high speed for 2-3 minutes. Remove from the blender and serve. Yields 375 ml.

SPICY COCONUT SAUCE

Saus Rendang
SPICY COCONUT SAUCE

30 ml peanut oil
50 g shallots (bawang merah), peeled, finely diced
10 g garlic, peeled, finely diced
10 g ginger, peeled, finely diced
10 g greater galangal, peeled, finely diced
20 g candlenuts, ground
1 lemon grass stalk, bruised
4 kaffir lime leaves
1 turmeric leaf
2 g coriander powder
375 ml red chili juice (see page 23)
250 ml coconut milk (see page 22)
salt

1   In a saucepan, heat the peanut oil and sauté the shallots, garlic, ginger and greater galangal for approximately 5 minutes until light brown.
2   Add the candlenuts, lemon grass, lime leaves, turmeric leaf and coriander powder. Continue to sauté for 2 minutes.
3   Pour in the chili juice and coconut milk, and season with the salt. Bring the mixture to the boil, reduce the heat and let it simmer until the sauce thickens, approximately 6-8 minutes. Stir the mixture from time to time.
4   Remove the pan from the heat and discard the lemon grass and lime leaves.
5   Pour the sauce into a blender and run machine at high speed for approximately 3-4 minutes until the sauce is smooth. Yields 625 ml.

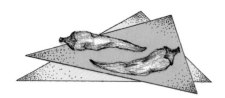

Saus Sambal Brambang
BRAMBANG SAUCE

260 g tomatoes, peeled, seeded, diced
20 g garlic, peeled, finely diced
120 g shallots (bawang merah), peeled, finely diced
20 g bird's eye chilies, seeded, diced
80 ml freshly squeezed lime juice
125 ml water
salt

1   Combine all the ingredients in a blender. Process for approximately 3-4 minutes until smooth.
2   Remove the pinkish sauce from the blender and refrigerate. Yields 500 ml.

NOTE: To make Sambal Brambang instead of Brambang Sauce, simply mix the above ingredients together without blending them. It should be left to marinate for an hour before use for the flavour to develop.

Saus Sambal Kecap
SWEET SPICY SOYA SAUCE

In this sauce, the bite of the chili cuts the heavy sweetness of the sweet soya sauce. It should always be served cold, and is a popular accompaniment to many dishes.

30 g shallots (bawang merah), peeled, finely diced
15 g garlic, peeled, finely diced
30 g red chilies, seeded, finely diced
10 g bird's eye chilies, seeded, finely diced
30 g tomatoes, peeled, seeded, diced
500 ml dark sweet soya sauce
45 ml freshly squeezed lime juice
salt

1   Combine all the ingredients and mix well.
2   Season with salt. Yields 500 ml.

SWEET SPICY SOYA SAUCE

Saus Gulai

INDONESIAN CURRY SAUCE

From Padang, the bustling port of west Sumatra, comes this hot curry sauce. Though several kinds of spices are used in the recipe, each spice carries its own distinct flavour which is easily detected in the sauce.

30 ml peanut oil
20 g shallots (*bawang merah*), peeled, finely diced
10 g garlic, peeled, finely diced
5 g ginger, peeled, finely diced
5 g greater galangal, peeled, finely diced
2 salam leaves
20 g candlenuts, ground
5 g turmeric root, finely diced
2 g anise powder
2 g cinnamon powder
2 g clove powder
1 g cardamom powder
30 ml tamarind water (*see* page 23)
90 ml red chili juice (*see* page 23)
500 ml coconut milk (*see* page 22)
salt

1 Heat the oil in a saucepan and sauté the shallots, garlic, ginger and greater galangal in the oil over high heat for 3-4 minutes until light brown. Stir frequently.
2 Add in the salam leaves, candlenuts, turmeric and powdered spices. Continue to sauté for another 2 minutes over reduced heat.
3 Pour in the tamarind water and chili juice, and slowly add in the coconut milk. Season with salt.
4 Bring the mixture to the boil, then reduce the heat and simmer for approximately 10 minutes, stirring constantly.
5 Withdraw the pan from the heat and discard the salam leaves.
6 Pour the sauce into a blender and process until smooth, approximately 3-4 minutes. Serve hot. Yields 500 ml.

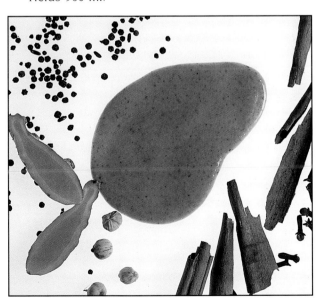

INDONESIAN CURRY SAUCE

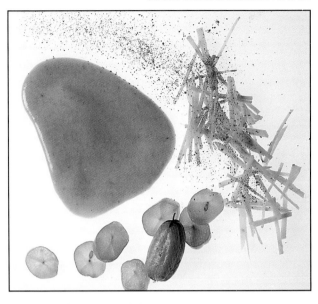

Saus Belimbing Wuluh

SOUR FINGER CARAMBOLA SAUCE

The sour *belimbing wuluh* is commonly used throughout Indonesia as a mild substitute for vinegar in fish and meat dishes. It is also eaten as a pickle or raw in salads. This sour sauce goes well with pork, lamb, poultry and fish.

30 ml peanut oil
40 g shallots (*bawang merah*), peeled, finely diced
5 g garlic, peeled, finely diced
5 g ginger, peeled, finely diced
5 g lemon grass stalk, finely diced
10 g shrimp paste
200 g sour finger carambolas, diced
20 g candlenuts, ground
5 g turmeric powder
60 ml red chili juice (*see* page 23)
375 ml coconut milk (*see* page 22)
salt

1 Heat the peanut oil in a saucepan. Sauté the shallots, garlic, ginger and lemon grass in the hot oil for 2 minutes without browning.
2 Add the shrimp paste and sour carambolas. Continue to sauté for another 2 minutes.
3 Add in the candlenuts and turmeric powder and sauté for an additional 2 minutes.
4 Pour in the chili juice and coconut milk and season lightly with salt. Bring the mixture to the boil, reduce the heat and simmer for approximately 10 minutes.
5 Pour the sauce into a blender and process for 2 minutes until smooth. Yields 625 ml.

Saus Dabu-dabu Manado

DABU-DABU SAUCE

This thin, fiery sauce is served uncooked and cold, even when accompanying hot dishes.

> 60 g red chilies, seeded, diced
> 10 g bird's eye chilies, seeded, diced
> 30 g shallots (bawang merah), peeled, finely diced
> 250 g tomatoes, peeled, seeded, diced
> 30 ml white vinegar
> 160 ml chicken stock, cold (see page 24)
> salt
> white pepper

1 Put the chilies, shallots, tomatoes and vinegar in a blender. Process until smooth.
2 Pour the mixture into a bowl, add in the chicken stock and season with salt and pepper. Mix well. Yields 500 ml.

NOTE: When chicken stock is mixed with the sauce, it can be served with meat or chicken dishes. If the sauce is to accompany fish dishes, use fish stock instead.

Saus Jeruk

ORANGE SAUCE

> 30 ml peanut oil
> 30 g shallots (bawang merah), peeled, finely diced
> 10 g garlic, peeled, finely diced
> 5 g greater galangal, peeled, finely diced
> 5 g ginger, peeled, finely diced
> 30 g candlenuts, ground
> 1 lemon grass stalk, crushed
> 15 g turmeric root, finely diced
> 2 g coriander powder
> 10 g brown sugar (gula Jawa)
> 125 ml coconut milk (see page 22)
> 250 ml unsweetened orange juice
> salt

1 Heat the oil in a saucepan and sauté the shallots, garlic, greater galangal and ginger for about 1-2 minutes, until the ingredients are light brown.
2 Add in the candlenuts, lemon grass, turmeric root, coriander powder and brown sugar. Sauté for a further 2 minutes.
3 Pour in the coconut milk and orange juice, and season with salt. Bring the mixture to the boil. Reduce the heat and let it simmer for about 20 minutes, stirring frequently.
4 Remove the pan from the heat and discard the lemon grass.
5 Pour the sauce into a blender and process for 2 minutes until smooth. Serve hot. Yields 375 ml.

Saus Asam Manis

SWEET SOUR SAUCE

This sauce is light red in colour. One should be able to taste the ginger in it. If not, increase the amount of ginger by 2-5 g at a time.

> 30 ml vegetable oil
> 40 g shallots (bawang merah), peeled, finely diced
> 5 g garlic, peeled, finely diced
> 20 g ginger, peeled, finely diced
> 250 g tomatoes, peeled, seeded, diced
> 40 g sugar
> 45 ml white vinegar
> 125 ml water
> salt

1 Heat the oil in a saucepan. Sauté the shallots, garlic and ginger in the hot oil for 2 minutes without browning.
2 Add in the tomatoes, sugar, white vinegar and water. Season with salt and bring to the boil. Reduce the heat and let the sauce simmer for 5 minutes.
3 Pour the sauce into a blender and process at high speed for 2 minutes until the sauce is smooth. Yields 500 ml.

Saus Kacang Madu

PEANUT HONEY SAUCE

Although lots of honey is produced in Indonesia, honey is rarely used in traditional cooking. Nonetheless, this sweet sauce makes a fine complement to chicken, duck or lamb. It is important that a strong-tasting honey be used, otherwise the peanut taste will predominate.

> 30 ml peanut oil
> 40 g shallots (bawang merah), peeled, finely diced
> 5 g garlic, peeled, finely diced
> 10 g ginger, peeled, finely diced
> 150 g peanuts, roasted, ground
> 10 g lemon grass stalk, finely diced
> 60 ml red chili juice (see page 23)
> 150 ml honey
> 375 ml water
> salt

1 Heat the oil in a saucepan and sauté the shallots, garlic and ginger in the hot oil for 2 minutes without browning.
2 Add in the peanuts and lemon grass and continue to sauté for 2 minutes.
3 Pour in the chili juice, honey and water. Season with salt and bring the mixture to the boil.
4 Reduce the heat and let the sauce simmer for approximately 8-10 minutes, stirring slowly.
5 Pour the sauce into a blender and process 2 minutes. The sauce should have a silky consistency. Yields 625 ml.

Saus Rica-rica

RICA-RICA SAUCE

This sauce hails from Manado in north Sulawesi, where it (or variations of it, but always featuring tomatoes) is used on practically everything. This particular Rica-rica Sauce is good, served hot or cold, with fish. It is also a fine accompaniment for poultry.

30 ml vegetable oil
30 g shallots (bawang merah), peeled, finely diced
10 g garlic, peeled, finely diced
5 g ginger, peeled, finely diced
60 g red chilies, seeded, finely diced
1 salam leaf
30 g candlenuts, ground
200 g tomatoes, peeled, seeded, diced
5 g turmeric powder
250 ml coconut milk (see page 22)
60 ml red chili juice (see page 23)
salt

1 Heat the oil in a saucepan. Add the shallots, garlic, ginger and chilies and sauté for 2-3 minutes without browning.
2 Add in the salam leaf and candlenuts, and continue to sauté for 2 minutes more.
3 Add in 150 g of the tomatoes and the turmeric powder, and sauté for another 2 minutes. Pour in the coconut milk and chili juice. Season with salt.
4 Bring the mixture to the boil, reduce the heat and simmer until the sauce thickens, approximately 8 minutes. Stir constantly.
5 Remove the pan from the heat and discard the salam leaf.
6 Pour the sauce into a blender and process until smooth, approximately 2-3 minutes.
7 Remove the sauce from the blender. Just before serving, add in the remaining diced tomatoes. Yields 625 ml.

NOTE: Should the sauce become too thick, add a small amount of chicken stock.

Saus Sambal Godok

WHITE BEANCURD SAUCE

30 ml peanut oil
30 g shallots (bawang merah), peeled, finely diced
10 g garlic, peeled, finely diced
10 g greater galangal, peeled, finely diced
4 salam leaves
15 g candlenuts, ground
100 g white beancurd, diced
40 g long beans, diced
90 ml red chili juice (see page 23)
250 ml coconut milk (see page 22)
salt

1 Heat the peanut oil in a saucepan. Add the shallots, garlic, greater galangal and salam leaves and sauté for 2 minutes without browning.
2 Add in the candlenuts and continue to sauté for 2 minutes.
3 Add in the beancurd and long beans, and sauté for 2 minutes more.
4 Pour in the chili juice and coconut milk, and season with salt. Bring to the boil, reduce the heat and simmer for approximately 10 minutes or until the sauce thickens.
5 Withdraw the pan from the heat and discard the salam leaves.
6 Pour the mixture into a blender and process at high speed until smooth. Serve hot. Yields 500 ml.

Saus Bumbu Rujak

SPICY RUJAK SAUCE

Use this *rujak* sauce with fish and beef dishes. It is yellow in colour and should be served hot.

30 ml peanut oil
10 g garlic, peeled, finely diced
30 g shallots (bawang merah), peeled, finely diced
10 g ginger, peeled, finely diced
10 g greater galangal, peeled, finely diced
5 g lemon grass stalk, finely diced
1 salam leaf
5 g white sugar
20 g candlenuts, ground
2 g turmeric powder
10 ml white vinegar
90 ml red chili juice (see page 23)
400 ml coconut milk (see page 22)
salt

1 Heat the peanut oil in a saucepan. Sauté the garlic and shallots until light brown, approximately 2-3 minutes.
2 Add in the ginger, greater galangal, lemon grass and salam leaf, continuing to sauté for a further 1-2 minutes without letting the new ingredients take colour.
3 Stir in the sugar, candlenuts and turmeric powder, and continue to sauté for another minute.
4 Pour in the vinegar, chili juice and coconut milk. Season with some salt. Then bring the mixture to the boil, reduce the heat and simmer for 8-10 minutes or until the sauce starts to thicken.
5 Remove the pan from the heat and discard the salam leaf.
6 Pour the sauce into a blender and purée at high speed for 2-3 minutes. Remove from the blender and serve. Yields 500 ml.

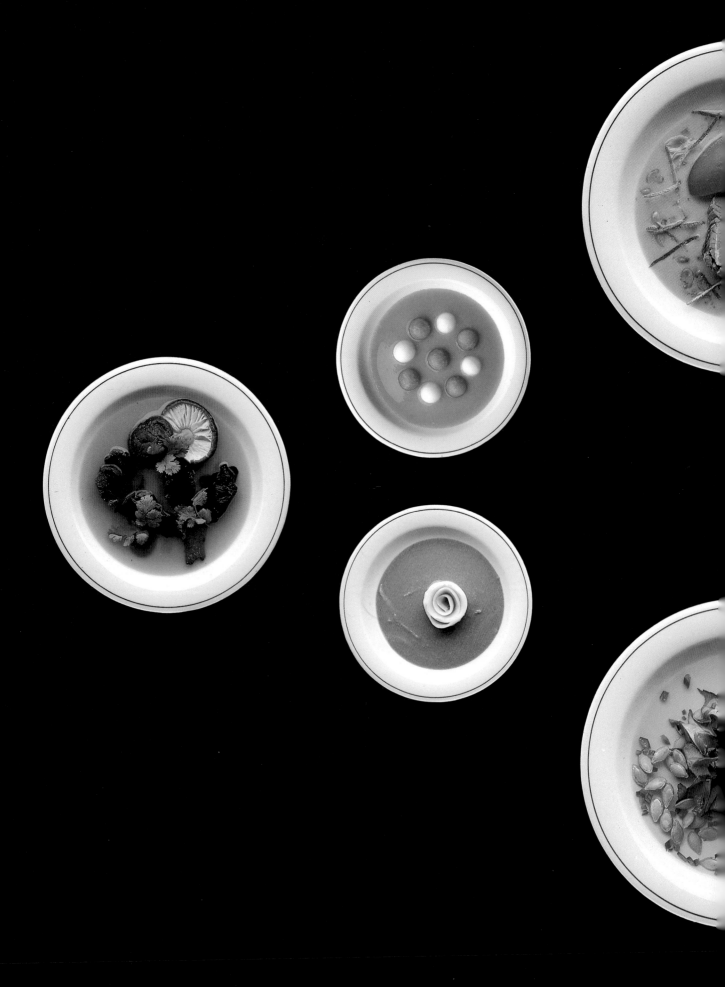

SOUPS AND APPETIZERS

SOUPS

Soto Jawa Timur

EAST JAVANESE CHICKEN SOUP

STEP 1: Chicken Soup
> 15 ml vegetable oil
> 10 g garlic, peeled, finely diced
> 5 g ginger, peeled, finely diced
> 5 g turmeric root, peeled, finely diced
> 2 g shrimp paste
> 320 ml chicken stock (see page 24)
> 375 ml coconut milk (see page 22)
> salt
> ground white pepper
> 120 g chicken meat, diced

1 Heat the vegetable oil in a shallow stockpot. Add in the garlic, ginger and turmeric root and sauté in the oil for 2 minutes without browning.
2 Stir in the shrimp paste and continue to sauté for approximately 2 minutes, until the paste has been thoroughly mixed in.
3 Pour in the chicken stock and gradually add in the coconut milk, stirring frequently. Season with salt and pepper, but use salt sparingly.
4 Bring the soup to the boil, then reduce the heat and let it simmer for 20 minutes, to absorb the flavours. Stir constantly to prevent the coconut milk from settling. Remove the pot from the heat.

STEP 2: Garnish and Presentation
> 40 g dried glass noodles, soaked in warm water for 20 minutes
> 40 g sour finger carambolas, sliced thinly
> 10 g shallots (bawang merah), peeled, sliced thinly, deep-fried

1 Arrange the glass noodles, sour finger carambola slices and fried shallots in individual soup plates.
2 Ladle in the soup made in Step 1 and serve immediately.

Sop Siwalan

PALM NUT SOUP

This beautifully mild soup features the fruit of the versatile Palmyra tree. If palm nuts are not available, use fresh water chestnuts instead.

> 30 ml vegetable oil
> 10 g shallots (bawang merah), peeled, finely diced
> 10 g garlic, peeled, finely diced
> 5 medium-sized red chilies, sliced
> 160 g chicken meat, skinned, diced
> 160 g palm nuts, boiled until crunchy — about 20 minutes
> 40 g carrot, peeled, finely diced
> 2 g nutmeg powder
> 1 litre chicken stock (see page 24)
> salt
> 1 nutmeg, grated

1 Heat the oil in a shallow stockpot and sauté the shallots, garlic and red chilies for 2 minutes, until they look glazy.
2 Stir in the chicken meat, palm nuts and carrots, and sauté for 2 minutes more.
3 Sprinkle the nutmeg powder over the mixture. Pour in the chicken stock and season with salt.
4 Bring the stock to the boil, reduce the heat and simmer for 10 minutes over low heat.
5 Remove from the heat and sprinkle the freshly grated nutmeg over the soup just before serving.

Sop Kacang Merah

RED KIDNEY BEAN SOUP WITH GINGER

STEP 1: Soup
> 10 ml peanut oil
> 40 g onions, peeled, finely diced
> 40 g shallots (bawang merah), peeled, finely diced
> 5 g garlic, peeled, finely diced
> 10 g ginger, peeled, finely diced
> 5 g greater galangal, peeled, finely diced
> 150 g red kidney beans, soaked overnight, boiled until soft — 45 minutes to 1 hour
> 500 ml clear chicken stock (see page 24)
> 125 ml coconut milk (see page 22)
> salt
> white pepper

1 Heat the peanut oil in a saucepan and sauté the onions, shallots, garlic, ginger and greater galangal until soft. Do not let them brown.
2 Add in the kidney beans, toss and continue to cook for another 2 minutes.
3 Pour the chicken stock over the mixture and bring to the boil. Reduce the heat and let the soup simmer, stirring often, until all the ingredients are soft.
4 Withdraw the pan from the heat; pour the soup into a blender and purée it until silky.
5 Return the soup to the pan and continue to cook, gradually adding in the coconut milk, for another 5 minutes. Season with salt and pepper.

STEP 2: Garnish and Presentation
> 20 g red kidney beans, soaked overnight, boiled until soft — 45 minutes to 1 hour
> 10 g ginger, cut into fine strips
> 10 g red chilies, cut into fine strips
> 4 sprigs coriander leaves

1 Divide the kidney beans into 4 equal parts and put a portion in each soup bowl. Arrange the ginger and red chili julienne in the bowls.
2 Ladle in the soup made in Step 1 and top each bowl with a sprig of coriander leaves.

Sop Cendawan Indonesia

INDONESIAN MUSHROOM SOUP

STEP 1: Broth

  15 *ml peanut oil*
  50 *g shallots (bawang merah), peeled, finely chopped*
  10 *g garlic, peeled, finely chopped*
  5 *g lemon grass stalk, finely chopped*
  10 *g fresh coriander leaves*
  50 *g dried black Chinese mushrooms, soaked in warm water*
     for 1 hour, chopped
  50 *g dried wood fungus, soaked in warm water for 1 hour,*
     chopped
  1 *litre chicken stock (see page 24)*
  ground white pepper
  ground nutmeg
  5 *g fresh ginger, chopped*
  salt

1 Heat the oil in a stockpot or saucepan and sauté the shallots in the hot oil until they look glazy.
2 Add in the garlic, lemon grass, coriander leaves, mushrooms and wood fungus and continue to sauté for 2-3 minutes.
3 Pour in the chicken stock and the remaining seasoning ingredients; add salt to taste. Bring the broth to the boil, then let it simmer for 1 hour, stirring occasionally.
4 Strain the liquid through a cheesecloth or fine wire sieve into another pot. Keep hot.

NOTE: In order to intensify the mushroom flavour of the soup, cook the chicken stock with 200 g of dried wood fungus for 30 minutes before using the stock for the soup.

STEP 2: Garnish and Presentation

  40 *g dried black Chinese mushrooms, soaked in warm water*
     for 1 hour
  40 *g dried wood fungus, soaked in warm water for 1 hour*
  4 *lemon grass stalks, peeled, washed*
  8 *sprigs coriander leaves*

1 Put a portion of the mushrooms and wood fungus in each soup plate.
2 Ladle in the broth made in Step 1 and garnish with the lemon grass stalks and coriander leaves.

Soto Solo Kasuhnanan

BEEF BROTH SOLO KASUHNANAN

This clear beef broth with fermented bean cake is named after the palaces of the ancient capital of Solo.

STEP 1: Beef Broth

  15 *ml vegetable oil*
  30 *g shallots (bawang merah), peeled, finely diced*
  5 *g garlic, peeled, finely diced*
  5 *g ginger, peeled, finely diced*
  1.5 *litres beef stock (see page 24)*
  2 *g coriander powder*
  2 *salam leaves*
  5 *g brown sugar (gula Jawa)*
  260 *g boneless beef — topside, top round or inside round*
  salt
  ground white pepper
  10 *g red chilies, stem removed, sliced into rings*

1 Heat the vegetable oil in a shallow stockpot and sauté the shallots, garlic and ginger in the oil for 2 minutes, without colouring.
2 Pour in the beef stock and add in the coriander powder, salam leaves and brown sugar.
3 Bring the soup to boiling point and then add in the beef. Season with salt and pepper.
4 Reduce the heat and let it simmer over low heat for approximately 40-50 minutes. From time to time skim the scum off the surface so that the broth remains clear.
5 When the beef is cooked, remove it from the broth and let it cool before slicing and putting to one side.
6 Pour the clear broth through a sieve and discard the remains.
7 Pour the broth back into the stockpot. Add in the sliced chilies and let it simmer for 2 minutes.

STEP 2: Garnish and Presentation

  40 *g red chilies, seeded, sliced into rings*
  40 *g stringbeans, cut into thin strips*
  40 *g beansprouts, cleaned*
  40 *g fermented bean cake, steamed for 5 minutes, cubed*
  4 *salam leaves*

1 Arrange a portion of the chilies, stringbeans, beansprouts, fermented bean cake and beef slices in each individual soup bowl.
2 Ladle in the broth made in Step 1, garnish with the salam leaves and serve immediately.

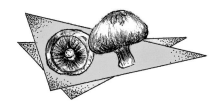

PUMPKIN LEAF SOUP WITH PRAWNS

BIRD'S NEST SOUP WITH QUAIL EGGS

Sop Daun Labu Udang Rebon

PUMPKIN LEAF SOUP WITH PRAWNS

This spicy, smooth soup has a strong taste of pumpkin leaves.

STEP 1: Soup

    30 *ml vegetable oil*
    20 *g shallots (bawang merah), peeled, finely diced*
    15 *g garlic, peeled, finely diced*
    10 *g shrimp paste*
    40 *g tomatoes, peeled, seeded, diced*
    60 *g young pumpkin leaves, cut into strips, blanched*
    625 *ml coconut milk (see page 22)*
    150 *g grey baby prawns, shelled, deveined*
    salt

1. Heat the oil in a shallow stockpot and sauté the shallots and garlic for 2 minutes, until glazy.
2. Stir in the shrimp paste and continue to sauté until the paste has been thoroughly mixed in.
3. Add in the diced tomatoes and young pumpkin leaves. Sauté for another 2 minutes.
4. Pour in the coconut milk and bring to the boil. Reduce the heat and simmer for 10 minutes. Stir from time to time to prevent the coconut milk from settling.
5. Season with salt. Then add in the baby prawns and continue to simmer for 2 minutes more.
6. Remove the soup from the stockpot and pour it into a blender. Purée the mixture at high speed for 2-3 minutes.

STEP 2: Garnish and Presentation

    2 *large prawns, cleaned, shell on, blanched for 1 minute*
    20 *g red chilies, seeded, finely diced*
    5 *g green chilies, seeded, finely diced*

1. Slice the prawns in half lengthwise and clean out the heads. Fill the cavity with the diced chilies.
2. Ladle the hot soup made in Step 1 into individual soup plates. Place a prawn on top for garnish.

Sop Sarang Burung Karangbolong

BIRD'S NEST SOUP WITH QUAIL EGGS

STEP 1: Soup

    560 *ml chicken stock, cold (see page 24)*
    100 *g chicken, minced or ground*
    2 *egg whites*
    20 *g shallots (bawang merah), peeled, chopped*
    10 *g garlic, peeled, chopped*
    10 *g celery stick, diced*
    10 *g leeks, diced*
    3 *lemon grass stalks, crushed*
    4 *bird's nests, whole, cleaned, soaked in warm water for a*
        short while
    salt
    pepper

1. Combine all the ingredients in a stockpot. Season with salt and pepper and bring to simmering point.
2. When all the ingredients have risen to the surface, after approximately 15 minutes, reduce the heat and simmer for another 30 minutes.
3. Strain the liquid carefully through a wet cheesecloth. The broth should be golden in colour. Reheat before serving.

STEP 2: Garnish and Presentation

    1 *bird's nest, soaked for 30 minutes in lukewarm water to*
        remove impurities
    1 *green bell pepper, cut into diamonds, blanched*
    6 *quail eggs, cooked in boiling salt water for 4 minutes,*
        shelled, halved
    20 *g carrots, peeled, finely diced, blanched*

1. Arrange the above garnish ingredients in individual soup bowls.
2. Remember to reheat the soup before ladling it into the bowls.

INDONESIAN MUSHROOM SOUP

BEEF BROTH SOLO KASUHNANAN

SPINACH COCONUT SOUP

Sop Bobor

SPINACH COCONUT SOUP

This is a rich, sweet-tasting soup. Water convolvulus leaves may be used instead of spinach for the soup.

STEP 1: Soup

30 ml vegetable oil
15 g onions, peeled, finely diced
5 g garlic, peeled, finely diced
10 g lesser galangal, peeled, finely diced
1 salam leaf
1 lemon grass stalk, crushed
3 g coriander powder
15 g brown sugar (gula Jawa)
500 ml chicken stock (see page 24)
250 ml coconut milk (see page 22)
100 g spinach leaves, stems removed
80 g young coconut meat, diced
salt

1 Heat the vegetable oil in a shallow stockpot. Sauté the onions, garlic and lesser galangal for 2 minutes without browning.
2 Add in the salam leaf, lemon grass, coriander powder and brown sugar. Sauté for another 2-3 minutes until the sugar has dissolved.
3 Pour in the chicken stock and gradually add in the coconut milk, stirring frequently. Bring to the boil.
4 Add in the spinach leaves and diced coconut meat. Season with salt. Reduce the heat and let the soup simmer over low heat for 15 minutes.
5 Remove the pot from the heat. Discard the salam leaf and lemon grass.
6 Pour the mixture into a blender and purée for 2-3 minutes.

NOTE: If fresh coconut is not available, use shredded, dried coconut flakes instead, but be sure to soak them first in lukewarm water for at least 10 minutes.

STEP 2: Garnish and Presentation

20 small young spinach leaves
80 g young coconut meat

1 Serve a portion of the soup made in Step 1 in each soup bowl.
2 Use young and tender spinach leaves and the coconut to garnish each bowl.

Sop Pelangi Pagi

CLEAR PRAWN SOUP WITH LEMON GRASS

STEP 1: Clarification

150 g red snapper fillet, skinned
20 g garlic, peeled
20 g carrot, peeled
20 g leeks, use bottom part only
2 egg whites
1 lemon grass stalk, crushed
1 bay leaf
10 ml chili juice (see page 23)
20 g tamarind pulp
750 ml clear fish stock, cold (see page 24)

1 Mince or grind the red snapper finely together with the garlic, carrots and leeks. Put the mixture into a bowl.
2 Stir in the egg whites, then add in the lemon grass, bay leaf, chili juice and tamarind pulp. Mix well.
3 Put this mixture in a stockpot, add in the cold fish stock and bring slowly to the boil, stirring the soup occasionally.
4 Reduce the heat and let the soup simmer until the solid ingredients float to the top, approximately 15 minutes.
5 Withdraw from the heat and using a large soup ladle, push the solid ingredients aside. Strain the liquid through cheesecloth or a fine wire sieve into another pot. Keep the broth hot.

NOTE: When preparing the stock for this recipe, use half the amount of fish and bones given in the recipe on page 24 and mix with an equal amount of prawns.

STEP 2: Garnish and Presentation

2 tomatoes, peeled, seeded, cut into diamonds
4 baby corns, blanched, cut into 1-cm pieces
1 lemon grass stalk, finely diced
12 sweet basil leaves (kemangi)
12 medium-sized prawns, shelled, cleaned, tail on, blanched
    for 2 minutes in the fish stock

1 Divide the garnish ingredients equally into 4 portions and arrange them in individual soup bowls.
2 Pour the warm soup made in Step 1 over the garnish and serve immediately.

Sop Kecipir dari Betawi
ASPARAGUS BEAN SOUP

This soup should be seasoned mildly to allow the aroma of the asparagus bean leaves to be fully appreciated. If asparagus beans are unavailable, use snowpeas instead; however, the snowpeas will take considerably less time than the asparagus beans to cook.

STEP 1: Asparagus Bean Broth
500 ml chicken stock (see page 24)
5 g salt
2 g sugar
150 g asparagus beans

1 Pour the stock into a stockpot, season with the salt and sugar, then bring it to the boil.
2 Drop the asparagus beans into the boiling water, reduce the heat and simmer for approximately 30-40 minutes.
3 Withdraw the pot from the heat and pour the mixture into a blender. Process for 2-3 minutes.
4 Strain the liquid through a fine sieve and discard the solid remains.

STEP 2: Soup
15 ml vegetable oil
10 g shallots (bawang merah), peeled, finely diced
60 g green asparagus beans, cut into 1-cm long pieces
10 g red chilies, seeded, finely diced
120 g asparagus beans, cut into triangles, blanched for 2-5 minutes
20 g pumpkin seeds, dried, roasted

1 In a shallow stockpot, heat the vegetable oil and sauté the shallots, green asparagus beans and chilies in the oil for 2 minutes. Stir constantly and do not let the ingredients take colour.
2 Pour in the asparagus bean broth made in Step 1 and simmer over low heat for 10 minutes.
3 Add the blanched asparagus beans and continue to simmer for 2 minutes more.
4 Sprinkle the roasted pumpkin seeds over the soup just before serving.

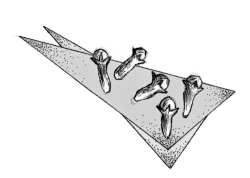

Soto Makassar
MAKASSAR SOUP

This is a traditional soup from Ujung Pandang in Sulawesi. Here is our own version of a fine-tasting beef soup with the interesting underlying sourness of kaffir lime juice.

STEP 1: Beef Broth
1.5 litres water
1 lemon grass stalk, crushed
2 garlic cloves, peeled
10 coriander leaves
5 g salt
160 g beef shoulder, boned

1 Pour the water into a shallow stockpot. Add in the lemon grass, garlic and coriander leaves. Season with the salt and bring to the boil.
2 Add in the beef and let it cook at reduced heat, approximately 45 minutes, until the meat is tender. (There should only be about 500 ml of liquid left after this step.)
3 Withdraw the pot from the heat and allow the meat to cool in the stock. Remove the beef and slice it.

STEP 2: Soup and Presentation
15 ml peanut oil
80 g raw peanuts, shelled, skinned
20 g shallots (bawang merah), peeled, finely diced
5 g garlic, peeled, finely diced
5 g ginger, peeled, finely diced
40 g candlenuts, chopped
45 ml salty soya sauce
2 g coriander powder
salt
30 ml freshly squeezed lime juice
20 g tomato, peeled, seeded, diced or cut into sections
2 g kaffir lime rind, finely sliced

1 In a separate pot, heat the peanut oil and cook the raw peanuts over low heat. Stir frequently until the peanuts become light brown in colour, approximately 3 minutes. Remove about half of the peanuts from the pot and keep aside.
2 Add in the shallots, garlic, ginger and candlenuts. Sauté for 2 minutes.
3 Stir in the soya sauce and add the coriander powder. Pour in the beef broth made in Step 1 and season lightly with salt. Taste and adjust.
4 Bring the soup to the boil, reduce the heat and simmer for 10 minutes only, to allow the flavour to be absorbed.
5 Stir in the lime juice, then remove the soup from the heat.
6 Pour the soup into a blender and run at high speed for 2-3 minutes.
7 Remove from the blender and ladle the soup into individual bowls. Garnish with the beef slices, the remaining peanuts, the tomatoes and lime rind.

PAPAYA SOUP

Sop Pepaya

PAPAYA SOUP

30 ml vegetable oil
20 g shallots (bawang merah), peeled, finely diced
5 g garlic, peeled, finely diced
10 g red chilies, seeded, finely diced
2 g bird's eye chilies, finely diced
2 g ginger, peeled, finely diced
2 g turmeric root, peeled, finely diced
10 g candlenuts, finely chopped
2 salam leaves
200 g young green papaya, peeled, seeded, cubed
l litre chicken stock (see page 24)
salt
16 unripe (white) papaya balls
20 ripe (yellow) papaya balls

1 Heat the vegetable oil in a shallow stockpot. Sauté the next 6 ingredients for 2-3 minutes without browning.
2 Add in the candlenuts and salam leaves and continue to sauté for another 2 minutes.
3 Add in the papaya and pour the chicken stock over the mixture. Season lightly with salt.
4 Bring the soup to the boil. Then reduce the heat and simmer for 10-15 minutes, stirring from time to time, until the papaya becomes soft.
5 Withdraw the pot from the heat. Discard the salam leaves.
6 Pour the soup into a blender and purée for 2-3 minutes at high speed.
7 Remove the soup from the blender, divide into 4 portions and garnish with the papaya balls.

CLEAR PRAWN SOUP WITH LEMON GRASS

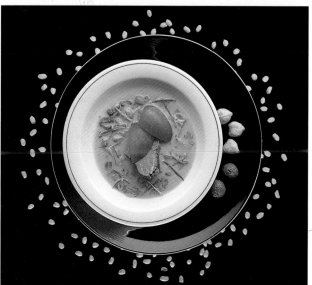

ASPARAGUS BEAN SOUP

MAKASSAR SOUP

APPETIZERS

Selada Bebek Danau Toba
DUCK BREAST TOBA

Lake Toba, a magnificent crater lake, lies in the highlands of Sumatra. Duck, a popular dish here, is frequently served with a fiery green chili sauce.

STEP 1: Fiery Green Chili Sauce
(Saus Bumbu Cabe Hijau)
   30 ml peanut oil
   40 g shallots (bawang merah), finely diced
   10 g garlic, finely diced
   100 g green chilies, seeded, finely diced
   1 lemon grass stalk
   10 g greater galangal, finely diced
   3 kaffir lime leaves
   40 g candlenuts, ground
   15 g turmeric powder
   60 ml tamarind water (see page 23)
   500 ml water
   salt

1   Heat the peanut oil in a frying pan. Sauté the shallots and garlic until they are light brown.
2   Add the chilies, lemon grass, greater galangal and kaffir lime leaves, and continue to sauté for 2 minutes.
3   Add in the ground candlenuts and turmeric powder. Continue to sauté for another 5 minutes.
4   Turn down the heat, stir in the tamarind water and simmer over a low flame for approximately 15-20 minutes, stirring frequently.
5   Pour in the water, increase the heat and cook until the sauce thickens, approximately 6-9 minutes.
6   Remove the lemon grass and lime leaves, and let the sauce cool. Yields 675 ml.

STEP 2: Cooking and Presentation
   2 x 250 g duck breasts
   salt
   pepper
   30 ml peanut oil
   250 ml Fiery Green Chili Sauce, cold
   80 g oyster or button mushrooms, sautéed in butter

1   Season the duck breasts with the salt and pepper.
2   Heat the peanut oil in a frying pan and place the duck breasts in the hot oil, skin side down.
3   Fry the duck over medium heat evenly on each side for approximately 5 minutes. Remove the meat from the pan and let it cool for 5 minutes.
4   Spread a layer of the sauce on each plate.
5   Slice the duck breasts and arrange the slices on the plates.
6   Garnish with the mushrooms.

Ikan Lidah Isi Tahu Sumedang
SOLE FILLETS ON RICA-RICA SAUCE

This dish is a combination of fish and sauce served hot with a cold garnish.

STEP 1: Poached Sole Fillets
   160 g sole meat, boned, diced
   80 g prawns, shelled, deveined
   80 g lobster meat
   5 g garlic, peeled, finely diced
   10 g shallots (bawang merah), peeled, finely diced
   1 egg
   60 ml cream (33% fat)
   salt
   ground white pepper
   20 g firm white beancurd, diced finely
   8 x 60 g sole fillets
   250 ml fish stock (see page 24)

1   Mince or grind the sole meat, prawns and lobster meat finely and put in a chilled bowl.
2   Work in the garlic, shallots, egg, cream, salt and pepper with a wooden spatula.
3   Fold in the beancurd and chill this mixture in a refrigerator for 2 hours.
4   Put the sole fillets, skin side down, on a board and spread with the seafood beancurd mixture. Fold the fillets into triangular shapes.
5   Place the fillets in a shallow pan just large enough to hold them.
6   Pour in the fish stock and cover with greased parchment or waxed paper.
7   Poach the fillets in the stock gently for 12-15 minutes. Remove from the heat and keep the fish warm in the stock.

STEP 2: Garnish and Presentation
   20 g red chilies, seeded, finely diced
   40 g yam bean, peeled, diced
   60 g mango, peeled, diced
   20 sweet basil leaves (kemangi)
   125 ml Rica-rica Sauce, hot (see page 39)

1   Mix the red chilies, yam bean and mango together to make a salad.
2   Place 2 poached sole fillets on each plate.
3   Garnish with the chili, yam bean and mango salad, the basil leaves and hot sauce.

Pepes Jamur

MUSHROOM AND CHICKEN EN COCOTTE

Most mushrooms in Java grow near Mount Dieng, where the climate is wet and humid. The traditional type, *jamur merang*, grows on old rice stalks left in padi fields after harvest. This is a recipe for a warm appetizer served on a cold spicy sauce.

STEP 1: Mushroom and Chicken Cocotte
4 white cabbage leaves
100 g chicken breast meat, cut into strips
50 g straw or button mushrooms, cut into strips
10 g shallots (bawang merah), peeled, cut into strips
10 g red chilies, seeded, cut into strips
1 egg, whisked
5 ml freshly squeezed lime juice
salt

1. Blanch the cabbage leaves in boiling water for 2 minutes. Remove and dip immediately into iced water.
2. Preheat the oven to 250°C. Then line 4 small soufflé moulds or coffee cups with 1 cabbage leaf each.
3. In a bowl, mix together the chicken strips, mushrooms, shallots and chilies.
4. Stir in the egg and lime juice. Season with the salt.
5. Pour the mixture into the moulds or cups and "cover" with the overhanging cabbage leaves.
6. Place the moulds in a roasting pan and pour in enough hot water to reach halfway up the moulds. Poach in the preheated oven for approximately 25 minutes.
7. Remove the moulds from the pan. Keep them warm.

STEP 2: Salad
20 g red chilies, seeded, cut into strips
20 g turnip, peeled, cut into strips
20 g carrot, peeled, cut into strips
20 g cucumber, seeded, cut into strips
20 g white cabbage, shredded
30 ml peanut oil
30 ml freshly squeezed lime juice
salt

1. Blanch the red chilies, turnips and carrots in boiling water for 2 minutes. Cool in iced water and drain.
2. Combine all the vegetables in a bowl.
3. Add in the peanut oil and lime juice, mix well and season with the salt.

STEP 3: Sauce and Presentation
20 g red chilies, seeded, diced finely
120 g mangoes, cubed
125 ml sugar syrup (see page 23)
45 ml freshly squeezed lime juice
30 ml water
salt

1. Combine all the ingredients together and blend for 3-4 minutes until smooth. Serve the sauce cold. Yields 250 ml.
2. Flip the cooked mushroom and chicken mixture out of the moulds and cut each in half. Pour some cold sauce on each plate and arrange 2 halves on the sauce.
3. Garnish with the salad made in Step 2.

Udang dengan Daun Pakis dan Saus Tauco

PRAWNS ON FERNTOP SALAD

Pakis are delicate fernlike plants which grow wild in the highlands of Bali, Java and particularly Sumatra. Here they are used in a recipe of our own invention. It is served cold.

STEP 1: Steamed Wrapped Prawns
100 g white perch or bass meat
100 g prawn meat
20 g shallots (bawang merah), peeled, finely diced
10 g garlic, peeled, finely diced
125 ml cream (33% fat)
salt
1 egg
20 g firm white beancurd, diced
20 g beansprouts, cleaned
8 x 100 g prawns, shelled, deveined

1. Chop the fish and prawn meat into fine pieces and put into a blender with the shallots, garlic and cream. Season with salt and blend until smooth, approximately 2-3 minutes.
2. Add in the egg and continue to blend for 30 seconds more.
3. Put this mixture into a cold bowl. Add the diced beancurd and beansprouts. Mix well with a wooden spatula.
4. Press this mixture around each prawn.
5. Place the prawns on a tray and steam them for 15 minutes. Remove from the steamer.

STEP 2: Salad and Presentation
40 g carrot, cut into strips, blanched
40 g beansprouts, blanched
40 g red chilies, cut into strips, blanched
185 ml Sumatran Black Bean Sauce, cold (see page 35)
20 ferntops

1. Mix the blanched vegetables with 60 ml of the Sumatran Black Bean Sauce to make a salad.
2. Pour a layer of the remaining sauce on each plate.
3. Place a portion of the salad on the sauce.
4. Slice the prawns and arrange the slices on the plates.
5. Garnish with the ferntops.

CHICKEN BREAST WITH FERNTOPS

Selada Ayam Bali
BALI CHICKEN SALAD

500 ml chicken stock (see page 24)
2 x 150 g boneless chicken breasts, skinned
20 g sweet basil leaves (kemangi)
20 g kaffir lime leaves
20 g long bean leaves
160 ml Bali Sauce, cold (see page 27)
20 g red chilies, finely diced

1 Heat up the chicken stock in a pan.
2 Gently poach the chicken breasts in the hot stock for 20 minutes. Remove the pan from the heat and let the meat cool in the stock.
3 Remove the breasts from the stock when cooled. Pat dry with a paper towel and cut each breast into 6-8 slices.
4 Clean and wash all the leaves. Put them in a bowl with the chicken. Add in the Bali Sauce and toss.
5 Arrange the leaves and meat on each plate. Sprinkle with the diced chilies.

BALI CHICKEN SALAD

Ayam Isi Tauge Bumbu Bali
CHICKEN BREAST WITH FERNTOPS

STEP 1: Beansprout Stuffing
250 g chicken meat, diced
60 ml cream (33% fat)
1 egg
10 g red chilies, seeded, diced
20 g beansprouts, cleaned
salt

1 Mince or grind the chicken meat until fine.
2 Place the minced chicken meat in a blender with the cream, and process for 1-2 minutes. Gradually add in the egg and blend together for a short while until mixture becomes very fine and smooth.
3 Put the chicken mixture in a bowl, add in the chilies and beansprouts and stir well with a wooden spatula. Season with the salt and set aside.

STEP 2: Poached Chicken Breasts
4 x 100 g boneless chicken breasts, skinned
500 ml chicken stock (see page 24)

1 Place the chicken breasts skin side down on a flat surface and make an incision with a small pointed knife in the breast from the breast tip to the wing
2 Fill a piping bag with the stuffing made in Step 1 and pipe it into the breasts until they have plumped out. Secure the incision to prevent the stuffing from coming out.
3 Place the stuffed breasts in a pan and pour in the chicken stock. Poach the breasts gently for approximately 15 minutes.
4 Take the pan from the heat and let the chicken breasts cool in the stock.
5 When cool, remove the breasts and slice evenly.

STEP 3: Garnish and Presentation
4 leeks
8-12 fern stalks with leaves and stems
125 ml Bali Sauce, cold (see page 27)

1 Blanch the leeks and ferns in boiling water for 2 minutes. Cool immediately by plunging into iced water.
2 Spread a layer of the cold Bali Sauce on each plate.
3 Place a leek on the sauce.
4 Arrange slices of the chicken breast next to the leek and garnish with a rolled fern stalk.

CALAMARE WITH CUCUMBER SAUCE

MANADONESE LOBSTER SALAD

DUCK BREAST ON BITTER GOURD SALAD

Lalaban Dada Bebek dengan Pare

DUCK BREAST ON BITTER GOURD SALAD

STEP 1: Roast Duck Breast

30 ml peanut oil
20 g shallots (bawang merah), peeled, diced
10 g garlic, peeled, diced
10 g lemon grass stalk, diced
5 g greater galangal, peeled, diced
2 g freshly ground cloves
2 g turmeric powder
12 sweet basil leaves (kemangi), chopped
2 x 300 g boneless duck breasts
salt

1 Heat the peanut oil in a frying pan. Sauté the shallots, garlic, lemon grass and greater galangal in the hot oil for 2-4 minutes until light brown.
2 Add the ground cloves, turmeric powder and basil leaves and continue to sauté for 2 minutes. Remove the pan from the heat and let the marinade cool.
3 Brush the marinade evenly onto both sides of the duck breasts. Let the meat marinate in the refrigerator for 5 hours. Then preheat the oven to 280°C.
4 Roast the duck breasts in the preheated oven for 5 minutes on each side. Remove from the oven and keep warm.

NOTE: If 300 g boneless duck breasts are not available, increase the number of breasts to make up the amount.

STEP 2: Spicy Peanut Sauce (Saus Bumbu Kacang)

30 ml peanut oil
100 g raw peanuts, shelled
60 g red chilies, seeded, diced
15 g bird's eye chilies, seeded, diced
45 g candlenuts, ground
5 g lesser galangal, peeled, chopped
15 g garlic, peeled, finely chopped
15 g shallots (bawang merah), peeled, finely chopped
60 ml freshly squeezed lime juice

1 Heat half of the peanut oil in a flat pan.
2 Add the peanuts and fry them until they are light brown, approximately 5 minutes. Take them out and drain off the excess oil.
3 Heat up the remaining peanut oil in the pan. Add the chilies, candlenuts, lesser galangal, garlic and shallots. Sauté for 3-5 minutes until light brown. Remove from the pan.
4 Combine the peanuts with the sautéed mixture and mince or grind this until fine.
5 Put the ground mixture in a frying pan, stir in the lime juice and boil for 5 minutes. (Use only freshly squeezed lime juice — bottled juice is too strong.) Then remove the sauce from the heat and let it cool. Yields 325 ml.

STEP 3: Salad and Presentation

40 g bitter gourd
80 g young coconut meat, cut into strips
20 sweet basil leaves (kemangi)
30 ml freshly squeezed lime juice
salt
160 ml Spicy Peanut Sauce, cold

1 Slice the bitter gourd into rounds. Take out the seeds and keep them, then blanch the bitter gourd for 1-2 minutes.
2 Combine all the ingredients, except the sauce, in a salad bowl. Season with salt.
3 Arrange portions of the salad on individual plates. Sprinkle the bitter gourd seeds over the salad.
4 Slice the duck breasts and arrange the slices next to the salad. Serve the sauce on the side.

Cumi-cumi dan Saus Ketimun

CALAMARE WITH CUCUMBER SAUCE

STEP 1: Cucumber Sauce

90 ml palm wine
10 g shallots (bawang merah), peeled, finely diced
375 ml fish stock (see page 24)
200 g cucumbers, peeled, seeded, cut
salt
5 ml freshly squeezed lime juice

1 Mix the palm wine with the shallots and bring to the boil in a pan. Boil until the liquid has reduced to two-thirds.
2 Pour in the fish stock and reduce again to two-thirds.
3 Blanch the cucumber in boiling salt water for 2 minutes. Then place in a blender with the palm wine mixture.
4 Blend together until well mixed and fine. Season with salt and the lime juice. Serve the sauce hot. Yields 500 ml.

STEP 2: Cooking and Presentation

15 ml peanut oil
240 g squid, body tube only, cleaned with ink sac removed,
        cut into strips
2 g ginger, peeled, finely diced
5 g garlic, peeled, finely diced
10 g shallots (bawang merah), peeled, finely diced
5 g red chilies, seeded, finely diced
5 g green chilies, seeded, finely diced
salt
160 ml Cucumber Sauce, hot
4 small cucumbers, each carved or turned into 12 pieces

1 Heat the oil in a frying pan. Sauté the squid together with the ginger, garlic, shallots and chilies in the hot oil for 3-5 minutes. Season with salt and keep hot.
2 Pour some of the hot sauce onto each plate. If desired, sprinkle on some diced cucumber skin.
3 Arrange a portion of the squid on the plates and garnish with the turned cucumbers.

Selada Udang Karang Gohu

MANADONESE LOBSTER SALAD

STEP 1: Papaya Salad
180 g young green papaya, peeled — half, cut into strips;
    half, carved or turned
5 g ginger, peeled, finely diced
20 g red chilies, seeded, finely diced
15 g sugar
30 ml white vinegar
30 ml water
salt

1   Combine all the ingredients and season with the salt. Let the salad marinate in the refrigerator for 2 hours.
2   Use a sieve or colander to drain off the liquid from the salad before serving.

STEP 2: Lobster Simmered in Coconut
250 ml coconut milk (see page 22)
5 g turmeric powder
5 g coriander powder
20 g shallots (bawang merah), peeled, finely diced
20 g leeks, finely diced
320 g shelled lobster (about 2 tails or 1 cold-water lobster)

1   Bring the coconut milk to the boil in a saucepan.
2   Add the turmeric, coriander, shallots and leeks and boil for 2 minutes. Reduce the heat to simmering point.
3   Put the lobster in the coconut milk and let it simmer for 15 minutes. The lobster meat should turn a light yellow colour.
4   Remove the pan from the heat and allow the lobster to cool in the liquid.
5   Then remove the lobster from the liquid and slice the meat evenly.

STEP 3: Garnish and Presentation
125 ml Spicy Bajak Sauce, hot (see page 27)
20 kenikir leaves

1   Put 2-3 tablespoons of the hot sauce on each plate.
2   Arrange the papaya salad made in Step 1 on the sauce.
3   Place the slices of lobster next to the salad.
4   Garnish with the kenikir leaves.

Selada Ikan Muara

SEAFOOD SALAD MUARA

STEP 1: Baked Seafood
15 ml vegetable oil
20 g shallots (bawang merah), peeled, finely diced
5 g garlic, peeled, finely diced
30 g candlenuts, ground
10 g brown sugar (gula Jawa)
15 g turmeric powder
30 ml water
salt
160 g perch or white bass fillets
160 g pomfret fillets
4 x 50 g prawns, shelled, deveined
86 g squid, only the body tube, washed, cleaned, ink sac
    removed, cut into rings

1   Heat the vegetable oil in a frying pan and sauté the shallots and garlic for 2-3 minutes.
2   Add in the candlenuts, brown sugar and turmeric powder. Continue to sauté for 2 minutes more.
3   Pour in the water, season with salt, then remove from the heat and let the marinade cool.
4   Preheat the oven to 350°C.
5   Cut 4 pieces of aluminium foil large enough to wrap up each type of fish or seafood. Brush the foil lightly with oil.
6   Place each type of seafood separately on the pieces of greased foil and brush the marinade evenly on all the seafood pieces.
7   Fold each piece of foil over its contents, forming a neat, tightly-sealed package.
8   Bake the wrapped seafood packages in the pre-heated oven as follows: perch or bass, approximately 8-10 minutes; pomfret, approximately 6 minutes; prawn, approximately 6 minutes; squid, approximately 10 minutes.
9   Open the packages and let the seafood cool. Slice the fish.

STEP 2: Salad and Presentation
80 g long beans, parboiled, cut into strips
80 g beansprouts, cleaned
20 g red chilies, seeded, cut into strips
90 ml Spicy Rujak Sauce (see page 39)
20 sweet basil leaves (kemangi)

1   Mix the long beans, beansprouts and chilies together to make a salad.
2   Place a portion of the salad on each plate.
3   Arrange the fish and seafood pieces on the salad.
4   Pour some of the sauce over half of the fish and seafood pieces and leave the other half without sauce.
5   Garnish with sweet basil leaves.

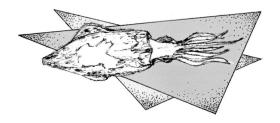

PIGEON BREAST ON PEANUT SALAD

Burung Dara dengan Selada Kacang

PIGEON BREAST ON PEANUT SALAD

STEP 1: Roast Pigeon Breasts
30 ml peanut oil
4 x 50 g boneless pigeon breasts
salt
pepper
4 x 20 g chicken livers

1   Preheat the oven to 250°C.
2   Heat 20 ml of the peanut oil in a flat pan.
3   Season the pigeon breasts with salt and pepper and brown them on both sides in the hot oil.
4   Put the pan into the preheated oven and roast the pigeon breasts until they are done as liked. (It will take about 5 minutes for medium.) While roasting, baste the meat frequently to keep it moist.
5   Remove the breasts from the pan and keep warm.

6   Season the chicken livers with salt and pepper.
7   Heat the remaining peanut oil in a pan and sauté the chicken livers in the hot oil for 3 minutes. Remove and keep warm.

STEP 2: Salad and Presentation
120 g fern stems, blanched, chopped
20 g peanuts, roasted, chopped
180 ml Peanut Sauce, cold (see page 29)
10 g red chilies, diced

1   Combine the fern stems, peanuts and 60 ml of the Peanut Sauce in a bowl. Mix well.
2   Spoon some of the remaining sauce on each plate and place a portion of the ferns and peanuts on it.
3   Slice the warm pigeon breasts and chicken livers. Arrange sices of the meat on the cold salad.
4   Sprinkle with the diced chilies.

Squid on Mango Coconut Sauce

Red Snapper Fillets with Mussels

Freshwater Prawn Cirebon

Kukus Cumi-Cumi dengan Saus Mangga

SQUID ON MANGO COCONUT SAUCE

This dish can be served as an appetizer, a salad, or even as a main course.

STEP 1: Poached Stuffed Squid

160 g snapper fillets, cubed
125 ml cream (33% fat)
10 g dried black wood fungus, soaked in warm water for 1 hour, cut into strips
1 red chili, seeded, diced finely
10 sweet basil leaves (kemangi), cut into strips
½ egg white
salt
4 squid, body tube only, washed, ink sac removed
500 ml fish stock (see page 24)

1   Put the cubed fish fillets in a blender with the cream. Blend until the mixture is silky.
2   Put the mixture in a cold bowl and stir in the black wood fungus, chili, sweet basil leaves and egg white. Mix well and season with salt.
3   Fill the squid with the fish and mushroom mixture. Secure the opening with a toothpick.
4   Preheat the oven to 180°C.
5   Warm the fish stock in a pan, add in the squid and cover with a buttered piece of parchment paper.
6   Poach the squid gently for 10 minutes in the preheated oven. The squid must be cooked over low heat and not for a very long time, otherwise the meat becomes rubbery.
7   Remove the pan from the oven and keep the squid warm in the stock.

STEP 2: Mango Coconut Sauce (Saus Mangga)

120 g mango flesh
60 g young coconut flesh
15 ml freshly squeezed lime juice
salt

1   Put the mango, coconut and lime juice in a blender and process until silky.
2   Remove from the blender and season with salt. Heat the sauce. Since mango spoils quickly, don't prepare this sauce too early. Yields 125 ml.

STEP 3: Garnish and Presentation

16 pieces ripe mango, turned or carved
4 wood fungus, soaked in warm water for 1 hour, sliced
120 g young coconut, scooped out with a spoon

1   Remove the squid from the fish stock and pat dry with paper towels. Slice each squid into 4-5 pieces.
2   Put 2 tablespoons of the Mango Coconut Sauce on each plate.
3   Arrange the squid slices on the sauce.
4   Garnish with the mango, wood fungus and young coconut.

Kakap Merah dengan Kerang Hijau

RED SNAPPER FILLETS WITH MUSSELS

STEP 1: Poached Snapper Fillets

120 g mussels
480 g red snapper fillets
10 sweet basil leaves (kemangi), cut into strips
salt
500 ml fish stock (see page 24)

1   Rinse the mussels, scrub off the beard and steam them until the shells open, approximately 3-5 minutes. Discard any which do not open. Rinse off any sand and extract the flesh from the shell. Clean and keep a few of the shells.
2   Place the snapper fillets side by side, skin side down, on a piece of cheesecloth.
3   Place a mussel in the middle of each fish fillet and sprinkle with the strips of basil leaves. Season with salt. Save the extra mussels for garnishing the dish.
4   Roll all the fillets in the cheesecloth into a sausage shape and tie the ends of the cloth with string.
5   Place the wrapped fillets in a pan just large enough to hold them. Pour in the fish stock.
6   Place the pan over low heat and simmer gently for 10 minutes.
7   Withdraw the pan from the heat and let the fillets cool in the stock.
8   Remove the roll from the stock. Discard the cheesecloth and slice the fillets.

STEP 2: Presentation

250 ml Pesmol Sauce, hot (see page 30)
20 sweet basil leaves (kemangi)

1   Pour some Pesmol Sauce on each plate.
2   Arrange the sliced fillets on the plate.
3   Garnish with the basil leaves and the remaining mussels and the cleaned shells.

Ikan Mas Bumbu Rujak

GOLDEN CARP WITH SPICY RUJAK SAUCE

500 ml fish stock (see page 24)
480 g golden carp fillets
12 cashewnut leaves, cut into fine strips
60 ml Spicy Rujak Sauce, cold (see page 39)
20 g young coconut meat, cut into strips
20 g ripe mango flesh, cut into strips
40 g water apples, cut into strips

1   Heat up the fish stock in a saucepan. Poach the golden carp fillets in the stock for 8-10 minutes
2   Remove the pan from the heat and let the fillets cool in the stock.
3   Arrange 3 cashewnut leaves on each plate.
4   Place a portion of the fillets on the plate and top with the cold sauce.
5   Garnish with the strips of fruit.

Udang Galah Sungging
FRESHWATER PRAWN CIREBON

Udang galah are popular all over Indonesia, and in Cirebon, in Java, the rivers are still filled with these prawns. In this recipe, the steamed prawns and Pesmol Sauce are served hot while the salad and Rujak Sauce are cold.

STEP 1: Steamed Prawns
>*30 g prawns, cleaned, shelled, finely chopped*
>*30 g white bass or snapper meat, boned, diced*
>*1 egg*
>*125 ml cream (33% fat)*
>*20 g carrot, peeled, finely diced*
>*10 g red chilies, finely diced*
>*10 g stringbeans, finely diced*
>*20 g celery sticks, finely diced*
>*10 x 50 g freshwater or jumbo prawns, heads removed,*
>   *deveined, shelled except for the tail*

1 Put the chopped prawns and fish meat in a blender. Process until very fine.
2 Gradually add in the egg, cream, carrots, chilies, stringbeans and celery and process until smooth.
3 Press about 30-50 g of the blended mixture on each freshwater prawn, following the contours of the prawn. Wrap each prawn in greased plastic wrap (cling film).
4 Steam the prawns for 10 minutes. Remove from the steamer, take off the plastic wrap and keep warm.

STEP 2: Salad and Presentation
>*30 g water chestnuts, diced*
>*30 g young green mango, diced*
>*20 g pineapple, diced*
>*20 g red chilies, diced*
>*20 ml Rujak Sauce, cold (see page 30)*
>*60 ml Pesmol Sauce, hot (see page 30)*
>*32 sweet basil leaves (kemangi)*

1 Combine the water chestnuts, young mango, pineapple and chilies into a salad. Toss lightly with the Rujak Sauce.
2 Put 3 teaspoons of hot Pesmol Sauce on each plate.
3 Slice each prawn in half and arrange the halves on the sauce.
4 Garnish with the basil leaves and the cold salad.

Selada Kakap dan Belut
SNAPPER AND EEL SALAD

In the night, farmers in Java and Bali go to their rice fields in hope of catching eels. Although smaller than the eels raised in pens, these wild eels are just as delicious. This salad is fiery hot in taste.

>*100 g white snapper fillets*
>*100 g red snapper fillets*
>*100 ml fish stock (see page 24)*
>*100 g smoked eel*
>*100 ml Dabu-dabu Sauce, cold (see page 38)*
>*80 g stringbeans, cut in strips*
>*50 g red chilies, cut in strips*
>*12 long bean leaves*
>*12 sweet basil leaves (kemangi)*

1 Preheat the oven to 180°C.
2 Poach the snapper fillets in the fish stock in the preheated oven for approximately 15 minutes. Remove the fish from the stock and let it cool.
3 Cut the fish and smoked eel into strips.
4 Pour a little Dabu-dabu Sauce onto each plate.
5 Toss the stringbeans, red chilies and long bean leaves together to make a salad, and arrange on the plates.
6 Place the strips of fish and eel on the plates next to the salad and garnish with the basil leaves.

Udang Raja dengan Acar Kuning
LOBSTER WITH YELLOW PICKLES

STEP 1: Boiled Lobster
>*1 litre water*
>*5 g salt*
>*150 g onions, peeled, cubed*
>*200 g carrots, peeled, cubed*
>*1 lemon grass stalk, bruised*
>*2 x 300 g spiny or rock lobster tails, or 1 x 600 g cold-water*
>   *lobster*

1 Put the water, salt, onions, carrots and lemon grass in a stockpot and bring to the boil.
2 Add the lobster and boil for 10 minutes.
3 Remove the lobster from the pot and discard the stock. Let the lobster cool, then break the lobster meat out of the shell and cut it into even slices Chill.

STEP 2: Garnish and Presentation
>*4 portions Yellow Pickles, cold (see page 126)*
>*16-20 sweet basil leaves (kemangi)*
>*125 ml Spicy Bajak Sauce, cold (see page 27)*

1 Place a portion of the pickles in the middle of each plate.
2 Arrange the cold lobster slices on the plate and garnish with the sweet basil leaves.
3 Spoon a little of the sauce onto the lobster slices.

STRINGBEAN SALAD WITH MUSSELS

Selada Buncis Karang Hijau

STRINGBEAN SALAD WITH MUSSELS

Mussels are found in the seabeds to the east and west of Jakarta. The flavour of these mussels is less strong than that of mussels found in colder waters.

45 ml peanut oil
20 ml palm wine
40 g shallots (bawang merah), peeled, finely diced
salt
2 g black peppercorns, crushed
10 ml fish stock (see page 24)
200 g mussels, cleaned, shelled
200 g stringbeans
100 g onions, peeled

1 Combine the first 5 ingredients in a bowl to make the vinaigrette. Mix well using a whisk. Chill.
2 Heat the fish stock in a small saucepan. Blanch the mussels in the hot stock for 2 minutes and leave them aside to cool.
3 Blanch the stringbeans and onions in boiling water for 1-2 minutes, then plunge them immediately into iced water, to retain crispness.
4 Cut the onions and some of the beans into strips and arrange them on individual plates with the whole beans, as illustrated. Pour the vinaigrette over the vegetables.
5 Garnish with the mussels.

NOTE: If red onions are available, they may be used to add colour to the dish.

WRAPPED PRAWNS

Selada Udang Bungkus Tahu

WRAPPED PRAWNS

STEP 1: Steamed Wrapped Prawns
100 g white perch or grouper, boned, skinned, diced
40 g prawns, shelled, deveined, diced
10 g shallots (bawang merah), peeled, finely diced
salt
80 ml cream (33% fat)
1 egg
60 g firm white or yellow beancurd, diced
6 x 60 g prawns, shelled, deveined

1   Mince or grind the diced fish and prawns finely, then put in a blender with the shallots and season with salt. Run the blender for 1 minute.
2   Gradually add in the cream and blend for another 30 seconds. With the blender still running, slowly add in the egg. Stop when the mixture is smooth.

3   Spoon the mixture into a bowl and fold in the beancurd cubes with a wooden spatula.
4   Press some of the fish beancurd mixture all round each prawn, then place them in a steamer. Cover with a lid and steam for about 15 minutes. Remove the prawns and keep them warm.

STEP 2: Garnish and Presentation
125 ml Sour Turmeric Sauce, hot (see page 35)
40 g firm white or yellow beancurd, cut into leaf shapes
20 g red chilies, cut into diamonds
20 g yam bean or water chestnuts, cut into leaf shapes

1   Put a layer of the hot sauce on each plate.
2   Slice the prawns evenly and arrange a portion of the slices on the sauce.
3   Garnish with the beancurd, chili and yam bean pieces.

Ikan Kembang Saus Bumbu Bali
MACKEREL ON BALI SAUCE

STEP 1: Baked Mackerel Fillets
4 x 120 g mackerel fillets, halved
15 ml peanut oil
15 g shallots (bawang merah), peeled, finely diced
5 g garlic, peeled, finely diced
60 ml chili juice (see page 23)
60 ml tomato juice
2 kaffir lime leaves
5 ml tamarind water (see page 23)
salt

1   Place the fillets in a shallow dish, skin side down.
2   Mix the remaining ingredients together and sprinkle this over the fillets. Let them marinate overnight in the refrigerator.
3   Preheat the oven to 300°C.
4   Brush a baking tray with a little peanut oil and heat it in the oven.
5   Place the fillets, skin side down, on the hot tray. Bake them in the oven for approximately 10 minutes.
6   Remove the tray from the oven and lift the fillets from the tray. Keep them warm.

STEP 2: Garnish and Presentation
20 g potatoes, boiled, diced
20 g pumpkin, boiled, diced
10 g red chilies, diced
1 kaffir lime leaf, finely shredded
120 ml Bali Sauce, hot (see page 27)

1   Combine the potatoes, pumpkin, red chilies and kaffir lime leaf together. Mix well and chill in the refrigerator.
2   Place the mackerel fillets on individual plates.
3   Garnish with the salad and dab with the hot sauce.

Dada Ayam Isi Tahu dengan Daun Kol
BEANCURD-STUFFED CHICKEN BREAST

Westerners may not think of Indonesia as a source of cabbage, but in fact much of the cabbage used in Southeast Asia is exported from the north Sumatran city of Medan, where the vegetable grows in abundance on Brastagi Mountain.

STEP 1: Chicken Beancurd Stuffing
160 g chicken breast meat
125 ml cream (33% fat)
1 egg, whisked
50 g firm white beancurd, finely diced
10 g red chilies, finely diced
5 g garlic, finely diced
salt

1   Dice the chicken meat and grind or mince it finely. Then, put it in a blender and process until very fine.
2   In a cold bowl, combine the chicken, cream and egg. Mix well.
3   Add in the beancurd and red chilies, and season with the garlic and salt. Set the stuffing mixture aside.

STEP 2: Steamed Chicken Breasts
2 x 140 g boneless chicken breasts, skinned
10 g shallots (bawang merah), peeled, sliced, deep-fried
3 g kaffir lime leaves, cut into fine strips
4-5 white cabbage leaves, blanched

1   With a small pointed knife, cut a lengthwise opening along the thin edge of the chicken breasts.
2   Put half of the stuffing made in Step 1 into a piping bag and pipe through the incision in the chicken breasts until they become round and full.
3   Spread the remaining stuffing on top of the chicken breasts to a thickness of 1 cm.
4   Sprinkle the deep-fried shallots and lime leaf julienne on top of the chicken breasts.
5   Wrap each chicken breast in blanched cabbage leaves. Place them in a steamer.
6   Steam the chicken for approximately 10-15 minutes. Remove from the heat and keep warm.

STEP 3: Salad and Presentation
40 g water apples, diced
40 g young green mango, peeled, diced
40 g water chestnuts, peeled, diced
40 g young green papaya, peeled, diced
15 g red chilies, finely diced
20 g sweet potato, finely diced
60 ml Rujak Sauce, cold (see page 30)
8 fresh whole kaffir lime leaves
125 ml Rica-rica Sauce, cold (see page 39)
3 g kaffir lime leaves, cut into fine strips

1   Combine the water apple, mango, water chestnut, green papaya, red chili and sweet potato pieces with the Rujak Sauce into a salad. Set this aside.
2   Cut each chicken breast into 4 triangles.
3   Put 2 whole lime leaves on each plate.
4   Use the Rica-rica Sauce and the salad to garnish each plate.
5   Top the salad with the lime leaf julienne.

NOTE: If kaffir lime leaves are not available, substitute sweet basil leaves.

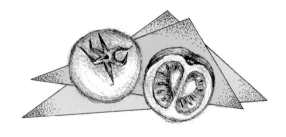

Pepes Ikan Emas Darawati

CARP WITH DARAWATI SAUCE

The Darawati area near Bandung in west Java is famous for its fish ponds. Virtually anyone who can afford it has one, even if it is half a hectare or less.

STEP 1: Baked Carp Fillets
20 g shallots (bawang merah), peeled, finely chopped
5 g garlic, peeled, finely chopped
20 g candlenuts, ground
5 g lemon grass stalk, finely diced
2 kaffir lime leaves, shredded
10 sweet basil leaves (kemangi), cut into strips
salt
400 g carp fillet, skinned, cut into 4 pieces

1   Blend the first 7 ingredients together and spread this mixture evenly on top of the fish fillets. Let the fish marinate overnight in the refrigerator.
2   Preheat the oven to 300°C.
3   Take the fish out of the marinade and put one fillet on top of a second with the marinated sides facing inwards.
4   Wrap each pair of fillets tightly in oiled aluminium foil and place the wrapped fillets on a baking tray.
5   Bake the fillets in the preheated oven for approximately 10 minutes. Then remove the fillets from the oven, unwrap the aluminium foil and let the fish cool completely.

STEP 2: Darawati Sauce (Saus Darawati)
15 ml peanut oil
15 g shallots (bawang merah), peeled, finely diced
5 g garlic, peeled, finely diced
1 lemon grass stalk, finely diced
5 g ginger, peeled, finely diced
30 g candlenuts, ground
5 g shrimp paste
125 ml chili juice (see page 23)
250 ml coconut milk (see page 22)
5 g tamarind pulp
6 sweet basil leaves (kemangi)
salt

1   Heat the oil in a frying pan and sauté the shallots, garlic, lemon grass and ginger for 3-4 minutes without browning.
2   Stir in the candlenuts and shrimp paste, and continue to sauté for a further 3 minutes until the shrimp paste has been absorbed in the mixture.
3   Add the chili juice, coconut milk, tamarind pulp and basil leaves, and season lightly with salt. Bring the mixture to the boil and let it cook slowly.
4   Remove from the heat as soon as the sauce begins to thicken. Leave it to cool. Yields 375 ml.

STEP 3: Garnish and Presentation
40 g shallots (bawang merah), peeled
125 ml Darawati Sauce, cold
80 g beansprouts, cleaned
10 g turmeric leaves, cut into very fine strips

1   Blanch the shallots in boiling water for 3 minutes. Remove and let them cool.
2   Pour a layer of Darawati Sauce on each plate.
3   Slice the fish fillets and place the slices on the sauce.
4   Garnish with the blanched shallots, the beansprouts and turmeric leaves.

Makanan Laut Pantai Selatan

SOUTH BEACH SEAFOOD MEDLEY

STEP 1: Sautéed Seafood
80 g white perch or snapper fillets, skinned
80 g pomfret, skinned, boned
80 g shelled spiny or rock lobster (approximately 1 tail)
80 g prawns, shelled, deveined
5 g turmeric powder
2 g coriander powder
5 g shallots (bawang merah), peeled, finely diced
5 g garlic, peeled, finely diced
125 ml coconut milk (see page 22)
30 ml peanut oil
salt

1   Cut the perch or snapper fillet, pomfret and lobster into medallions. Place these in a shallow dish with the prawns.
2   Sprinkle the seafood with the turmeric, coriander, shallots and garlic. Pour in the coconut milk, mix well and let the seafood marinate at room temperature for 30 minutes.
3   Drain off the coconut milk marinade.
4   Heat the peanut oil in a frying pan and sauté the seafood over high heat for 2-3 minutes until light brown. Remove from the pan.

STEP 2: Garnish and Presentation
160 g young green papaya, scooped out with a melon baller, blanched
160 g chayote, parboiled, sliced
4 sprigs kenikir leaves
125 ml Spicy Beansprout Sauce, hot (see page 30)

1   Arrange the blanched papaya and chayote in a circle on each plate.
2   Place the sautéed seafood in the centre.
3   Garnish with the kenikir leaves and the hot sauce.

NOTE: The kenikir leaves may be replaced with chervil or tarragon leaves.

FISH AND
SEAFOOD

FISH AND SEAFOOD

Ikan Lidah Pantai Florida

SOLE FLORIDA BEACH

STEP 1: Pan-fried Sole

> 4 x 320 g sole, head, skin and maw removed
> salt
> 40 g shallots (bawang merah), peeled, finely diced
> 40 g spring onions, peeled, finely diced
> 15 g turmeric powder
> 60 ml peanut oil

1. Season the sole with salt. Sprinkle the shallots, spring onions and turmeric powder on both sides of the fish.
2. Heat the peanut oil in a frying pan and fry the sole on each side for 3-4 minutes. Remove from the pan and keep warm.

STEP 2: Garnish and Presentation

> 15 ml peanut oil
> 20 g shallots (bawang merah), peeled, sliced into strips
> 10 g garlic, peeled, sliced into strips
> 20 g red chilies, seeded, sliced into strips
> 40 g Candied Mango, sliced into strips (see page 123)
> 2 cup leaves, sliced into strips
> 250 ml White Beancurd Sauce, hot (see page 39)

1. Heat the peanut oil in a frying pan. Add in the shallots, garlic and chilies and sauté for 2 minutes without browning.
2. Add the mango and cup leaves. Sauté for another minute and remove from the heat. Keep warm.
3. Spoon some of the White Beancurd Sauce on the plate.
4. Place a sole on the sauce and arrange the sautéed garnish next to the fish.

Lele Sembilang Tapos

CATFISH EEL TAPOS

STEP 1: Steamed Catfish Eel Fillets

> 8 x 80-100 g catfish eel fillets, skin on
> salt
> 30 ml Rica-Rica Sauce, cold (see page 39)
> 2 carrots, sliced thinly lengthwise into medium-sized pieces,. blanched

1. Place the catfish eel fillets, skin side down, on a flat surface. Season lightly with salt and brush with the Rica-rica Sauce. Top each fillet with the blanched carrot strips.
2. Roll each fillet into a tight roll and fasten the ends with a toothpick or skewer.
3. Place the rolled fillets in a steamer and steam for approximately 10-14 minutes. Remove and keep warm.

STEP 2: Garnish and Presentation

> 20 g candied snakefruit sections
> 20 g tomatoes, peeled, seeded, quartered
> 15 ml mango juice
> 160 ml Rica-rica Sauce, hot (see page 39)
> 16 sweet basil leaves (kemangi)

1. In a bowl, combine the snakefruit and tomatoes. Mix in the mango juice. Set this salad aside.
2. Pour some of the hot Rica-rica Sauce onto the centre of each plate.
3. Cut the steamed fillets into approximately 2-cm rolls and arrange these on top of the sauce.
4. Garnish with the fruit and tomato salad and the sweet basil leaves.

NOTE: After catfish eel has been steamed, its black skin tends to stick to utensils or fingers and will come off easily; to avoid this peeling off of skin, be sure to wet utensils or fingers with water.

Gurame Tauco Sumatra

CARP IN BLACK BEAN SAUCE

Most traditional fish farming was carried out in west Java and it is relatively new to west Sumatra. This particular dish has a fairly strong flavour.

> 600-750 g carp fillets, cut into 12 pieces of 50-60 g
> 15 ml freshly squeezed lime juice
> salt
> 15 ml vegetable oil
> 60 ml fish stock (see page 24)
> 180 ml Sumatran Black Bean Sauce (see page 35)
> 80 g cucumbers, turned or cut into wedges, blanched
> 15-20 long beans, blanched
> 3 red chilies, seeded, cut into diamonds

1. Place the fillets in a shallow dish and sprinkle with the lime juice and salt. (Do not use bottled lime juice — it is too strong in taste). Marinate for 20 minutes.
2. Heat the oil in a shallow frying pan. Sauté the carp fillets over high heat on both sides quickly for 1-2 minutes, to give them colour.
3. Drain off all the oil. Pour in the fish stock and Black Bean Sauce. Simmer the carp in this liquid over low heat for 2-4 minutes. Remove from the heat.
4. Heat more oil in another pan and sauté the blanched cucumbers for 2 minutes, tossing constantly. Season with salt. Remove and keep warm.
5. Set 3-4 carp pieces on each plate and garnish with the remaining sauce in the pan, the cucumbers, long beans and chilies.

Buntil Ikan Emas dan Daun Talas

GOLDEN CARP IN TARO LEAVES

The light bitterness of the taro and kenikir leaves is a pleasant contrast to the sweet sour sauce.

STEP 1: Steamed Golden Carp Fillets
8 x 50 g golden carp fillets
8 taro leaves large enough to wrap the fish fillets, blanched
salt
turmeric powder
5 g red chilies, seeded, finely diced
5 g green chilies, seeded, finely diced
2 kenikir leaves, finely chopped

1. Place each carp fillet on a blanched taro leaf.
2. Season the fillets with salt and turmeric powder.
3. Sprinkle the chilies and chopped kenikir leaves over the fish.
4. Fold the taro leaf over and wrap into tight packets.
5. Steam the fish in a steamer for approximately 6-8 minutes. Turn off the heat but keep the fish hot.

STEP 2: Garnish and Presentation
180 ml Sweet Sour Sauce, hot (see page 38)
½ cup kenikir leaves

1. Pour some of the hot sauce on each plate.
2. Slice the steamed fillets diagonally into triangles, or squares.
3. Arrange the fillets on top of the sauce and garnish with the kenikir leaves.

Ikan Sembilang Labu Siam Pedas

CATFISH EEL WITH WHITE BEANCURD

From the front the *ikan sembilang*, or *lele* as it is sometimes called, looks like a catfish; from the rear, it looks like an eel. Despite its ugly look, it is a tasty fish which inhabits the estuaries of many of Indonesia's rivers, flitting between the sea and the river. If *ikan sembilang* is not available, catfish may be used.

STEP 1: Catfish Eel Stuffing
120 g catfish eel fillets, minced
40 g prawns, shelled, deveined, minced
20 g shallots (bawang merah), peeled, finely diced
1 g turmeric powder
40 g bitter gourd, diced
20 g young coconut meat, diced
1 egg, whisked
60 ml cream (33% fat)
salt
ground white pepper

1. Place the minced fish and prawn in a blender. Add the shallots and season with the turmeric powder. Process for 2-3 minutes until smooth. Remove and place in a cold bowl.
2. Add the bitter gourd and coconut meat to the mixture and mix in the egg. Stir well with a wooden spoon.
3. Add in the cream slowly, then season with salt and pepper. Blend well with a wooden spatula until the cream is well mixed in.
4. Chill for 1 hour in a refrigerator before using.

STEP 2: Steamed Catfish Eel Fillets
8 x 100 g catfish eel fillets, leave black skin on
salt
10 g red chilies, seeded, cut into fine strips

1. Place 4 of the catfish eel fillets, skin side down, on a flat surface and season with salt.
2. With a spatula, spread the stuffing made in Step 1 evenly over the fillets. Sprinkle the chili strips over the stuffing, then place the remaining fillets, skin side up, over this and wrap tightly with kitchen plastic wrap.
3. Place the wrapped fillets in a steamer and steam for approximately 15-20 minutes. Switch off the steamer but keep the fish hot.

STEP 3: Spicy Chayote Sauce (Saus Labu Siam Pedas)
15 ml peanut oil
20 g shallots (bawang merah), peeled, finely diced
5 g garlic, peeled, finely diced
5 g greater galangal, peeled, finely diced
60 g red chilies, seeded, finely diced
1 salam leaf
-375 ml coconut milk (see page 22)
100 g chayote, parboiled, diced
salt

1. Heat the peanut oil in a saucepan. Sauté the shallots, garlic, greater galangal and chilies in the oil for 3-4 minutes until the ingredients are light brown.
2. Add in the salam leaf and coconut milk. Bring to the boil.
3. Add in the parboiled chayote. Season with some salt and reduce the heat. Simmer for 10 minutes.
4. Remove the pan from the heat and discard the salam leaf before pouring the mixture into a blender.
5. Blend the sauce for 2-3 minutes until smooth. Serve hot. Yields 500 ml.

STEP 4: Garnish and Presentation
180 ml Spicy Chayote Sauce, hot
80 g firm white beancurd, cubed or cut into shapes

1. Pour some of the hot sauce on each plate.
2. Place the steamed fish on the sauce.
3. Garnish with the beancurd.

CATFISH EEL TAPOS

GOLDEN CARP IN TARO LEAVES

CARP IN BLACK BEAN SAUCE

Catfish Eel with White Beancurd

Red Snapper from East Java

Fried Coconut Prawns

Udang Perkasa
FRIED COCONUT PRAWNS

The combination of fried spinach leaves, prawns and the light, sweet hot sauce is something new in Indonesian cuisine.

STEP 1: Vegetable Garnish

1 egg white
5 g cornflour
12 spinach leaves
250 ml vegetable oil
15 ml peanut oil
40 g shallots (bawang merah), peeled, finely chopped
20 g red chilies, seeded, cut into strips
120 g canned sweetcorn kernels, drained
salt

1 Using a whisk, beat the egg white together with the cornflour until thoroughly mixed, but not stiff, approximately 1 minute. Dip the spinach leaves into the batter mixture.
2 Heat the vegetable oil in a pan to 280°C. Fry the spinach leaves in the hot oil for 1 minute until crisp. Remove and keep warm. (Save the oil for frying the prawns later on.)
3 Heat the peanut oil in a frying pan. Sauté the shallots and chilies in this oil for 1 minute without browning.
4 Add in the sweetcorn kernels and sauté for another minute. Season with salt, remove from the heat and keep warm.

STEP 2: Sambal Sauce (Saus Sambal Goreng)

15 ml peanut oil
40 g shallots (bawang merah), peeled, finely diced
5 g garlic, peeled, finely diced
20 g candlenuts, ground
40 g tomatoes
1 lemon grass stalk, crushed
3 salam leaves
20 g brown sugar (gula Jawa)
120 ml chili juice (see page 23)
250 ml coconut milk (see page 22)
15 ml vinegar
salt

1 Heat the peanut oil in a saucepan. Add the shallots and garlic, and sauté for 3 minutes until light brown.
2 Add the candlenuts, tomatoes, lemon grass and salam leaves; then stir in the brown sugar. Sauté for a further 2 minutes.
3 Pour in the chili juice, coconut milk and vinegar. Bring the mixture to the boil, reduce the heat and simmer until the sauce thickens, approximately 5-7 minutes. Season with salt.
4 Remove the pan from the heat and discard the lemon grass and salam leaves.
5 Pour the sauce into a blender and process until smooth, approximately 3-4 minutes. Yields 500 ml.

STEP 3: Coconut Prawns and Presentation

8 x 40-60 g prawns, shelled, deveined, tail on
30 ml freshly squeezed lime juice
salt
50 g flour
1 egg, whisked
100 g grated coconut
vegetable oil left over from Step 1
160 ml Sambal Sauce, hot

1 Sprinkle the prawns with the lime juice and season with salt. Then dust the prawns with the flour and dip them into the beaten egg. Finally, roll the prawns in the grated coconut.
2 In a deep pan, heat the vegetable oil to 280°C. Deep-fry the prawns quickly for 3-4 minutes, then place them on kitchen paper to allow the oil to drip off. Serve hot.
3 Place 3 deep-fried spinach leaves on each plate.
4 Slice the prawns lengthwise and arrange them on the plates.
5 Sprinkle with the grated coconut and serve with the sautéed vegetables from Step 1 and hot Sambal Sauce.

Ikan Pedang Nelayan
SWORDFISH ON PUMPKIN SAUCE

In most parts of the world, swordfish is an expensive game fish. In Indonesia, they're often just hauled out with nets. If you can't get swordfish, use marlin.

4 x 180-200 g pieces of swordfish steaks, boned
5 g lemon grass stalk, finely diced
anise powder
salt
45 ml peanut oil
80 g pumpkin, cut into any shape desired, blanched
80 g chayote, cut into any shape desired, blanched
180 ml Pumpkin Sauce, hot (see page 29)
4 pumpkin leaves, blanched
12-16 star anise

1 Season the swordfish steaks with the lemon grass, anise powder and salt.
2 Heat half of the peanut oil in a frying pan to 200°C. Pan-fry the fish on each side for approximately 4-5 minutes. Withdraw the pan from the heat.
3 Using a different frying pan, heat the remaining oil and sauté the pumpkin and chayote over medium heat, tossing well, for 2-3 minutes. Season with salt. Remove from the heat and keep warm.
4 Pour some of the hot sauce on each plate. Top the sauce with the pumpkin leaves.
5 Arrange the sautéed vegetables on the pumpkin leaves and sprinkle a few star anise over them.
6 Slice the fish steaks open from the side, lengthwise, into 2 flat steaks.
7 Place them on the plate so that the pan-fried side shows as well as the inner section of the fish steak.

Kakap Merah Banyuwangi

RED SNAPPER FROM EAST JAVA

Probably the best known fish throughout Indonesia, *kakap merah* is excellent whether grilled, steamed, baked or pan-fried. Any other good-tasting member of the snapper family can be used as a substitute.

STEP 1: Pan-fried Red Snapper Fillets
20 g red chilies, seeded, finely diced
20 g green chilies, seeded, finely diced
10 g shallots (bawang merah), peeled, finely diced
5 g garlic, peeled, finely diced
rind of 1 lime, finely diced
10 ml freshly squeezed lime juice
4 x 120 g red snapper fillets, skin on
30 ml vegetable oil

1   Combine the first 6 ingredients to make the marinade. Mix well.
2   Place the snapper fillets in a dish, skin side down, add the marinade and marinate for 2 hours.
3   Heat the vegetable oil in a frying pan. Place the marinated fillets skin side down in the pan and fry on each side for 2-3 minutes. Remove and keep warm.

STEP 2: Garnish and Presentation
15 ml vegetable oil
50 g beansprouts, cleaned
40 g red chilies, seeded, cut into strips
40 g green chilies, seeded, cut into strips
salt
160 ml Banyuwangi Sauce, hot (see page 31)

1   Heat the vegetable oil in a frying pan. Stir-fry the beansprouts and chilies in the hot oil, tossing constantly, for 2-3 minutes. Season with salt. Remove and keep warm.
2   Pour a layer of the hot sauce on each plate.
3   Slice each fillet into 6 pieces and place these slices on the sauce.
4   Garnish with the sautéed vegetables.

Udang Windu Surabaya

TIGER PRAWNS SURABAYA

Several prawn species are popular in Indonesia: the *udang putih* — banana or white prawn, the freshwater *udang galah* — giant blue prawn — which is often raised in ponds, and the *udang windu*, featured in this recipe.

STEP 1: Chili Prawn Sauce (Saus Sambal Udang)
30 ml vegetable oil
30 g shallots (bawang merah), peeled, finely diced
10 g garlic, peeled, finely diced
10 g ginger, peeled, finely diced
10 g greater galangal, peeled, finely diced
5 g shrimp paste
100 g prawns, shelled, diced
1 lemon grass stalk, crushed
20 g candlenuts, ground
125 ml chili juice (see page 23)
125 ml coconut milk (see page 22)
salt

1   Heat the oil in a saucepan. Sauté the shallots, garlic, ginger and greater galangal for 2 minutes in the oil, without letting the ingredients brown.
2   Add the shrimp paste, prawns, lemon grass and candlenuts. Continue to sauté for 2-3 minutes until light brown.
3   Pour in the chili juice and coconut milk, season lightly with salt, then bring to the boil. Reduce the heat and let the sauce simmer, stirring frequently, until it thickens, approximately 8-10 minutes.
4   Remove the pan from the heat and discard the lemon grass stalk.
5   Pour the sauce into a blender and purée until smooth, approximately 3 minutes. Serve hot. Yields 375 ml.

STEP 2: Cooking and Presentation
30 ml peanut oil
20 x approximately 40 g tiger prawns, cleaned, shelled,
    deveined, tail on, head removed
20 g shallots (bawang merah), peeled, cut into fine strips
10 g ginger, peeled, cut into fine strips
20 g red chilies, seeded, cut into fine strips
20 g young green mango, cut into fine strips
salt
180 ml Chili Prawn Sauce, hot

1   Heat the peanut oil in a large frying pan, preferably a wok, to 220-240°C.
2   Sauté the prawns, shallots, ginger, chilies and green mango strips quickly over high heat for 2-3 minutes. Season with salt. Serve immediately otherwise the prawns will dry out.
3   Put some of the hot sauce on a deep plate or large soup plate.
4   Arrange the sautéed prawns and vegetables on the sauce.

FILLET OF HALIBUT MADURA

Kukus Ikan Sebelah Madura
FILLET OF HALIBUT MADURA

STEP 1: Poached Halibut Fillets
    4 Indian halibuts, skinned
    20 g red chilies, in julienne strips
    20 g sweet basil leaves (kemangi), washed, stems removed
    ground white pepper
    125 ml fish stock (see page 24)

1 Cut each halibut into 4 fillets.
2 Place 8 of the fillets on a flat surface and sprinkle with the chili strips. Top with the basil leaves and season with the ground pepper. Put the remaining 8 fillets on top.
3 Place the fillets in a flat pan and poach gently in the fish stock for 5-8 minutes.
4 Remove from the stock and cut the fillets into diamonds. Keep them warm.

STEP 2: Garnish and Presentation
    40 g shallots (bawang merah), peeled
    40 g potatoes, peeled, cubed or in balls
    40 g carrots, peeled, cubed or in balls
    20 g long beans, diced
    10 ml peanut oil
    3 g garlic, peeled, finely diced
    180 ml Banyuwangi Sauce, hot (see page 31)
    60 ml Sour Turmeric Sauce, hot (see page 35)
    2 long beans, blanched

1 Blanch the shallots, potatoes, carrots and long beans in salt water for ½-1 minute.
2 Heat the peanut oil in a pan. Sauté the blanched vegetables with the garlic for 2 minutes in the hot oil. Remove and keep warm.
3 Pour the Banyuwangi Sauce in a circular fashion in the centre of each plate and add 1 tablespoon of Sour Turmeric Sauce on top.
4 Arrange the cut fillets on the sauces.
5 Garnish with the sautéed vegetables and the blanched long beans tied in a knot.

Ikan Ekor Kuning Sungai Musi
FUSILIER WITH MINT NOODLES

The *ikan ekor kuning* is a particularly attractive fish with a bright yellow tail fin, and it is one of the prime products of Indonesia's burgeoning aquaculture. Any small perch can be used as a substitute.

STEP 1: Pineapple Sauce (Saus Nanas)
    30 ml vegetable oil
    40 g shallots (bawang merah), peeled, finely diced
    5 g lemon grass stalk, finely diced
    250 ml freshly blended pineapple juice
    210 ml chili juice (see page 23)
    60 ml tamarind water (see page 23)
    salt

1 Heat the vegetable oil in a saucepan. Add the shallots and lemon grass and sauté for 2 minutes without browning.
2 Pour in the pineapple juice, chili juice and tamarind water. Season with salt.
3 Bring the mixture to the boil, reduce the heat and simmer for approximately 5-7 minutes, stirring occasionally.
4 Remove the pan from the heat and pour the mixture into a blender. Process until smooth. Yields 375 ml.

STEP 2: Cooking and Presentation
    480 g fusilier fillets
    10 g turmeric powder
    10 g ginger, peeled, finely diced
    15 g rice flour
    30 ml peanut oil
    10 g red chilies, cut into strips
    160 g cooked broad egg noodles
    250 ml Pineapple Sauce, hot
    10 g mint leaves

1 Let the fusilier fillets marinate in the turmeric powder and ginger for 1 hour.
2 Dust the fillets lightly with the rice flour.
3 Heat half of the peanut oil until very hot in a frying pan. Sauté the fillets quickly, about 2-3 minutes on each side, in the oil. Remove and keep warm.
4 Sauté the chili strips in the remaining peanut oil for a minute. Add the cooked noodles and sauté for 1 minute. Remove from the pan.
5 Put a little of the hot Pineapple Sauce on each plate.
6 Arrange the noodles and sautéed fish fillets on the sauce. Garnish with the mint leaves.

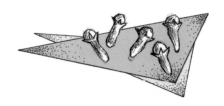

FRIGATE MACKEREL SOUTHWEST JAVA

GREY MULLET WITH SWEETCORN

FUSILIER WITH MINT NOODLES

Ikan Tongkol Krakatau

FRIGATE MACKEREL SOUTHWEST JAVA

In general, mackerels are well known throughout Southeast Asia, and the frigate mackerel especially so in Indonesia. If this variety is not available, any other mackerel will do for this recipe.

STEP 1: Pan-fried Mackerel Steaks
> *4 x 150-160 g pieces of frigate mackerel steaks, skinned,*
> *boned*
> *80 ml tamarind water (see page 23)*
> *15 ml freshly squeezed lime juice*
> *salt*
> *25 ml peanut oil*

1   Place the mackerel steaks in a bowl and pour the tamarind water and lime juice over them. Let the mackerel marinate in the refrigerator for 1 hour.
2   Remove the mackerel steaks from the marinade and pat them dry with kitchen paper towels. Season with salt.
3   Heat the peanut oil in a frying pan to 220°C. Pan-fry the mackerel steaks quickly on each side for approximately 4-5 minutes. Remove and keep warm.

STEP 2: Vegetables and Presentation
> *20 ml peanut oil*
> *20 g shallots (bawang merah), peeled, finely diced*
> *5 g greater galangal, peeled, finely diced*
> *5 g shrimp paste*
> *5 g red chilies, seeded, finely diced*
> *40 g young green mango, cut into fine strips*
> *40 g white radish, cut into fine strips*
> *salt*
> *375 ml coconut milk (see page 22)*
> *8 white radish leaves, blanched*

1   In a saucepan, heat the peanut oil and sauté the shallots and greater galangal without colouring for about 1 minute.
2   Mix in the shrimp paste and chilies. Sauté over medium heat for 2 minutes.
3   Add in the mango and radish strips and continue to sauté for 2 minutes more. Season with salt.
4   Pour in the coconut milk and bring the mixture to the boil. Reduce the heat and simmer for approximately 4-5 minutes. Remove from the heat and keep the contents warm.
5   Ladle the vegetables into a large soup plate and put a small portion of it on individual plates.
6   Slice each of the mackerel steaks and arrange the pieces in a crescent on the plate.
7   Garnish with the radish leaves and serve immediately.

Ikan Belanak Isi Jagung Semarang

GREY MULLET WITH SWEETCORN

Ikan belanak is very similar to the grey mullet found in the West. Although, it is not widely used in Indonesia, it is a fine, sweet seasonal fish.

STEP 1: Grey Mullet Stuffing
> *100 g grey mullet fillet, minced*
> *10 g shallots (bawang merah), peeled, finely diced*
> *5 g garlic, peeled, finely diced*
> *10 g grated coconut*
> *1 egg white*
> *90 ml cream (33% fat)*
> *salt*
> *20 g canned sweetcorn kernels, drained*

1   Place the minced fish in a blender and purée until smooth, about 3-4 minutes. Transfer the fish to a cold bowl.
2   Add the shallots, garlic, coconut and egg white to the bowl. Mix well with a wooden spoon.
3   Add in the cream, season with salt and mix in the sweetcorn kernels. Blend the cream well into the mixture.
4   Place the stuffing in a refrigerator and let it rest for 1 hour before using.

STEP 2: Cooking and Presentation
> *4 x 200 g grey mullet fillets, skin on*
> *salt*
> *pepper*
> *15 ml peanut oil*
> *60 g canned sweetcorn kernels, drained*
> *10 g red chilies, seeded, cut into fine strips*
> *4-8 cup leaves, blanched*
> *160 ml Pesmol Sauce, hot (see page 30)*

1   Place two of the fillets, skin side down, on a flat surface and season with salt and pepper.
2   With a spatula, spread the stuffing made in Step 1 evenly on the fillets, then place the remaining fillets, skin side up, over the stuffing. Press the fish to make the fillets look even.
3   Wrap the stuffed fillets in kitchen plastic wrap and place the fish in a steamer. Steam for approximately 15 minutes. Turn off the heat but keep the fish hot.
4   Heat the peanut oil in a frying pan. Sauté 40 g of the sweetcorn kernels and the chilies for 2 minutes. Season with salt. Remove from the heat.
5   Spoon the vegetables into the cup leaves. Tie these into bundles using pieces of chives or lemon grass.
6   Pour some of the hot Pesmol Sauce on each plate.
7   Cut the steamed fillets small enough to have 3-4 pieces per serving.
8   Arrange the pieces on the plates.
9   Put the stuffed cup leaves on the sauce. Garnish with the remaining sweetcorn kernels.

Pindang Ekor Kuning
FUSILIER ON PINDANG SAUCE

This fish is served with a mild and light sweet sauce.

STEP 1: Poached Fusilier Fillets
250 ml fish stock (see page 24)
640 g fusilier fish fillets
salt
pepper

1 Preheat the oven to 180°C.
2 Heat the fish stock in a pan just large enough to hold the fillets.
3 Season the fillets with salt and pepper, and put them in the pan. Cover with a piece of buttered parchment paper and poach in the preheated oven for approximately 10-12 minutes. Remove and keep the fish warm in the stock.

STEP 2: Pindang Sauce (Saus Pindang)
15 ml peanut oil
25 g shallots (bawang merah), peeled, chopped finely
25 g red chilies, seeded, finely chopped
25 g green chilies, seeded, finely chopped
25 g candlenuts, ground
500 ml coconut milk (see page 22)
100 g starfruit, chopped
10 g ginger, peeled, finely chopped
5 g greater galangal, peeled, finely chopped
5 g turmeric powder
1 salam leaf
1 lemon grass stalk
salt

1 Heat the peanut oil in a frying pan and sauté the shallots and chilies for 2 minutes in the oil.
2 Add in the candlenuts and continue to sauté until the ingredients are light brown in colour.
3 Pour in the coconut milk and bring the mixture to the boil, stirring frequently.
4 Add in the starfruit, ginger, greater galangal, turmeric powder, salam leaf and lemon grass.
5 Let the sauce simmer for approximately 8-10 minutes, until it starts to thicken.
6 Remove from the heat and discard the lemon grass and salam leaf.
7 Pour the sauce into a blender and process until smooth, about 2-3 minutes. Remove from the blender and keep warm. Yields 500 ml.

STEP 3: Garnish and Presentation
160 ml Pindang Sauce, hot
24 mint leaves
120 g yam bean, peeled, cut into diamonds
80 g red chilies, seeded, cut into diamonds

1 Pour some of the Pindang Sauce on each plate.
2 Arrange a portion of the poached fusilier fillets on the sauce.
3 Garnish with the mint leaves, yam bean and chilies.

Ikan Kembung Lelaki dengan Saus Kunyit
MACKEREL WITH TURMERIC SAUCE

Ikan kembung, or mackerel, is a favourite fish throughout Indonesia and it is good grilled, steamed or baked. Here, it is accompanied with a spicy turmeric sauce and a slightly sour, hot shallot relish.

STEP 1: Turmeric Sauce (Saus Kunyit)
15 ml peanut oil
20 g shallots (bawang merah), peeled, finely diced
5 g garlic, peeled, finely diced
5 g greater galangal, finely diced
5 g ginger, peeled, finely diced
15 g turmeric powder
80 ml red chili juice (see page 23)
375 ml coconut milk (see page 22)
salt

1 In a saucepan, heat the peanut oil and sauté the shallots, garlic, greater galangal and ginger in the oil for 2-3 minutes, stirring constantly, without browning.
2 Add the turmeric powder and continue sautéing over low heat for another minute.
3 Pour in the chili juice and coconut milk. Season with salt. Bring the mixture to the boil, reduce the heat and simmer for approximately 10 minutes.
4 Remove from the heat. Do not blend or strain this sauce. Serve hot. Yields 375 ml.

STEP 2: Cooking and Presentation
8 x 100-120 g striped mackerel fillets, skin on
salt
30 ml freshly squeezed lime juice
30 ml peanut oil
180 ml Turmeric Sauce, hot
80 g Chili Tomato Pickles, cold (see page 127)
10 g turmeric leaves, cut into fine strips

1 Place the mackerel fillets in a shallow dish and season with salt and the lime juice. Marinate for ½ hour.
2 Remove the mackerel from the marinade and brush lightly with the oil.
3 Place the fillets on a hot grill or griddle, skin side down first, and cook on each side for approximately 3-4 minutes. Remove the fish from the heat and keep warm.
4 Cut the mackerel fillets into triangles or diamonds and arrange some pieces on each plate.
5 Pour the hot sauce between the fish pieces.
6 Set the pickles on the sauce and garnish with the turmeric leaf strips.

BARBECUED RED SNAPPER

Kakap Merah Bakar Belimbing Wuluh
BARBECUED RED SNAPPER

800 g-1 kg red snapper fillets, red skin on
salt
ground white pepper
30 ml peanut oil
120 g sour finger carambolas, sliced
40 g yam bean, peeled, cut into shapes
5 g red chilies, sliced
180 ml Sour Finger Carambola Sauce, hot (see page 37)

1 Cut the red snapper fillets into 8 even 100-125 g pieces or medallions.
2 Season the fish with salt and pepper. Brush lightly with half of the oil.
3 Place the fish on a rack over a hot barbecue and cook each side for approximately 2-3 minutes. Remove from the barbecue and keep hot.
4 Heat the remaining oil in a frying pan. Sauté the sour finger carambolas, yam bean and chilies over medium heat for 1 minute, tossing well. Season with salt. (The yam bean and carambola should be crunchy and crisp.) Remove from the heat.
5 Pour some of the sauce on each plate.
6 Arrange the sautéed vegetable garnish on the sauce and place a few pieces of the fish on the sauce.

LOBSTER MOUSSE ON PANCAKE NET

SPINY LOBSTER TELUK BAYUR

FUSILIER ON SHRIMP SAUCE

Udang Barong Teluk Bayur
SPINY LOBSTER TELUK BAYUR

Every morning fishermen bring in their catch of spiny lobster to the west Sumatran port of Teluk Bayur. If cooked properly, the meat is as firm and succulent as that of any cold-water lobster.

STEP 1: Steamed Lobster
4 x 150-200 g spiny or rock lobster tails, shelled
2 g coriander leaves, finely chopped
20 g shallots (bawang merah), peeled, finely diced
10 g leeks, finely diced
20 g candlenuts, ground
250 ml coconut milk (see page 22)

1 Place the lobster tails on a shallow dish.
2 In a bowl, combine the coriander, shallots, leeks and candlenuts. Pour in the coconut milk and mix well with a whisk.
3 Pour this mixture over the lobster and let it marinate for 4 hours in a refrigerator.
4 Remove the marinated lobster from the marinade and wrap each tail tightly with kitchen plastic wrap. Tie up the ends with twine or kitchen string.
5 Place the lobsters in a steamer, steam for approximately 15-18 minutes. Remove and keep hot.

NOTE: If Atlantic or cold-water lobsters are used, the meat in two claws is roughly equivalent in amount to that in a tail, so half the number of lobsters are required.

STEP 2: Teluk Bayur Sauce (Saus Santan Teluk Bayur)
15 ml peanut oil
20 g shallots (bawang merah), peeled, finely diced
2 g garlic, peeled, finely diced
5 g ginger, peeled, finely diced
5 g greater galangal, peeled, finely diced
5 g red chilies, seeded, finely diced
5 g shrimp paste
500 ml coconut milk (see page 22)
salt

1 Heat the peanut oil in a saucepan. Sauté the shallots, garlic, ginger and greater galangal in the oil over low heat for 2-3 minutes, without browning. Stir constantly.
2 Add the red chilies and shrimp paste and continue to saute for 2 minutes more.
3 Pour in the coconut milk, season lightly with salt and bring the mixture to the boil. Let it simmer for approximately 8 minutes until the sauce thickens.
4 Pour the sauce in a blender and process it for 2 minutes. Serve hot. Yields 250 ml.

STEP 3: Vegetables and Presentation
15 ml peanut oil
40 g young coconut meat, diced
80 g Candied Mango — 8 slices left whole; the remainder diced (see page 123)
salt
180 ml Teluk Bayur Sauce, hot

1 Heat the peanut oil in a frying pan and sauté the diced coconut and mango in it, tossing well, for 2-3 minutes. Season with salt. Remove from the heat and keep hot.
2 Pour some of the hot sauce across each plate.
3 Put a small mound of the sautéed fruit next to the sauce.
4 Unwrap the lobsters and slice them into scallop shapes.
5 Set the lobster scallops on the sauce and garnish with the mango slices.

Ikan Bakar Bakasem
FUSILIER ON SHRIMP SAUCE

STEP 1: Shrimp Sauce (Saus Udang)
60 g peeled shrimps
10 g brown sugar (gula Jawa)
15 ml white vinegar
salt
15 ml vegetable oil
20 g shallots (bawang merah), peeled, finely diced
5 g garlic, peeled, finely diced
·10 g ginger, peeled, finely diced
½ lemon grass stalk, finely diced
1 kaffir lime leaf
20 g turmeric root, finely diced
50 g tomatoes, peeled, seeded, diced
250 ml coconut milk (see page 22)

1 Combine the raw shrimps with the brown sugar, white vinegar and salt. Marinate for 4 hours.
2 Heat the vegetable oil in a saucepan. Sauté the shallots, garlic, ginger, lemon grass, lime leaf and turmeric root in the hot oil for 3-4 minutes without browning.
3 Stir in the marinated shrimp mixture and continue to sauté for 2 minutes.
4 Add the tomatoes and coconut milk. Bring the mixture to the boil and simmer until the sauce thickens, approximately 8 minutes.
5 Remove from the heat and discard the lime leaf.
6 Pour the sauce into a blender and process until fine. Remove and keep warm. Yields 375 ml.

STEP 2: Cooking and Presentation
4 x 150 g fusilier fish fillets
salt
pepper
15 ml vegetable oil
160 ml Shrimp Sauce, hot
20 g red chilies, finely diced
4 sweet basil leaves (kemangi)

1 Season the fish fillets with salt and pepper.
2 Brush the fillets lightly with the oil, then place in a hot pan, skin side down, and cook evenly on both sides for 3 minutes each. Remove and keep warm.
3 Pour a little of the hot sauce on each plate.
4 Place the cooked fillets on top of the sauce.
5 Garnish with the chilies and basil leaves.

Roti Jala dengan Udang Raja

LOBSTER MOUSSE ON PANCAKE NET

In northern Sumatra, a favourite snack is *roti jala*, a type of pancake, topped with lamb curry. Here is a new version with lobster mousse.

STEP 1: Lobster Mousse

200 g lobster meat
10 g shallots (bawang merah), peeled, finely chopped
20 g ginger, peeled, finely chopped (set aside a little for seasoning the scallops)
5 g coriander powder (set aside a little for the scallops)
15 ml chili juice (see page 23)
salt
pepper
1-2 egg whites
125 ml cream (33% fat)
4-5 mustard green leaves, blanched
4 x 10-15 g scallops

1 Dice the raw lobster meat and put it into a blender. Add in the shallots, ginger and coriander powder and chili juice. Season with salt and pepper.
2 Blend for 3-4 minutes until smooth.
3 Remove the mixture from the blender and place it in a bowl. Refrigerate until the mixture is cold.
4 Work the egg whites and cream into the mixture with a wooden spatula. Set the mousse aside.
5 Line 4 soufflé moulds or small coffee cups with some of the blanched mustard green leaves.
6 Season the scallops with the remaining coriander powder and ginger.
7 Wrap the scallops one by one with the remaining pieces of mustard green leaves.
8 Half-fill the moulds or cups with the mousse mixture. Add 1 wrapped scallop and top with more of the mousse until the mould or cup is almost filled. Fold the leaves over to make a cover.
9 Poach the mousse gently in a waterbath in the oven at 180°C for approximately 15 minutes. Remove and keep warm.

STEP 2: Pancake Net (Roti Jala)

50 g white flour
1 egg
10 g ginger, peeled, finely grated
100 ml coconut milk (see page 22)

1 Combine the ingredients to form a pancake batter. Make sure the batter is thin. If it is too thick, add more coconut milk.
2 Take a small empty can and pierce 3 holes, about 1-2 mm in diameter, in the bottom in a triangle formation.
3 Heat a teflon pan (or a flat pan with very little oil). Pour the batter into the perforated can and spin the pancake batter into the pan in a net fashion.
4 Fry the pancake for 1 minute on either side.

NOTE: This recipe makes 10-12 roti jalas of approximately 15-20 g each.

STEP 3: Presentation

4 Pancake Nets
36 fresh white or green asparagus tips, blanched
4 small red chilies, stem on, slit from halfway down to the tip, seeded
160 ml Chili Basil Sauce, hot (see page 28)

1 Place a pancake net on each preheated plate.
2 Free the mousse from the moulds, cut each mousse in half and place the halves on top of the pancake.
3 Garnish with the asparagus tips and chilies.
4 Serve the sauce on the side.

NOTE: A thin crepe can be used in place of a roti jala.

Ikan Kembung Perempuan

MACKEREL WITH TOMATOES

8 x 30-40 g short-bodied mackerel fillets, skin on
80 ml green chili juice (see page 23)
80 ml coconut milk (see page 22)
salt
45 ml peanut oil
60 g green chilies, sliced
40 g tomatoes, peeled, seeded, diced
20 g dried Chinese black mushrooms, soaked, sliced
5 g ginger, peeled, finely diced
180 ml Green Chili Sauce, hot (see page 30)

1 Place the mackerel fillets in a shallow dish and pour over the chili juice and coconut milk. Let them marinate in the refrigerator for 1 hour.
2 Remove the fillets from the marinade and dry them with kitchen paper towels. Season lightly with salt.
3 Brush the fillets with a little oil and place the fish, skin side down first, on a rack over a barbecue. Cook each side for approximately 2 minutes. Remove from the barbecue and keep hot.
4 Heat the remaining oil in a frying pan and sauté the green chilies over medium heat, stirring constantly, for 2 minutes.
5 Add in the tomatoes and mushrooms and season with salt and the ginger. Continue to sauté for another minute. Remove from the heat.
6 Pour some of the hot Green Chili Sauce on each plate. Spoon the sautéed vegetables on the sauce.
7 Set the fish on the vegetables. Arrange 2 slices per plate, with one piece skin side up and the other skin side down.

NOTE: Bigger mackerel fillets may be used but be sure to increase the cooking time.

CATFISH EEL WITH PECEL SAUCE

Cobek Lele Saus Pecel

CATFISH EEL WITH PECEL SAUCE

STEP 1: Poached Catfish Fillets

25 g shallots (bawang merah), peeled, finely chopped
10 g garlic, peeled, finely chopped
10 g red chilies, seeded, finely chopped
16 sweet basil leaves (kemangi), cut into strips
5 g turmeric powder
5 ml tamarind water (see page 23)
salt
4 x 120 g catfish fillets, skin on, halved
250 ml fish stock (see page 24)

1 Combine the first 7 ingredients to make the marinade. Mix well.
2 Place the fillets skin side down in a shallow pan.
3 Sprinkle the marinade over the fillets and let them marinate in the refrigerator for 2 hours.

4 Preheat the oven to 180°C, then take the fillets out of the refrigerator.
5 Roll up each fillet and fasten with a skewer.
6 Place the fillets in a pan and pour in the fish stock.
7 Poach the fillets in the preheated oven for approximately 15 minutes.
8 Remove the fillets from the oven and keep them warm in the stock.

STEP 2: Garnish and Presentation

120 ml Sweet Spicy Pecel Sauce, hot (see page 31)
100 g mango flesh, scooped out with a melon baller
100 g young coconut meat, cut into strips
24 turmeric leaves, cut into fine strips

1 Spread some of the hot sauce on each plate.
2 Slice the catfish fillets and arrange 2-3 slices by the sauce.
3 Garnish with the mango and coconut flesh and turmeric leaf strips.

Udang Saus Opor

KING PRAWNS IN COCONUT SAUCE

25 g shallots (bawang merah), peeled, finely chopped
10 g garlic, peeled, finely chopped
30 g red chilies, — 10 g finely chopped; 20 g cut into rounds
25 g candlenuts, ground
5 g ginger, peeled, finely chopped
1 lemon grass stalk, finely chopped
salt
24 x 40 g king prawns, cleaned, shelled, deveined
15 ml peanut oil
60 g ripe mango flesh, scooped out with a melon baller
30 g young green papaya flesh, scooped out with a melon baller
60 ml fish stock (see page 24)
180 ml coconut milk (see page 22)

1 Combine the shallots, garlic, finely chopped chilies, candlenuts, ginger, lemon grass and salt to make the marinade. Mix well.
2 Put the cleaned prawns in a shallow bowl and sprinkle with the marinade. Let them marinate in the refrigerator for 2 hours.
3 After 2 hours, drain off all the marinade from the prawns
4 Heat the peanut oil in a frying pan and sauté the prawns over high heat for 2 minutes.
5 Add in the mango and papaya balls, fish stock and coconut milk. Simmer for 2 minutes.
6 Remove from the heat. Take the prawns out of the sauce and arrange 5-6 of them on each plate.
7 Place a few mango and papaya balls next to the prawns.
8 Put a spoonful of sauce on the plate, sprinkle with the sliced chilies and serve immediately.

81

Sotong Kukus dengan Saus Kenikir

SQUID WITH GREEN SAUCE

The kenikir leaf gives a light green tint to the sauce in this dish.

STEP 1: Poached Stuffed Squid

> 16 mussels
> 100 g white perch, skinned, boned, cubed
> 60 ml cream (33% fat)
> ½ egg white
> 10 g dried black Chinese mushrooms, soaked in warm water for 1 hour, cut into strips
> 15 g red chilies, seeded, cut into strips
> 12 sweet basil leaves (kemangi), cut into strips
> salt
> ground white pepper
> 4 x 120 g squid, body tube only, washed, ink sac removed
> 250 ml fish stock (see page 24)

1 Clean and steam the mussels as described on page 58. Extract the mussels from their shells and set aside.
2 Mince or grind the perch until fine, then process in a blender for 2 minutes.
3 Keeping the blender running, gradually add in the cream and process for another minute. Then work in the egg white slowly, but blend only for another 5 seconds until the mixture becomes smooth.
4 Transfer the mixture to a cold bowl. Add the mussels, black mushrooms, chilies and basil leaves. Mix well with a wooden spatula, season and place in a refrigerator for 2 hours.
5 After 2 hours, remove the mixture from the fridge and use it to stuff the squid.
6 Roll each squid in a piece of cheesecloth and tie up the ends.
7 Heat the fish stock in a pan just big enough to hold the squid. Put in the squid and let them simmer in the stock for 15 minutes.
8 Withdraw the pan from the heat. Take the squid out of the stock (save the stock for making the sauce), untie the cheesecloth and slice the squid in half lengthwise.

STEP 2: Green Sauce (Saus Kenikir)

> 10 g kenikir leaves
> 20 g spinach leaves
> 185 ml fish stock left over from Step 1
> 20 g shallots (bawang merah), peeled, finely chopped
> 5 g garlic, peeled, finely chopped
> 15 g red chilies, seeded, finely chopped
> 40 g coconut meat
> 12 sweet basil leaves (kemangi)
> 90 ml red chili juice (see page 23)

1 Blanch the kenikir and spinach leaves in boiling water for 2 minutes.
2 Bring the fish stock to the boil in a saucepan, then add in the shallots, garlic, chilies, coconut meat, basil leaves and chili juice. Cook until all the ingredients are soft, around 10-12 minutes.

3 Pour the contents of the pan into a blender. Add in the blanched kenikir and spinach leaves and blend until smooth.
4 Remove the sauce from the blender. Taste and adjust the seasoning if necessary. Serve hot. Yields 375 ml.

STEP 3: Garnish and Presentation

> 20 g brown sugar (gula Jawa)
> 30 ml tamarind water (see page 23)
> 15 g red chilies, seeded, diced
> 5 g bird's eye chilies, sliced
> 80 g water apples, sliced
> 125 ml Green Sauce, hot

1 Dissolve the brown sugar in the tamarind water and add in the chilies.
2 Pour this mixture over the water apple slices. Toss well.
3 Place a portion of the water apple slices on each plate.
4 Arrange the squid slices next to the fruit and garnish with the hot sauce.

Ikan Bawal Putih Saus Sambal Godok

STEAMED WHITE POMFRET

One of the most highly prized fish, the white or silver pomfret has delicious flesh which comes off easily from its bones. It also requires very little cooking time. Plaice or any flat fish may be used as a substitute for pomfret, but the flavour is not the same.

> 4 x 300 g white pomfrets, cleaned
> 20 g lesser galangal, peeled, finely diced
> 20 g shallots (bawang merah), peeled, finely diced
> salt
> 60 ml red chili juice (see page 23)
> 180 ml White Beancurd Sauce, hot (see page 39)
> 10 g sweet basil leaves (kemangi), finely chopped
> 120 g Chili Tomato Pickles (see page 127)

1 Place the pomfrets in a shallow dish and add the lesser galangal and shallots. Season with salt and pour on the chili juice.
2 Leave the fish to marinate in the refrigerator for 1 hour.
3 Drain off the marinade and place the marinated fish in a dish in a steamer and steam for approximately 15-18 minutes.
4 Turn off the heat but keep the fish hot.
5 Pour some of the hot sauce on individual serving plates.
6 Sprinkle the chopped basil leaves on the sauce.
7 Set a pomfret on the sauce and garnish with the pickles.

Ikan Bawal dari Bengkulu
BENGKULU BLACK POMFRET

Although black pomfret ranks second to its white variety, it is still a very good fish.

> 4 x 250-300 g black pomfrets, cleaned
> 5 g ginger, peeled, finely diced
> 30 ml freshly squeezed lime juice
> salt
> 45 ml peanut oil
> 10 g shallots (bawang merah), peeled, finely diced
> 5 g lesser galangal, peeled, finely diced
> 20 g red chilies, seeded, cut into fine strips
> 5 g ginger, peeled, cut into fine strips
> 120 g water convolvulus, stems on
> ground white pepper
> 180 ml Bengkulu Sauce, hot (see page 35)

1 Place the pomfrets in a shallow dish, sprinkle the ginger on top and pour in the lime juice.
2 Let the fish marinate in the refrigerator for 1 hour.
3 Remove the pomfrets from the marinade and dry them with kitchen paper towels. Season with salt.
4 Heat half of the peanut oil in a frying pan to 220°C. Pan-fry the pomfrets on each side for approximately 4 minutes. Remove and keep hot.
5 In a large frying pan, heat the remaining oil and sauté the shallots, lesser galangal, chilies and ginger quickly for 1 minute over high heat, until the shallots are light brown.
6 Add in the water convolvulus, season with some salt and pepper and continue to sauté over high heat for another minute. Remove immediately from the pan.
7 Place a portion of the sautéed vegetables on each plate and arrange a pomfret next to the vegetables.
8 Serve with the hot Bengkulu Sauce.

Ikan Garoupa Saus Tauge Pedas
GROUPER ON SPICY BEANSPROUT SAUCE

> 4 x 160 g grouper fillets
> 20 g shallots (bawang merah), peeled, finely diced
> 5 g garlic, peeled, finely diced
> salt
> 30 ml peanut oil
> 250 ml Spicy Beansprout Sauce, hot (see page 30)
> 120 g fresh coconut meat, cut into strips
> 20 mint sprigs

1 Sprinkle the fillets with the shallots and garlic. Season with salt.
2 Heat the peanut oil in a frying pan. Fry the fillets quickly on each side for 2 minutes. Remove.
3 Place the grouper fillets on individual plates.
4 Pour some of the hot sauce next to the fillets.
5 Garnish with the coconut strips and mint sprigs.

Ikan Ekor Kuning Isi Udang Windu
FUSILIER AND TIGER PRAWN

STEP 1: Poached Fusilier Fillets
> 40 g candlenuts, ground
> 10 g shallots (bawang merah), peeled, finely diced
> 2 g garlic, peeled, finely diced
> 2 g turmeric powder
> 60 ml coconut milk (see page 22)
> 12 x 40-50 g fusilier fish fillets, skin on
> salt
> 12 x 30 g tiger prawns, shelled, deveined
> 500 ml fish stock (see page 24)

1 In a bowl, combine the candlenuts, shallots, garlic, turmeric powder and coconut milk. Mix well with a wooden spoon. The marinade should be a slightly thick paste.
2 Place the fusilier fillets, skin side down, on a flat surface. Season lightly with salt, then brush the marinade on the fish.
3 Place 1 prawn on each fillet and fold the fillet over so that it forms a tight triangular parcel. Secure the ends with a toothpick.
4 Place the fillets in a pan and pour in the fish stock.
5 Poach the fillets for approximately 5-7 minutes. Turn off the heat but keep the fillets hot in the stock.

STEP 2: Garnish and Presentation
> 30 ml peanut oil
> 80 g asparagus beans, blanched, sliced
> 40 g coconut meat, cut into strips
> salt
> 180 ml Sweet Sour Sauce, hot (see page 38)
> 10 g kenikir leaves, finely chopped

1 In a frying pan, heat the peanut oil and sauté the asparagus beans and coconut meat quickly for 2 minutes without browning. Season with salt, then remove from the heat and keep hot.
2 Pour some of the hot sauce on one side of each plate and place 2-3 poached fusilier fillets on the sauce.
3 Arrange the sautéed asparagus beans and coconut in the centre of the plate. Sprinkle on the chopped kenikir leaves.

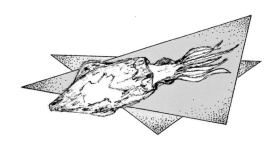

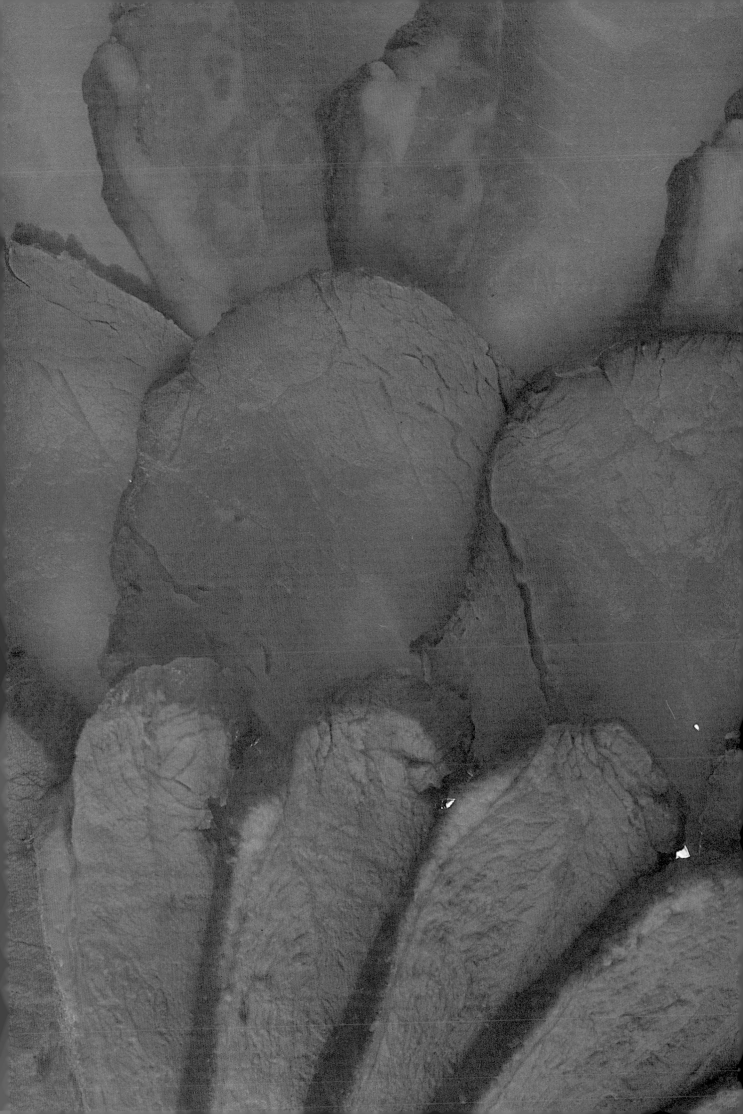

MEAT AND
POULTRY

MEAT

Gulai Korma Kambing

MELAYU LAMB STEW

STEP 1: Lamb Stew
30 ml peanut oil
90 g shallots (bawang merah), peeled, finely diced
20 g garlic, peeled, finely diced
1 lemon grass stalk, finely diced
10 g ginger, peeled, finely diced
600 g boneless leg of lamb, cubed
5 g white pepper powder
2 g coriander powder
2 g nutmeg powder
2 g fennel seeds, crushed
100 g tomatoes, peeled, seeded, diced
1 litre coconut milk (see page 22)
salt
500 ml lamb stock (see page 24)

1. Preheat the oven to 180°C.
2. Heat the peanut oil in a braising pan. Add in the shallots, garlic, lemon grass and ginger. Sauté, stirring constantly, for 2-3 minutes. Do not let the ingredients colour.
3. Add the lamb cubes and continue to sauté over high heat until the meat is browned.
4. Season with the pepper, coriander, nutmeg and fennel. Sauté for 2 minutes more.
5. Add in the tomatoes and pour in the coconut milk. Season with salt. Put on the lid of the braising pan and place it in the preheated oven.
6. Braise the meat for approximately 60-90 minutes, stirring occasionally with a wooden spoon. Use the lamb stock to thin the sauce when it gets too thick or starts to stick to the bottom of the pan.
7. Remove from the oven and keep the stew warm.

NOTE: Instead of lamb leg, a cheaper cut such as lamb shoulder may be used, but a longer braising time is needed.

STEP 2: Garnish and Presentation
15 ml peanut oil
4 young green mangoes, sliced, blanched
nutmeg powder
salt
9-12 sprigs coriander leaves
12 dried black Chinese mushrooms, soaked in warm water for
    1 hour, sliced, sautéed in oil
3 tomatoes, peeled, seeded, quartered

1. Heat the peanut oil in a frying pan, add in the green mangoes and season with nutmeg powder and salt. Sauté the mangoes for 1-2 minutes.
2. Ladle the lamb stew into serving plates.
3. Garnish with the sautéed green mango, coriander sprigs, sautéed mushrooms and tomato quarters.

Daging Sapi Muda Saus Ebi

VEAL WITH DRIED SHRIMP SAUCE

STEP 1: Dried Shrimp Sauce (Saus Ebi)
30 ml peanut oil
50 g dried shrimps, ground
40 g shallots (bawang merah), peeled, finely chopped
20 g garlic, peeled, finely chopped
10 g ginger, peeled, finely chopped
10 g greater galangal, peeled, finely chopped
1 lemon grass stalk, finely chopped
5 g turmeric root, finely diced
15 g candlenuts, ground
30 g brown sugar (gula Jawa)
30 ml chili juice (see page 23)
30 ml tamarind water (see page 23)
500 ml coconut milk (see page 22)
salt

1. Heat the peanut oil in a saucepan. Sauté the dried shrimps, shallots and garlic until light brown.
2. Add the ginger, greater galangal and lemon grass. Continue to sauté for 2 minutes more.
3. Add the turmeric, candlenuts and brown sugar, and sauté for another 2 minutes.
4. Pour in the chili juice, tamarind water and coconut milk, and season with salt. Bring the mixture to the boil. Then reduce the heat and simmer for approximately 10 minutes, stirring frequently.
5. Pour the sauce into a blender and process for 2-3 minutes until smooth. Serve hot. Yields 500 ml.

STEP 2: Cooking and Presentation
500 g veal fillet, fat and sinew removed
4 tablespoons direndam marinade (see page 23)
salt
45 ml peanut oil
120 g bitter gourd, sliced, blanched
250 ml Dried Shrimp Sauce, hot
20 g red chilies, seeded, cut into diamonds, blanched
20 g green chilies, seeded, cut into diamonds, blanched

1. Preheat the oven to 180°C.
2. Brush the veal fillet with the marinade and season with salt.
3. Heat 30 ml of the peanut oil in a roasting pan. Put the veal fillet into the pan and roast in the oven for approximately 18-20 minutes, basting occasionally in order to prevent the meat from drying out. Remove and keep warm.
4. Heat the remaining oil in a frying pan and sauté the bitter gourd for 1 minute.
5. Spread a thin layer of the hot sauce on each plate.
6. Slice the fillet into 4 portions. Place the slices on the sauce.
7. Garnish with the sautéed bitter gourd, and sprinkle with the chilies.

Daging Sapi Muda dan Pete Cina
VEAL FILLET WITH JAVANESE PARKIA

Veal loin or pork fillets can also be used in this recipe.

STEP 1: Roast Veal Fillets
4 x 160 g pieces veal fillet, fat and sinew removed
10 g lemon grass stalk, finely diced
5 g garlic, peeled, finely diced
1 g turmeric powder
salt
15 ml peanut oil

1   Place the veal fillets on a plate and rub with the lemon grass, garlic and turmeric powder.
2   Put the veal in a refrigerator and let it marinate for 2 hours.
3   Season the veal with salt just before cooking.
4   Preheat the oven to 200°C.
5   Heat the peanut oil in a small roasting pan or tray and put the fillets into the pan. Sear each side for 1 minute.
6   Put the pan into the preheated oven and roast the meat for approximately 15-18 minutes. Baste occasionally to keep the meat moist.
7   Remove the fillets from the roasting pan and keep them warm.

STEP 2: Garnish and Presentation
25 ml peanut oil
160 g sweet potatoes, cut into diamonds, blanched
10 g brown sugar (gula Jawa)
salt
80 g Javanese parkia pods, blanched
5 g shallots (bawang merah), peeled, finely diced
250 ml Honey Chili Sauce, hot (see page 31)
20 g Javanese parkia seeds

1   Heat 15 ml of the peanut oil in a shallow frying pan. Sauté the sweet potatoes and brown sugar in the oil for 3-4 minutes, tossing frequently, until the sugar has dissolved completely and coated the potatoes. Season with a little salt and remove the pan from the heat.
2   In another pan, heat the remainder of the oil and sauté the parkia and shallots for 2 minutes, tossing from time to time. Season with a dash of salt and remove from the heat.
3   Pour some of the hot Honey Chili Sauce onto each plate.
4   Cut each veal fillet into 1-cm thick slices and place the slices in a line next to the sauce.
5   Garnish the plate with the sautéed sweet potatoes and parkia.
6   Sprinkle the green parkia seeds on the sauce.

Daging Bistik Jawa
ROAST JAVANESE BEEF FILLET

STEP 1: Roast Beef Fillet
720 g beef fillet, fat and sinew removed
2 g coriander powder
2 g nutmeg powder
5 g lemon grass stalk, finely diced
salt
30 ml peanut oil

1   Preheat the oven to 160°C.
2   Season the beef fillet with the coriander powder, nutmeg powder, lemon grass and salt.
3   Pour the oil into a roasting pan and heat it to a high temperature on the stove top. Sear the meat quickly on all sides in the pan.
4   Transfer the pan to the preheated oven and roast the fillet, basting frequently until it is cooked as liked (about 25 minutes, for medium).
5   Remove the pan from the oven and let the meat rest in the pan for 10 minutes before cutting.

STEP 2: Sweet Beef Sauce (Saus Bistik Jawa)
30 ml peanut oil
30 g shallots (bawang merah), peeled, finely diced
10 g garlic, peeled, finely diced
10 g candlenuts, ground
15 g coriander seeds, ground
5 g nutmeg powder
375 ml dark sweet soya sauce
125 ml beef stock (see page 24)

1   Heat the peanut oil in a saucepan and sauté the shallots and garlic for 2 minutes without browning.
2   Add in the candlenuts, coriander and nutmeg. Continue to sauté for another minute.
3   Pour in the sweet soya sauce and beef stock. Bring the mixture to the boil, then reduce the heat. Simmer slowly for 10 minutes, stirring from time to time. The sauce should be syrupy in consistency and served hot. Yields 500 ml.

STEP 3: Garnish and Presentation
8 small round aubergines (terung engkol), halved, or 400 g
_   aubergine, sliced_
50 g shallots (bawang merah), peeled
50 g carrot, peeled, carved
50 g young green papaya, peeled, carved
15 ml peanut oil
250 ml Sweet Beef Sauce, hot
4 sprigs coriander leaves

1   Blanch the aubergines, shallots, carrot and papaya in turn in boiling water for 2 minutes. Drain.
2   Heat the peanut oil in a frying pan. Add in the vegetables and sauté briefly for 1 minute without colouring. The vegetables should remain crunchy.
3   Spread some of the sauce on each plate.
4   Slice the roast beef into 8-12 pieces and place 2-3 slices on the sauce on each plate.
5   Garnish with the vegetables and coriander.

Melayu Lamb Stew

Veal with Dried Shrimp Sauce

Veal Fillet with Javanese Parkia

Roast Javanese Beef Fillet

Beef with Marinated Beansprouts

Hot and Sour Lamb Medallions

Kambing Gaya Asam Pedas

HOT AND SOUR LAMB MEDALLIONS

STEP 1: Baked Wrapped Lamb Medallions
    30 ml peanut oil
    5 g garlic, peeled, finely diced
    20 g shallots (bawang merah), peeled, finely diced
    20 g straw or button mushrooms, sliced
    30 g leeks, cut into fine strips
    10 g chilies, cut into fine strips
    salt
    6 x 60 g lamb medallions
    turmeric powder
    2 g ginger, peeled, finely diced
    8 white cabbage leaves approximately 10 x 10 cm in size,
        blanched

1   In a frying pan, heat half the peanut oil and sauté the garlic and shallots for 2 minutes, until glazy.
2   Add in the mushrooms, leeks and chilies and season with salt. Continue to sauté for 2 minutes more. Remove from the heat and let the mushroom-leek mixture cool at room temperature. Set aside.
3   Season the lamb with a little turmeric powder, salt and the ginger.
4   Preheat the oven to 200°C.
5   Heat the remaining oil in a pan over heat. Put the meat in the pan and sear quickly on each side for 30 seconds. Remove immediately from the pan.
6   Place each lamb medallion on a cabbage leaf. Top each piece with a portion of the mushroom-leek mixture. Fold the leaf over and wrap the lamb tightly into a small parcel.
7   Place the wrapped lamb medallions on a greased baking tray and put the tray in the preheated oven. Bake the lamb for approximately 8-10 minutes. Remove and keep warm.

STEP 2: Hot Sour Sauce (Saus Kunyit Asam Pedas)
    30 ml peanut oil
    20 g shallots (bawang merah), peeled, finely diced
    5 g garlic, peeled, finely diced
    5 g ginger, peeled, finely diced
    2 g greater galangal, peeled, finely diced
    30 g candlenuts, ground
    2 g turmeric powder
    2 kaffir lime leaves
    30 ml red chili juice (see page 23)
    60 ml tamarind water (see page 23)
    250 ml coconut milk (see page 22)
    salt

1   Heat the peanut oil in a saucepan and sauté the next 4 ingredients for 2-3 minutes, stirring frequently to prevent browning.
2   Add in the candlenuts, turmeric powder and lime leaves. Continue sautéing for 2 minutes more.
3   Pour in the chili juice, tamarind water and coconut milk. Season with salt. Bring the mixture to the boil, reduce the heat and simmer for 6-8 minutes.

4   Remove the pan from the heat and discard the lime leaves.
5   Pour the sauce into a blender and purée for 2-3 minutes. Remove and serve hot. Yields 375 ml.

STEP 3: Presentation
    250 ml Hot Sour Sauce, hot.
    25 g long bean leaves, cut into fine strips but 4 left whole
    4 cabbage leaves, blanched
    6 red chilies, seeded, cut into fine strips

1   Pour some of the hot sauce on each plate.
2   Slice the lamb medallions in half. Arrange on the sauce.
3   Garnish with a long bean leaf, a cabbage leaf and the shredded chilies and bean leaves.

Empal Basah dengan Urap Tauge Kedele

BEEF WITH MARINATED BEANSPROUTS

This dish offers an interesting taste combination of hot spiced beef with a cold spicy sour sauce which is contrasted with the bitterness of the papaya leaves. The double procedure of simmering (or boiling) beef and then pan-frying in order to seal in the meat juices is widely practised in many places in Indonesia.

    600 g beef fillet, fat and sinew removed
    2 g coriander powder
    2 g cumin powder
    salt
    750 ml beef stock (see page 24)
    20 ml peanut oil
    250 ml Sambal Brambang (see page 36)
    160 g Coconut-marinated Beansprouts (see page 122)
    8 papaya leaves, blanched

1   Season the beef fillet with the coriander, cumin and salt. Rub the spices well into the meat.
2   Heat the beef stock in a stockpot and bring to the boil. Reduce the heat to simmering point.
3   Put the fillet in the stock and let it simmer for 25-30 minutes. Remove and let the meat rest for 5-7 minutes before slicing it thinly.
4   In a frying pan, heat the peanut oil and sear the meat slices over high heat on both sides for 15-20 seconds. Serve immediately.
5   Pour some of the sambal onto each plate.
6   Arrange the marinated beansprouts to one side of the sauce.
7   Place the beef slices on the sauce.
8   Garnish with the papaya leaves.

Panggang Kambing Isi

LAMB WITH SPICY VEAL STUFFING

STEP 1: Spicy Veal Stuffing

100 g boneless veal shoulder or leg, finely minced
20 g shallots (bawang merah), peeled, finely diced
2 g garlic, peeled, finely diced
1 egg
125 ml cream (33% fat)
5 g salt
1 g white pepper powder
5 g red chilies, seeded, finely diced
5 g carrot, finely diced

1   Combine the minced veal, shallots and garlic in a blender. Blend until smooth, approximately 2-3 minutes.
2   Remove the mixture from the blender and put it in a cold bowl. Use a wooden spatula to mix in the egg thoroughly.
3   Slowly add in the cream, then season with the salt and pepper. Add the chilies and carrot and mix until the cream is blended well into the mixture.
4   Place this stuffing in a refrigerator and let it rest for 1 hour before using.

STEP 2: Lamb Marinade

45 ml peanut oil
40 g shallots (bawang merah), peeled, finely diced
10 g garlic, peeled, finely diced
1 lemon grass stalk, finely diced
10 g ginger, peeled, finely diced
10 g greater galangal, peeled, finely diced
40 g candlenuts, ground
10 g turmeric powder
5 g black peppercorns, crushed
salt

1   Heat the peanut oil in a frying pan and sauté the shallots and garlic for 2-3 minutes, stirring constantly.
2   Add the lemon grass, ginger and greater galangal. Continue to sauté for another 2-3 minutes.
3   Stir in the candlenuts, turmeric powder and black peppercorns, and season with salt. Continue sautéing for another 3 minutes.
4   Remove from the heat and let the mixture cool at room temperature before using.

STEP 3: Roast Stuffed Lamb Racks

4 x 400 g lamb racks, with about 6-7 rib bones
4 mustard green leaves, blanched
30 ml peanut oil

1   Bone the lamb racks but leave the rib bones attached to the meat. Use a sharp knife to make an incision between the rib bones and the roll of meat, but do not separate the two.
2   Flap down the roll of meat so that it is at right angles to the rib bones. Flatten the meat part with a cleaver or chopper to approximately 1.5 cm in thickness. Top the meat part with a blanched mustard green leaf.

3   Use a wooden spatula to spread the stuffing made in Step 1 on the mustard green leaf.
4   Fold the lamb meat over the stuffing towards the rib bones into a tight sausage shape. Tie the roll with twine or string.
5   Place the rolled lamb in a pan and pour the marinade made in Step 2 over it. Let the lamb marinate in a refrigerator for 2 hours.
6   Preheat the oven to 180°C, then remove the lamb from the fridge and drain off the excess marinade.
7   Heat the peanut oil in a roasting pan and place the lamb rolls in the pan. Sear them quickly on all sides until golden brown.
8   Place the roasting pan in the preheated oven and roast for 10 minutes, basting frequently to keep the meat moist.
9   Remove the lamb from the pan and keep it warm for 5 minutes in order to retain the meat juices.

STEP 4: Presentation

250 ml Peanut Honey Sauce, hot (see page 38)
10 g black peppercorns
2 red chilies, sliced
2 green chilies, sliced

1   Pour a thin layer of the sauce on each plate.
2   Cut each lamb roll into 3-4 slices and place these pieces on the sauce.
3   Sprinkle the peppercorns over the sauce and garnish with the chilies.

Daging Saus Ubi Jalar

BEEF ON SWEET POTATO SAUCE

4 x 150 g pieces beef fillet, fat and sinew removed
salt
pepper
75 ml peanut oil
120 g ferntops
80 g sweet potatoes, blanched, cut into balls with a melon baller
250 ml Sweet Potato Sauce, hot (see page 28)
10 bird's eye chilies, diced

1   Season the beef fillet with salt and pepper.
2   Use 60 ml of the oil to brush on the meat.
3   Cook the meat under a medium-hot grill or on a griddle for 3 minutes each side. Remove and keep warm.
4   Heat the remaining oil in a frying pan. Sauté the ferntops and sweet potatoes over medium heat for 1-2 minutes. Season with salt, remove from the heat and keep warm.
5   Pour some of the hot sauce in the centre of each plate. Sprinkle the diced chilies on the sauce.
6   Arrange the vegetables around the sauce.
7   Slice each piece of beef in half and arrange the slices on the sauce.

NOTE: The meat may be fried instead of grilled.

Bakar Iga Kambing Bengkulu
LAMB FILLET BENGKULU

STEP 1: Pan-fried Lamb Fillets
10 g coriander powder
10 g kaffir lime leaves, finely chopped
5 g nutmeg powder
4 x 150 g pieces lamb fillet
salt
15 ml peanut oil

1   Combine the first 3 ingredients to make the marinade.
2   Put the lamb fillets in the marinade and let them sit overnight in the refrigerator.
3   Drain off the excess marinade and season the fillets with salt.
4   Heat the peanut oil in a pan to 200°C and sauté the fillets on each side for approximately 4 minutes.

STEP 2: Garnish and Presentation
15 ml peanut oil
160 g young green papaya, peeled, sliced into thin strips
10 g red chilies, seeded, diced
salt
250 ml Bengkulu Sauce, hot (see page 35)
4 young papaya leaves, blanched
20 carved potatoes, boiled in turmeric water (see page 123)
20 kaffir lime leaves

1   Heat the peanut oil in a pan and sauté the papaya julienne and red chilies for 2 minutes. Season with salt.
2   Spread a layer of the hot sauce on each plate.
3   Spoon a portion of the sautéed papaya into each papaya leaf and arrange this on the sauce.
4   Slice the lamb fillets and arrange the slices around the papaya julienne.
5   Garnish the dish with the potatoes and lime leaves.

Iga Babi Saus Dabu-dabu Manado
GRILLED PORK CHOPS NORTH SULAWESI

STEP 1: Grilled Pork Chops
30 ml dark sweet soya sauce
30 ml tomato juice
20 g shallots (bawang merah), peeled, finely diced
5 g garlic, peeled, finely diced
2 g ginger, peeled, finely diced
pinch of nutmeg powder
4 x 140-160 g boneless pork chops
salt
15 ml peanut oil

1   In a bowl, combine the first 6 ingredients and blend well with a whisk.
2   Brush this marinade on the pork chops and let them marinate in a refrigerator for 2 hours.
3   Drain off the excess liquid and season the meat with salt. Brush the meat lightly with the peanut oil.
4   Place the pork chops on a hot griddle or under a hot grill and cook on each side for 5-6 minutes. Keep warm.

STEP 2: Garnish and Presentation
120 ml Dabu-dabu Sauce, cold (see page 38)
100 g Sambal Brambang (see page 36)
8 kaffir lime leaves

1   Spoon a little of the Dabu-dabu Sauce on each plate.
2   Place a portion of the sambal next to the sauce.
3   Slice the grilled chops and arrange the meat on the sambal.
4   Garnish with the lime leaves.

BEEF ON SWEET POTATO SAUCE

LAMB MEDALLIONS IN FIERY SPICES

LAMB WITH SPICY VEAL STUFFING

Kambing Bumbu Bajak

LAMB MEDALLIONS IN FIERY SPICES

STEP 1: Grilled Lamb Medallions

> 30 ml peanut oil
> 20 g shallots (bawang merah), peeled, finely diced
> 2 g garlic, peeled, finely diced
> 5 g red chilies, seeded, finely diced
> 20 g peanuts, ground, deep-fried
> 30 ml dark sweet soya sauce
> 5 ml freshly squeezed lime juice
> 15 ml tamarind water (see page 23)
> 30 ml water
> 12 x 50 g lamb medallions, fat and sinew removed
> salt

1 Heat half of the peanut oil in a saucepan and sauté the shallots, garlic and red chilies until slightly browned.
2 Add in the peanuts and continue to sauté for another minute.
3 Pour in the sweet soya sauce, lime juice, tamarind water and water. Simmer this marinade mixture for 5-7 minutes.
4 Withdraw the pan from the heat and let the marinade cool completely before using.
5 Season the lamb medallions with salt and brush the marinade on both sides of the meat.
6 Brush the remaining oil on the medallions and cook them under a grill or on a hot griddle for 2-3 minutes on each side. Remove and keep warm.

STEP 2: Garnish and Presentation

> 15 ml peanut oil
> 80 g potato balls, scooped with a melon baller, boiled in
>   turmeric water (see page 123)
> salt
> 250 ml Spicy Bajak Sauce, hot (see page 27)
> 4 Stuffed Mustard Green Leaves, hot (see page 119)
> 4 mustard green leaves, blanched

1 Heat the oil in a frying pan and add in the turmeric potato balls. Sauté for 2 minutes without browning, then season with salt. Remove the pan from the heat.
2 Pour some of the hot sauce onto each plate and place 2 or 3 medallions on the sauce.
3 Garnish with the sautéed potato balls, stuffed mustard greens and a blanched mustard green leaf.

NOTE: The meat may be fried instead of grilled.

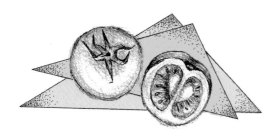

Daging Masak Tauco

MEDALLIONS OF BEEF TAUCO

STEP 1: Tomato Tauco Sauce (Saus Tomat Tauco)

> 30 ml peanut oil
> 40 g shallots (bawang merah), peeled, finely diced
> 10 g garlic, peeled, finely diced
> 20 g red chilies, seeded, finely diced
> 20 g green chilies, seeded, finely diced
> 200 g tomatoes, peeled, seeded, diced
> 160 ml fermented yellow soya beans
> 250 ml water

1 In a saucepan, heat the peanut oil and sauté the shallots, garlic and chilies in the oil for 2-3 minutes, without browning, stirring constantly.
2 Stir in the tomatoes, fermented soya beans and water. Bring the mixture to the boil and then reduce the heat and simmer for 5-6 minutes.
3 Taste the sauce and adjust if necessary. The fermented soya beans will make the sauce salty and this may be adjusted by adding a small amount of water if it is too salty. Remove from the heat.
4 Pour the sauce into a blender and process for 2-3 minutes until smooth. Remove from blender and keep hot. Yields 375 ml.

STEP 2: Tauco Beef Medallions

> 8-12 x 60 g beef medallions
> salt
> 20 black peppercorns, crushed
> 30 ml peanut oil
> 200 ml Tomato Tauco Sauce, hot

1 Season the beef medallions with the salt and peppercorns.
2 Heat the peanut oil in a frying pan.
3 Place the beef in the pan and sear quickly over high heat for 30 seconds on either side.
4 Pour the Tomato Tauco Sauce into the pan, reduce the heat and let the meat simmer for 4-5 minutes, so that the beef absorbs the flavour of the sauce.

STEP 3: Garnish and Presentation

> 40 g tomatoes, peeled, seeded, diced
> 5 g green chilies, seeded, finely diced
> black peppercorns
> 12 kaffir lime leaves

1 Take the beef medallions out of the sauce and arrange the meat in the centre of individual plates.
2 Pour the sauce over the meat.
3 Mix the diced tomatoes with the chilies. Put a mound of this to one side of the meat. Sprinkle on some black peppercorns and garnish with the lime leaves.

Lidah Sapi Bumbu Kuning

OX TONGUE IN COCONUT MILK

STEP 1: Boiled Ox Tongue
> 2 litres water
> 10 g garlic cloves, peeled, crushed
> 20 g shallots (bawang merah), peeled, crushed
> 10 g ginger, peeled, crushed
> 1 leek, use the bottom half only
> 1 x 800 g piece ox tongue

1   Pour the water into a stockpot and bring to the boil. Drop the garlic, shallots, ginger and leek into the boiling water.
2   Add in the ox tongue. Reduce the heat and simmer for approximately 1½-2 hours, until the tongue is cooked. To check whether the ox tongue is ready, remove it from the hot stock and pinch the tip with your thumb and forefinger. If your fingers go through the meat easily, then it is done.
3   Remove the ox tongue from the stock and cool it in cold water.
4   Quickly peel off and discard the thick outer skin.
5   Slice the tongue into 1-cm thick slices. Keep hot.

STEP 2: Sauce and Presentation
> 30 ml peanut oil
> 20 g shallots (bawang merah), peeled, finely diced
> 2 g garlic, peeled, finely diced
> 5 g ginger, peeled, finely diced
> 10 g turmeric root, finely diced
> 20 g candlenuts, ground
> 1 g coriander powder
> 500 ml coconut milk (see page 22)
> 120 g leeks, sliced into rounds
> 20 g red chilies, seeded, sliced into rounds
> 1 g cumin powder
> salt
> 2 spring onion stalks, cut into 4-cm lengths

1   In a deep frying pan, heat half of the peanut oil and sauté the shallots, garlic, ginger and turmeric root for 2 minutes, stirring constantly to prevent browning the ingredients.
2   Mix in the candlenuts and coriander powder and continue to sauté for 2 minutes more.
3   Pour in the coconut milk and bring the mixture to the boil. Put the ox tongue slices in the coconut mixture and simmer for 5-8 minutes. Remove from the heat and keep the meat warm in the sauce.
4   Meanwhile, heat the remaining peanut oil in a separate frying pan. Add the leeks and red chilies, and season with the cumin powder and salt. Sauté, tossing well, for 2 minutes. Remove the pan from the heat and keep the vegetables warm.
5   Pour some of the strained coconut sauce onto each plate.
6   Arrange the tongue slices on the sauce.
7   Garnish with the sautéed leeks, red chilies and spring onions.

NOTE: If fresh turmeric root is not available, substitute with 2 g turmeric powder.

Paha Kambing Panggang Sambal Kecap

ROAST MARINATED LEG OF LAMB

This is an interesting dish, served hot, with a cold sauce.

STEP 1: Roast Rolled Leg of Lamb
> 45 ml peanut oil
> 20 g shallots (bawang merah), peeled, finely diced
> 35 g garlic, peeled, finely diced
> 10 g ginger, peeled, finely diced
> 5 g clove powder
> 5 g coriander powder
> 5 g turmeric powder
> 2 lemon grass stalks, crushed
> 2 kaffir lime leaves
> 2 g black peppercorns, ground
> salt
> 600 g boneless leg of lamb

1   Pour 30 ml of the peanut oil into a bowl. Add the shallots, garlic, ginger, clove, coriander and turmeric powder. Stir briskly with a whisk until the ingredients are well mixed.
2   Add in the lemon grass, lime leaves and peppercorns. Season this marinade with some salt.
3   Place the lamb in a large bowl. Pour the marinade over the lamb, turning the meat over a few times so that the marinade is distributed evenly on the meat. Place in the refrigerator for 12 hours.
4   Preheat the oven to 180°C. Then remove the marinated lamb from the fridge, season with a little salt and roll up the meat. Secure the roll with kitchen string.
5   Heat 15 ml of the peanut oil in a roasting pan and roast the meat in the oven for approximately 30-40 minutes, turning the roll from time to time. Baste constantly to keep the meat moist. When done, remove the roast from the oven and keep hot.

STEP 2: Garnish and Presentation
> 15 ml peanut oil
> 120 g chayote, blanched, cubed
> salt
> 120 ml Sweet Spicy Soya Sauce, cold (see page 36)
> 4 kaffir lime leaves
> 1 tomato, peeled, seeded, quartered
> black peppercorns
> 4 lemon grass stalks, finely peeled

1   Heat the peanut oil in a frying pan and sauté the chayote for 2 minutes. Season with salt. Remove the vegetable from the pan and keep hot.
2   Untie the string from the lamb roll and slice the meat into 8 even slices.
3   Pour a little of the cold sauce onto each plate.
4   Arrange 2 slices of lamb on the sauce and garnish with the sautéed chayote, the lime leaf, a tomato quarter, black peppercorns and lemon grass.

PORK FILLET WITH CARAMBOLA

Daging Babi Belimbing Wuluh

PORK FILLET WITH CARAMBOLA

Two types of carambola are featured in this recipe: the small and sour-tasting *belimbing wuluh*, which serves as the base for the sauce, is counteracted by the sweetness of the relatively larger starfruit (*belimbing manis*), which is more commonly eaten raw, as a dessert, but is used here as a garnish.

> 4 x 140 g pieces pork fillet, fat and sinew removed
> coriander powder
> turmeric powder
> salt
> pepper
> 30 ml peanut oil
> 2 medium-sized starfruit
> 3 sour finger carambolas, sliced
> 250 ml Sour Finger Carambola Sauce, hot (see page 37)
> 60 g black glutinous rice or wild rice, cooked
> 2 red chilies, halved

1   Season the pork fillets with a little coriander, turmeric, salt and pepper.
2   Heat half of the peanut oil in a frying pan and fry the fillets in the hot oil on each side for 6-7 minutes, basting occasionally with the oil.
3   Remove the meat from the pan and keep warm.
4   Slice the starfruit to get the star cross-section. Heat the remaining peanut oil in a flat frying pan and quickly sauté the starfruit and sour finger carambola slices for 1 minute on each side. Season with salt. Remove the pan from the heat.
5   Pour some of the hot sauce onto each plate.
6   Slice the pork fillets into finger-thick slices and arrange them in a line on top of the sauce. Garnish with the sautéed fruit, cooked black glutinous rice and chili half.

NOTE: Soak the glutinous rice grains for 2-3 hours before cooking, or the cooked rice will be very hard.

Paha Kambing Jawa Timur Saus Pecel

LAMB LEG WITH PECEL SAUCE

STEP 1: Roast Lamb Leg
> 60 ml peanut oil
> 30 g shallots (bawang merah), peeled, finely diced
> 30 g onion, peeled, finely diced
> 20 g garlic, peeled, finely diced
> 20 g candlenuts, ground
> 600 g boneless lamb leg, rubbed with salt inside, tied firmly

1   Heat half of the oil in a frying pan. Add in the shallots, onions, garlic and candlenuts and sauté for 3-4 minutes until golden brown. Leave to cool.
2   Rub the lamb leg with the mixture. Let it marinate for 4 hours in a refrigerator.
3   Preheat the oven to 200°C.
4   Heat the remaining oil in a roasting pan.
5   Place the lamb leg in the pan and roast it in the oven for 30-40 minutes, basting frequently.
6   Remove the lamb leg from the oven and the roasting pan, and let it rest for 10 minutes.

STEP 2: Garnish and Presentation
> 500 ml water
> 50 g carrot, peeled, cut into fine strips
> 50 g long beans, cut into thin lengths
> 50 g cucumber, peeled, seeded, cut into fine strips
> 50 g water convolvulus
> 20 g beansprouts, cleaned
> 250 ml Sweet Spicy Pecel Sauce, hot (see page 31)
> 120 g fermented bean cake, fried, cut into shapes
> 10 g sweet basil leaves (kemangi)

1   Bring the water to the boil. Boil the carrot, long beans and cucumber for 1 minute in the water.
2   Add in the water convolvulus and beansprouts. Continue to boil for another minute. Drain.
3   Pour some of the hot sauce on each plate. Place portions of the vegetables on the sauce.
4   Slice the lamb leg and place on the vegetables. Garnish with bean cake, basil and remaining sauce.

OX TONGUE IN COCONUT SAUCE

BEEF BRAINS WITH BITTER GOURD

ROAST MARINATED LEG OF LAMB

Otak Godok dengan Pare

BEEF BRAINS WITH BITTER GOURD

Indonesians by and large love to eat brains and other offal. In this recipe, the natural sweetness of the brains is contrasted with the bitterness of the bitter gourd.

STEP 1: Beef Brains in Sauce

4 x 120 g beef brains
1 litre water
salt
2 salam leaves
500 ml White Beancurd Sauce (see page 39)

1   Soak the beef brains in very cold water for 6 hours to clean off all the blood and impurities. The water should be changed hourly and the brains will become very white as a result.
2   Pour the litre of water into a pot. Sprinkle in some salt and drop the salam leaves into the water. Bring the water to simmering point.
3   Add in the washed beef brains and continue to simmer for 5 minutes.
4   Remove the brains from the water and cool them off in iced water. When cool, peel off the fine transparent outer skin.
5   Pour the White Beancurd Sauce into a separate pot and bring it to a simmer. Put the brains in the sauce and cover the pot with a lid. Simmer for approximately 5-7 minutes. Stir occasionally, so that the brains absorb the flavour of the sauce.
6   Remove the pot from the heat and keep the brains warm in the sauce.

STEP 2: Vegetables and Presentation

30 ml vegetable oil
20 g bitter gourd, sliced, blanched
40 g tomatoes, peeled, seeded, sliced
20 g red chilies, seeded, diced
salt
white pepper
8 salam leaves
12 spring onions

1   In a frying pan, heat the vegetable oil and sauté the bitter gourd, tomatoes and chilies for 2 minutes, stirring frequently. Season with salt and pepper.
2   Spoon some of the sauce from the pot onto each plate.
3   Take the beef brains out of the pot and place them whole on the sauce.
4   Garnish the plate with the sautéed tomatoes, chilies, bitter gourd, the salam leaves and spring onions.

NOTE: Even after blanching, bitter gourd remains extremely bitter, hence, only a small amount is needed for this dish.

Daging Malbi

BRAISED BEEF MALBI

STEP 1: Braised Beef

60 ml peanut oil
30 g shallots (bawang merah), peeled, finely diced
10 g garlic, peeled, finely diced
600 g beef (top or bottom round or topside), cubed
5 g ginger, peeled, finely diced
5 g greater galangal, peeled, finely diced
30 g brown sugar (gula Jawa)
1 salam leaf
salt
125 ml tomato juice
500 ml coconut milk (see page 22)
60 ml dark sweet soya sauce
500 ml beef stock (see page 24)

1   Preheat the oven to 180°C.
2   Heat the peanut oil in a deep braising pan on top of the stove. Add the shallots and garlic and sauté until they are light brown, about 2-3 minutes.
3   Add in the beef and continue to sauté over high heat until all the meat has been seared a light brown.
4   Reduce the heat and add in the ginger, greater galangal, brown sugar and salam leaf. Continue to sauté an additional 2-3 minutes, then season with salt.
5   Stir in the tomato juice, coconut milk and sweet soya sauce.
6   Cover the braising pan with a lid and place it in the preheated oven. Cook for 1½-2 hours, gradually adding as much of the stock as necessary to prevent the sauce from becoming too thick and sticking.
7   Remove the pan from the oven and keep warm.

STEP 2: Vegetables and Presentation

15 ml peanut oil
6 small round aubergines (terung engkol), quartered,
    blanched for 2 minutes in salt water
60 g yam bean, blanched, cubed
60 g long beans, blanched, cut into thin lengths
40 g tomatoes, peeled, seeded, diced

1   In a separate pan, heat the oil and sauté all the vegetables in the hot oil for 2-3 minutes. Season with salt.
2   Serve the braised beef on individual plates and garnish with the sautéed vegetables.

NOTE: If small aubergines are not available, use 300-350 g aubergine cut in 1-cm cubes and blanched.

Gulai Kambing Pangandaran
BONELESS LAMB RACK PANGANDARAN

This recipe features a fiery, spicy accompanying sauce which is served cold with the hot lamb dish.

STEP 1: Roast Rolled Lamb Racks
4 x 150 g boneless lamb racks
10 g shallots (bawang merah), peeled, finely diced
5 g garlic, peeled, finely diced
20 g candlenuts, ground
5 g ginger, finely diced
1 lemon grass stalk, finely diced
2 g turmeric powder
salt
pepper
20 ml vegetable oil

1 Using a cleaver or chopper, slightly flatten the lamb racks.
2 In a bowl, combine the next 5 ingredients. Mix well. Rub this mixture on both sides of the lamb.
3 Sprinkle on the turmeric powder, salt and pepper. Let the lamb marinate overnight in a refrigerator.
4 Preheat the oven to 180°C. Then remove the marinated lamb from the refrigerator.
5 Roll each piece into a sausage shape and tie with string.
6 Put the oil in a roasting pan and heat it in the oven. Place the lamb rolls in the pan and roast for approximately 8-10 minutes. Occasionally baste the lamb with the dripping to keep the meat moist.
7 Withdraw the pan from the oven and let the lamb rest in the pan for 3-4 minutes before cutting.

STEP 2: Garnish and Presentation
15 ml vegetable oil
8 long beans, blanched
4 perkedels (see pages 118, 119)
250 g Brambang Sauce (see page 36)

1 Heat the oil in a pan and sauté the beans for 2 minutes, then fry the perkedels for 4 minutes.
2 Slice the lamb rolls and arrange them on individual plates.
3 Garnish with the long beans and perkedel, and serve with the cold sauce.

Otak Sapi Muda Bukit Tinggi
BRAISED CALF BRAINS BUKIT TINGGI

4 x 120-140 g calf brains
500 ml beef stock (see page 24)
60 ml white vinegar
salt
4 mustard green leaves, blanched
250 ml Indonesian Curry Sauce, hot (see page 37)
10-15 g turmeric leaves, cut into very fine strips
80 g vegetable pickles, cold (see pages 126-7)

1 Clean the brains as described in Beef Brains with Bitter Gourd (see page 98).
2 Pour the beef stock into a stockpot and add in the vinegar. Season with salt. Bring the stock to the boil, reduce the heat to simmering point.
3 Add the calf brains to the stock and simmer for 6-8 minutes.
4 Remove the brains from the stock and cool them in iced water.
5 Peel off the transparent outer skin and discard this, then wrap each brain in a mustard green leaf and place the wrapped pieces in a small saucepan.
6 In a separate pan, heat up the Indonesian Curry Sauce until it simmers. Pour this sauce over the wrapped calf brains and simmer them gently for approximately 2-4 minutes.
7 Remove the brains from the sauce and cut each parcel in half.
8 Place 2 pieces on each plate and pour the sauce over the meat.
9 Garnish the plates with the strips of turmeric leaves and vegetable pickles.

Kambing Kecap Saus Gulai
LAMB CHOPS GULAI

45 ml dark sweet soya sauce
10 g shallots (bawang merah), peeled, finely diced
2 g garlic, peeled, finely diced
5 ml freshly squeezed lime juice
salt
12 x 50-60 g lamb chops
30 ml peanut oil
8 spring onions, use lower half only
4 cabbage leaves, cut into squares
1 g anise powder
250 ml Indonesian Curry Sauce, hot (see page 37)

1 Mix the sweet soya sauce with the shallots, garlic, lime juice and salt.
2 Brush this mixture on both sides of the lamb chops and let them marinate in the refrigerator for 2 hours.
3 Dip the marinated lamb chops in some peanut oil, place them on a hot griddle or under a hot grill and cook on both sides for approximately 3-4 minutes, until medium-done. Remove and keep warm.
4 In a flat frying pan, heat the remaining peanut oil and sauté the spring onions and cabbage for 1-2 minutes. Season with the anise, toss well and continue to sauté for another 2 minutes. Withdraw the pan from the heat.
5 Pour the hot sauce onto the plates.
6 Set 3 lamb chops on the sauce on each plate and garnish with the sautéed vegetables.

BEEF ON SPICY COCONUT SAUCE

VEAL WITH GREEN CHILI SAUCE

Daging Bakar Kecap Saus Rendang
BEEF ON SPICY COCONUT SAUCE

STEP 1: Grilled Beef Fillet

20 g shallots (bawang merah), peeled, finely diced
5 g garlic, peeled, finely diced
10 g red chilies, seeded, finely diced
5 ml freshly squeezed lime juice
30 ml dark sweet soya sauce
salt
4 x 160 g pieces beef fillet, fat and sinew removed
30 ml vegetable oil

1 Combine all the ingredients, except for the fillet and oil, in a bowl. Mix well.
2 Brush this marinade on both sides of the fillets and marinate in the fridge for 1 hour.
3 Drain off the marinade and season the beef with a little salt.
4 Dip the meat into the vegetable oil and then cook it under a hot grill or over a hot griddle for 4 minutes on each side. Remove the meat from the heat and keep it warm.

STEP 2: Garnish and Presentation

30 ml vegetable oil
120 g beansprouts, cleaned
10 g red chilies, seeded, cut into strips
salt
coriander powder
250 ml Spicy Coconut Sauce, hot (see page 36)
4 mustard greens, blanched, cut into half

1 Heat the oil in a frying pan and add the beansprouts and chilies. Sauté the vegetables in the oil briskly for 2 minutes. Season with salt and a dash of coriander powder. Remove from the heat.
2 Pour a portion of the hot sauce onto each plate.
3 Arrange the meat on the sauce. Garnish with the sautéed vegetables and the mustard greens.

Daging Sapi Muda Saus Cabe Hijau
VEAL WITH GREEN CHILI SAUCE

8 x 60 g veal medallions, fat and sinew removed
3 g ginger, peeled, finely diced
3 g greater galangal, peeled, finely diced
salt
30 ml peanut oil
12 dried black Chinese mushrooms, soaked in warm water for
1 hour
8 Red Chilies with Veal Stuffing (see page 118)
250 ml chicken stock (see page 24), or water
250 ml Green Chili Sauce, hot (see page 30)
2 green chilies, seeded, diced

1 Season the veal medallions with the ginger and greater galangal. Leave the meat to marinate in a refrigerator for 1 hour before using.
2 Take the meat out of the refrigerator and season with salt.
3 Use half the amount of peanut oil to brush on the meat. Grill the veal medallions on each side for approximately 3-4 minutes under a hot grill or on a hot griddle. Remove and keep warm.
4 Heat the remaining oil in a separate frying pan and add in the black mushrooms. Season with salt. Sauté, tossing well, for 2 minutes. Remove from the heat but keep the mushrooms warm.
5 Poach the stuffed chilies in chicken stock for approximately 4-5 minutes. Remove from the stock and cut in half.
6 Spoon 3 tablespoons of the hot sauce onto each plate. Slice the medallions in half and place on the sauce.
7 Place the stuffed chilies in the centre of each plate. Garnish with the sautéed mushrooms and sprinkle with the diced chilies.

LAMB LOIN AND PUMPKIN

Kambing Labu Merah

LAMB LOIN AND PUMPKIN

4 x 150 g pieces lamb loin, cut off a rack, boned, fat and
*   sinew removed*
2 g anise powder
salt
pepper
30 ml peanut oil
60 g shallots (bawang merah), peeled, finely diced
120 g pumpkin, diced, blanched
250 ml Pumpkin Sauce, hot (see page 29)
20 g roasted pumpkin seeds
10 g green chilies, seeded, diced
12 star anise
4 kaffir lime leaves

1   Season the lamb with the anise, salt and pepper.
2   Heat half of the peanut oil in a frying pan. Sauté the lamb at 180°C for approximately 10 minutes, turning the meat occasionally. Remove and keep warm.
3   In a flat frying pan, heat the remaining oil and sauté the shallots and diced pumpkin for 2-3 minutes. Stir constantly. Season with some anise and salt. Remove from the pan and keep warm.
4   Pour some of the hot Pumpkin Sauce onto each plate.
5   Slice each lamb loin into 8-10 pieces and arrange the slices in a circle on the sauce.
6   Place the sautéed shallots and pumpkin in the centre of the plate, ringed by the lamb slices. Sprinkle with the pumpkin seeds and diced chilies.
7   Garnish with the star anise and lime leaf.

Iga Kambing Saus Ubi Jalar

LAMB RACK ON SWEET POTATO SAUCE

Good quality New Zealand lamb is highly recommended due to its fine taste, but if you prefer a stronger-tasting lamb, use the British or French.

STEP 1: Roast Lamb Racks

> 4 x 250-300 g lamb racks, on the bone, fat cover removed, fat and meat tissue between the rib bones should be cut out from the tips of the bones approximately 2 cm down
> 5 g greater galangal, peeled, finely diced
> 1 lemon grass stalk, diced
> 2 g turmeric powder
> 1 garlic clove, peeled, finely diced
> salt
> 15 ml peanut oil

1 Preheat the oven to 200°C.
2 Season the lamb racks with the greater galangal, lemon grass, turmeric powder, garlic and salt.
3 Pour 15 ml of the peanut oil into a roasting pan and heat it very hot on the stove top.
4 Place the lamb racks in the roasting pan and sear quickly, approximately 1 minute, on each side.
5 Then roast the meat in the preheated oven for about 10-12 minutes, basting frequently, until the lamb is medium-done.
6 Remove the racks from the oven and keep them warm.

STEP 2: Vegetables and Presentation

> 30 ml peanut oil
> 40 g sweet potato, diced, blanched
> 40 g bamboo shoots, diced, blanched
> salt
> pepper
> 250 ml Sweet Potato Sauce, hot (see page 28)

1 Heat the peanut oil in a frying pan. Sauté the sweet potatoes and bamboo shoots together for about 2-3 minutes. Season with salt and pepper.
2 Carve one chop off each lamb rack and leave the rest whole.
3 Form a pattern on the individual plates with the hot sauce.
4 Set the whole lamb rack on the sauce.
5 Place the sautéed vegetables next to the lamb rack and arrange the remaining lamb chop on the vegetables.

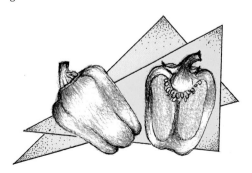

Daging Panggang Banda Aceh

BEEF FILLET BANDA ACEH

STEP 1: Fiery Acehnese Sauce (Saus Bumbu Aceh)

> 100 g dry shredded coconut flakes
> 15 ml peanut oil
> 20 g shallots (bawang merah), peeled, finely diced
> 10 g garlic, peeled, finely diced
> 30 g red chilies, seeded, finely diced
> 30 g green chilies, seeded, finely diced
> 3 g bird's eye chilies, seeded, finely diced
> 1 lemon grass stalk, bruised
> 10 g tamarind pulp
> 5 g clove powder
> 5 g coriander powder
> 5 g white pepper powder
> pinch of turmeric powder
> 500 ml water
> salt

1 Sauté the dry shredded coconut flakes in a hot pan without any fat or oil until they are light brown. Remove from the pan.
2 Heat the oil in the pan and sauté the shallots, garlic, chilies and lemon grass for 2 minutes.
3 Stir in the tamarind paste and clove, coriander, pepper and turmeric powder, together with the roasted coconut flakes. Continue to sauté for 2 minutes more.
4 Add in the water and bring to the boil. Season with salt, then reduce the heat. Let the mixture simmer for approximately 20 minutes.
5 Withdraw the pan from the heat and discard the lemon grass.
6 Pour the sauce into a blender and purée at high speed for 2-3 minutes. Remove from the blender and serve. Yields 750 ml.

STEP 2: Grilled Beef Fillet

> 4 x 150 g pieces beef fillet, fat and sinew removed
> salt
> 4 tablespoons direndam marinade (see page 23)
> 160 g pumpkin, skinned, seeded, blanched, cubed
> 15 ml vegetable oil

1 Season the fillet with the salt and brush on the marinade.
2 Grill the beef on each side for approximately 4 minutes. Remove from the grill and keep the meat warm.
3 Sauté the pumpkin in the oil and season with salt.

STEP 3: Presentation

> 250 ml Fiery Acehnese Sauce, hot
> 12 Stuffed Mustard Green Leaves, hot (see page 119)
> 10 g red chilies, seeded, finely diced

1 Spoon a little of the hot sauce onto each plate.
2 Place the fillet on top of the sauce and garnish with the Stuffed Mustard Green Leaves and sautéed pumpkin.
3 Sprinkle the diced red chilies over the dish.

Rendang Kambing Kota Baru

LAMB IN SPICY COCONUT SAUCE

STEP 1: Braised Lamb Loins

  30 ml peanut oil
  20 g shallots (bawang merah), peeled, finely diced
  2 g garlic, peeled, finely diced
  40 g candlenuts, ground
  2 g turmeric powder
  2 g coriander powder
  1 lemon grass stalk, finely diced
  salt
  4 x 150 g lamb loin chops, fat and sinew removed
  4 large white cabbage leaves, blanched
  500 ml Spicy Coconut Sauce, hot (see page 36)

1 Pour the peanut oil into a bowl. Add the shallots, garlic and candlenuts. Sprinkle the turmeric and coriander powder over the mixture. Add the lemon grass and season with salt. Mix well, using a whisk, until the mixture becomes a thick paste. (To adjust the consistency of the marinade, add more candlenuts to make the paste thicker; if it is too thick, add more peanut oil.)
2 Brush this marinade evenly on the lamb and let it marinate in a refrigerator for 2 hours.
3 Preheat the oven to 180°C. Then remove the lamb from the refrigerator.
4 Sear the lamb at high heat in a frying pan for 1 minute on each side.
5 Remove the meat from the pan and wrap each piece tightly in a blanched cabbage leaf.
6 Place the wrapped lamb in a small braising pan and pour the hot Spicy Coconut Sauce over the meat. Cover with the lid and braise in the preheated oven for 10 minutes, stirring occasionally. Withdraw the pan from the heat, but leave the meat in the pan.

NOTE: During the braising process, the thickness of the sauce may cause the meat to stick to the bottom of the pan and consequently burn. Add a little lamb stock to free the meat.

STEP 2: Garnish and Presentation

  15 ml peanut oil
  100 g straw mushrooms, quartered
  60 g long beans, blanched
  1 g turmeric powder
  salt
  15 ml lamb stock (see page 24)

1 In a shallow frying pan, heat the peanut oil and add the mushrooms and long beans. Season with the turmeric powder and salt. Sauté quickly, tossing well, for 2 minutes.
2 Pour in the lamb stock and continue sautéing until the liquid has evaporated.
3 Remove the lamb loins from the braising pan and slice each into 2 pieces. Arrange the pieces in the middle of the plate. Pour the remaining sauce over the meat and garnish with the sautéed vegetables.

Daging Sapi Muda Bungkus Daun Talas

VEAL FILLET IN TARO LEAVES

The large, dark green taro leaves impart a slightly bitter flavour to the veal; no other leaf will do the same.

STEP 1: Veal Fillets

  20 g shallots (bawang merah), peeled, finely diced
  30 g candlenuts, ground
  15 g turmeric powder
  2 g coriander powder
  250 ml coconut milk (see page 22)
  5 g salt
  4 x 120 g pieces veal fillet, fat and sinew removed
  15 ml peanut oil
  4 taro leaves, blanched in boiling salt water for 1-2 minutes

1 Combine the shallots, candlenuts, turmeric powder, coriander powder, coconut milk and salt in a bowl to make the marinade. Mix well.
2 Place the veal fillets in an earthenware dish and pour the marinade mixture on top.
3 Leave the meat to marinate for 1 hour.
4 Preheat the oven to 180°C.
5 Heat the peanut oil in a frying pan.
6 Remove the pieces of veal from the marinade and sear quickly over high heat in the hot oil for 1 minute on each side. Then wrap the meat in the taro leaves.
7 Place the wrapped meat on a slightly oiled baking sheet and bake for approximately 8-10 minutes in the preheated oven.
8 Remove the meat from the oven and keep warm.

STEP 2: Garnish and Presentation

  15 ml peanut oil
  80 g snowpeas, blanched
  80 g carrots, peeled, carved, blanched
  40 g water apples, cut into strips
  salt
  250 ml Spicy Coconut Sauce, hot (see page 36)
  8 cashewnut leaves

1 Heat the peanut oil in a frying pan. Sauté the snowpeas, carrots and water apples in the oil for 1 minute. Season with salt and keep warm.
2 Spread a layer of the hot sauce on each plate.
3 Cut each veal fillet into 4 slices and place the pieces on the sauce.
4 Garnish with the sautéed vegetables and cashewnut leaves.

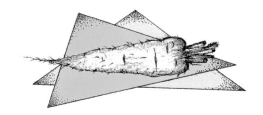

POULTRY

Dada Bebek Saus Jeruk

DUCK BREAST ON ORANGE SAUCE

STEP 1: Roast Duck Breasts

> 4 x 200 g boneless duck breasts
> 5 g ginger, peeled, finely diced
> 5 g lemon grass stalk, finely diced
> salt
> ground white pepper
> 15 ml peanut oil

1   Season the duck breasts with the ginger, lemon grass, salt and pepper. Let them marinate for 2 hours, then preheat the oven to 200°C.
2   Heat the oil in a frying pan and sear the duck breasts for 1-2 minutes on each side until brown.
3   Place the pan in the oven for 8-10 minutes. Turn the breasts over frequently and baste. Remove from the oven and keep warm.

STEP 2: Garnish and Presentation

> 250 ml Orange Sauce, hot (see page 38)
> 10 g green peppercorns
> 10 ml peanut oil
> 160 g oyster mushrooms
> 40 g dried black Chinese mushrooms, soaked in warm water
>   for 1 hour, sliced
> salt

1   Cover the plate with the hot Orange Sauce and sprinkle the peppercorns on the sauce.
2   Slice each breast very thinly and arrange the slices on the sauce.
3   Heat the peanut oil in a flat, wide frying pan. Sauté the oyster and black mushrooms for 2 minutes, stirring constantly. (Oyster mushrooms are very fine and delicate and require very little cooking time.) Season with salt, remove from the heat and serve immediately with the duck.

CHICKEN BREAST ON SPICED PEANUTS

CHICKEN ON HONEY CHILI SAUCE

DUCK IN PEANUT PINEAPPLE SAUCE

Ayam Sumbawa

CHICKEN ON HONEY CHILI SAUCE

Much of the best Indonesian honey comes from the volcanic island of Sumbawa, where bees gather nectar from the flower-festooned forests.

STEP 1: Grilled Chicken Breasts
60 ml honey
20 g shallots (bawang merah), peeled, finely diced
5 g garlic, peeled, finely diced
15 ml tamarind water (see page 23)
4 x 150-160 chicken breasts, boned except for the wing
25 ml peanut oil

1 Combine the honey, shallots, garlic and tamarind water in a bowl. Stir well with a whisk.
2 Brush this marinade on either side of the chicken breasts and let them marinate for 2 hours in a refrigerator.
3 After the chicken breasts have marinated, quickly dip them into the peanut oil.
4 Using a hot griddle or a charcoal or gas grill, cook the chicken at a high temperature on each side for approximately 4 minutes. Remove the meat from the grill and keep warm.

STEP 2: Garnish and Presentation
20 ml peanut oil
80 g asparagus beans, sliced
40 g candied nutmeg
10 g red chilies, seeded, cut into strips
salt
250 ml Honey Chili Sauce, hot (see page 31)

1 Heat the oil in a frying pan and sauté the asparagus beans, candied nutmeg and chilies quickly, tossing well, for 2 minutes. Season with salt. Remove the pan from the heat.
2 Spread the hot Honey Chili Sauce on the plates.
3 Arrange the sautéed vegetable mixture on the sauce.
4 Cut each chicken breast lengthwise into 2 and place the slices on the sauce and vegetables.

Itik Danau Laut Tawar

DUCK IN PEANUT PINEAPPLE SAUCE

STEP 1: Braised Duck
1 x 1.5-2 kg duck
20 g garlic, peeled, finely diced
20 g ginger, peeled, finely diced
110 ml freshly squeezed lime juice
salt
30 ml peanut oil
80 ml freshly squeezed pineapple juice
500 ml Peanut Sauce, hot (see page 29)
80 g fresh pineapple, diced

1 Take the duck, split it down the middle lengthwise and remove the backbone completely with a sharp knife. Then joint the duck and put all the pieces in a bowl.
2 Sprinkle the garlic and ginger over the duck. Pour 80 ml of lime juice over the meat and let it marinate in the refrigerator for 4-5 hours.
3 Preheat the oven to 180°C. Then take the duck out of the marinade and dry it with kitchen paper towels. Season with salt and set aside.
4 Heat the peanut oil in a small roasting pan over high heat and add in the duck pieces. Sear the meat quickly on each side for approximately 1-2 minutes, or until the meat is light brown.
5 Put the pan in the preheated oven and roast for approximately 10 minutes. Turn the pieces over from time to time and baste frequently.
6 Remove the pan from the oven, turn the oven down to 160°C, and drain off the fat and oil from the pan. Leave the duck pieces in the pan.
7 Pour the remaining lime juice, the pineapple juice, Peanut Sauce and diced pineapple into the pan with the duck. Return the pan to the oven and braise for 45 minutes.
8 After braising, remove the duck pieces, leaving the sauce in the pan.
9 Remove all bones from the duck breasts, except the wing bone. Then cut each duck breast into thin slices lengthwise, and split the legs into 3-4 pieces. Set aside and keep warm.
10 Take the sauce out of the pan, process in a blender for 2-3 minutes until it becomes a fine purée. Keep the sauce hot.

STEP 2: Garnish and Presentation
15 ml peanut oil
40 g raw peanuts, shelled
1 g cinnamon powder
salt
20 g green chilies, seeded, diced
40 g yam bean, turned or carved

1 Heat the oil in a frying pan and sauté the peanuts until golden brown. Season with the cinnamon and salt.
2 Pour a layer of the warm sauce from Step 1 on each plate. Sprinkle on the sautéed peanuts and diced chilies.
3 Arrange 2 pieces of the duck leg with some slices of the duck breast on the sauce.
4 Garnish with the yam bean.

Semur Ayam Bumbu Kacang

CHICKEN BREAST ON SPICED PEANUTS

STEP 1: Semur Marinade
15 ml peanut oil
10 g shallots (bawang merah), peeled, finely diced
2 g garlic, peeled, finely diced
2 g ginger, peeled, finely diced
1 g nutmeg powder
60 ml tomato juice
30 ml dark sweet soya sauce

1 In a pan, heat the peanut oil and sauté the shallots, garlic and ginger without letting them brown.
2 Add in the nutmeg powder, tomato juice and sweet soya sauce. Bring the mixture to the boil, reduce the heat and simmer until the marinade thickens.
3 Remove the pan from the heat, pour the marinade into a bowl and set it aside to cool.

STEP 2: Roast Chicken Breasts
4 x 150 g chicken breasts, boned except for the wing
salt
20 ml peanut oil

1 Place the chicken breasts in a bowl or dish and pour the marinade made in Step 1 over the meat. Place in a refrigerator to marinate for 2 hours.
2 Preheat the oven to 180°C. Then take out the marinated chicken breasts, drain off the excess liquid and season them with salt.
3 Heat the peanut oil in a shallow roasting pan or tray inside the preheated oven. Place the chicken breasts in the pan and roast for approximately 5-8 minutes, turning occasionally and basting frequently. (The chicken breasts may stick to the bottom of the roasting pan, so loosen the meat carefully when turning the breasts or removing them from the pan.)
4 Remove the pan from the oven and keep warm.

STEP 3: Garnish and Presentation
20 ml peanut oil
4 small round aubergines (terung engkol), quartered, or
*   300 g sliced aubergines, blanched in salt water*
salt
120 g Candied Mango, cut into slivers (see page 123)
250 ml Peanut Sauce, hot (see page 29)
20 g peanuts, shelled, peeled, deep-fried, finely chopped

1 Heat the peanut oil in a shallow frying pan and sauté the blanched aubergines for 2 minutes, stirring constantly. Season with salt.
2 Stir in the candied mango and continue to sauté for another minute. Remove and keep warm.
3 Pour some of the hot Peanut Sauce onto each plate. Sprinkle the chopped peanuts on the plate.
4 Cut each roast chicken breast, from the tip to the round end, into 3-5 long slices. Place the slices on the plate and garnish with the sautéed aubergines and mango.

Ayam Paniki

CHICKEN PANIKI

The original recipe for this hails from Manado in north Sulawesi.

STEP 1: Spring Chickens
60 ml peanut oil
25 g shallots (bawang merah), peeled, finely diced
10 g garlic, peeled, finely diced
50 g red chilies, seeded, finely diced
10 g lemon grass stalk, finely diced
5 g ginger, peeled, finely diced
15 g turmeric powder
2 kaffir lime leaves
500 ml coconut milk (see page 22)
salt
4 x 180-220 g boned spring chickens, each cut into 6-8 pieces

1 Heat 30 ml of the peanut oil in a large saucepan. Add in the shallots, garlic, chilies, lemon grass and ginger. Sauté for 2 minutes without browning.
2 Add the turmeric powder and kaffir lime leaves, and continue to sauté for 2 minutes more.
3 Pour in the coconut milk and bring to the boil, stirring frequently. Season with salt.
4 Preheat the oven to 280°C and heat the remaining peanut oil in a roasting pan in the oven.
5 Place the chicken pieces in the saucepan. Cover with a lid and simmer for approximately 5 minutes.
6 Remove the half-cooked chicken from the sauce and keep the sauce warm over low heat.
7 Place the chicken pieces in the oil heated in the roasting pan and roast the chicken in the preheated oven for approximately 8-10 minutes, basting from time to time. Then remove the roasting pan from the oven and take out the chicken pieces. Keep warm.
8 Remove the saucepan from the heat and discard the kaffir lime leaves.
9 Pour the sauce into a blender and process until smooth. Remove and keep warm.

STEP 2: Garnish and Presentation
15 ml peanut oil
3 starfruit, cut into sections
2 red chilies, cut into rings
12 melinjo leaves — 4 cut into fine strips; 8 blanched
salt

1 Heat the peanut oil in a frying pan and sauté the starfruit, chilies and melinjo leaf strips for 1 minute. Season with salt, then remove from the heat.
2 Spread some of the warm sauce on each plate.
3 Arrange the chicken pieces in the middle of the plate, on the sauce.
4 Garnish with the sautéed starfruit slices, chili rings and strips of melinjo leaves. Top with the blanched melinjo leaves.

QUAILS ON CURRIED VEGETABLES

Burung Puyuh Ujung Kulon

QUAILS ON CURRIED VEGETABLES

20 ml dark sweet soya sauce
20 ml palm wine
10 ml vegetable oil
15 g garlic, peeled, finely chopped
salt
4 quails
120 g glass noodles, soaked 5 minutes, cut into short lengths
4 dried black Chinese mushrooms, soaked for 1 hour, sliced
20 g peanuts, chopped
40 g chicken liver, boiled for 2-3 minutes, chopped
20 g shallots (bawang merah), peeled, finely diced
200 g chicken breast meat, diced
10 g ginger, peeled, finely diced
10 coriander leaves
20 ml peanut oil
4 portions Curried Vegetables (see page 123)

1 Mix the sweet soya sauce, palm wine, vegetable oil and 5 g garlic together to make the marinade. Season with salt.
2 Brush this marinade onto the quails and leave them to marinate for 1 hour.
3 Combine the noodles with the black mushrooms, peanuts, chicken liver, shallots and chicken breast. Mix well and add in the rest of the garlic, the ginger, coriander and salt to make the stuffing.
4 Preheat the oven to 200°C. Then stuff the marinated quails with the noodle filling. Secure the opening with a toothpick.
5 Place the quails in a roasting pan and brush them with some peanut oil. Roast them in the preheated oven for approximately 20 minutes.
6 Remove the quails from the oven and cut each in half. Arrange these on the Curried Vegetables. The vegetables used on page 123 can be varied according to taste.

PIGEON BREAST ON NUTMEG SAUCE

CHICKEN BREAST BANTEN

PEANUT HONEY CHICKEN

Ayam Kintuk Banten

CHICKEN BREAST BANTEN

STEP 1: Fried Chicken Breasts

4 x 120 g boneless chicken breasts, skinned
15 g turmeric powder
20 g candlenuts, ground
20 g shallots (bawang merah), peeled, finely diced
10 g garlic, peeled, finely diced
10 g lemon grass stalk, finely diced
10 g greater galangal, peeled, cut into fine strips
10 g sweet basil leaves (kemangi)
salt
30 ml peanut oil

1 Use a small, pointed knife to slice each chicken breast open lengthwise. Spread them out on a flat surface.
2 Mix together the next 6 ingredients.
3 Sprinkle the mixture on the open chicken breasts. Top with the basil leaves and season with salt.
4 Fold the chicken breasts back into their original shape. Secure the opening with a toothpick.
5 Heat the oil in a frying pan and fry the chicken breasts on each side for approximately 4-5 minutes. Remove from the pan and keep warm.

STEP 2: Banten Coconut Sauce (Saus Kintuk Banten)

30 ml peanut oil
20 g shallots (bawang merah), peeled, finely diced
5 g garlic, peeled, finely diced
30 g torch ginger, diced
50 g sour finger carambolas, diced
2 g nutmeg powder
5 g sugar
30 ml tamarind water (see page 23)
60 ml chili juice (see page 23)
250 ml coconut milk (see page 22)
salt

1 Heat the peanut oil in a saucepan. Sauté the shallots and garlic in the hot oil for 2 minutes.
2 Add in the torch ginger and sour finger carambola, and continue to sauté for another 2 minutes.
3 Add the nutmeg powder and sugar, and sauté for a further 2 minutes.
4 Pour in the tamarind water, chili juice and coconut milk. Season with salt and bring the mixture to the boil. Reduce the heat and simmer for approximately 10 minutes, stirring frequently.
5 Remove from the heat and pour the mixture into a blender. Process at high speed for 2-3 minutes until the sauce becomes smooth. Remove from the blender and keep warm. Yields 375 ml.

STEP 3: Garnish and Presentation

250 ml peanut oil
50 g dried glass noodles
250 ml Banten Coconut Sauce, hot
80 g leeks, sliced, blanched
20 g red chilies, seeded, diced
basil leaves

1 Heat the peanut oil in a pan to 350°C. Fry the dried glass noodles in the hot oil, stirring frequently, until they are light brown and crispy. This should happen very quickly.
2 Remove the noodles from the hot oil and drain them on kitchen paper. Keep warm.
3 Pour some of the hot sauce onto each plate.
4 Set the deep-fried noodles on the sauce.
5 Slice the chicken breasts vertically into 4 and place the slices by the deep-fried noodles.
6 Garnish with the leeks, diced chilies and basil leaves.

Ayam Saus Kacang Madu

PEANUT HONEY CHICKEN

This is a very tasty dish on a sweet spicy sauce which is well complemented by the fruit salad.

STEP 1: Sautéed Chicken Breasts

4 x 150-160 g chicken breasts, boned except for the wing
30 ml red chili juice (see page 23)
20 g shallots (bawang merah), peeled, finely diced
5 g ginger, peeled, finely diced
salt
30 ml peanut oil
250 ml Peanut Honey Sauce (see page 38)

1 Place the chicken breasts in a shallow dish.
2 In a bowl, combine the chili juice, shallots and ginger. Stir well with a whisk.
3 Pour this marinade over the chicken breasts and put them in a refrigerator to marinate for 4 hours.
4 Remove the marinated chicken breasts from the marinade and drain off the excess liquid. Season them with salt.
5 Heat the oil in a frying pan and sauté the chicken on each side for approximately 3-4 minutes, turning occasionally and basting with the oil. Remove from the pan and keep hot.
6 Pour out all the excess fat from the pan. Then, using the same pan, deglaze with the Peanut Honey Sauce and keep this boiling for 2 minutes. Withdraw the pan from the heat and keep the sauce hot.

STEP 2: Garnish and Presentation

15 ml peanut oil
40 g mangosteen segments
20 g water apples, sliced
10 g young green mango, finely sliced
salt

1 Heat the peanut oil in a frying pan and add in all the fruits. Sauté quickly for 1 minute and season lightly with salt. Remove from the heat.
2 Spread some of the hot Peanut Honey Sauce on each plate.
3 Cut the chicken breasts open, butterfly style, and arrange on top of the sauce.
4 Garnish with the sautéed fruits.

Dada Burong Dara dan Saus Pala

PIGEON BREAST ON NUTMEG SAUCE

Pigeon is a favourite dish on the island of Timor, where people go hunting for them in the rugged rock formations and wide expanses of bush.

STEP 1: Sautéed Pigeon Breasts
60 ml dark sweet soya sauce
20 g shallots (bawang merah), peeled, finely diced
5 g red chilies, seeded, finely diced
30 ml freshly squeezed lemon juice
16-20 x 30-40 g boneless pigeon breasts
salt
30 ml peanut oil
250 ml Nutmeg Sauce (see page 31)

1   Pour the sweet soya sauce into a bowl and add in the shallots, chilies and lemon juice. Stir the marinade well with a whisk.
2   Place the pigeon breasts in another bowl.
3   Pour the marinade over the pigeon breasts and let them marinate in the refrigerator for 4 hours to allow the meat to absorb the flavour.
4   Remove the marinated meat from the refrigerator and season with salt.
5   Heat the peanut oil in a frying pan. Sauté the pigeon breasts quickly on each side for approximately 2 minutes. Remove the meat from the pan and keep warm.
6   Drain off the oil from the pan and pour in the Nutmeg Sauce. Boil quickly for 2-3 minutes; withdraw the pan from the heat but keep the sauce hot.

STEP 2: Garnish and Presentation
15 ml peanut oil
40 g beansprouts, cleaned
5 g carrot, peeled, cut into strips
10-15 g kenikir leaves

1   Heat the peanut oil in a pan. Add in the beansprouts and carrots. Sauté, tossing quickly, for 2 minutes. Season with salt. Remove the vegetables from the heat and keep warm.
2   Spread some of the hot sauce in the centre of each plate.
3   Place the sautéed vegetables on the sauce.
4   Place 4-5 pigeon breasts on and around the vegetables.
5   Garnish with the kenikir leaves.

Burung Dara Isi Saus Semur

PIGEONS ON SPICED SOYA SAUCE

STEP 1: Roast Stuffed Pigeons
4 x 100 g pigeons, boned except for the legs
salt
300 g chicken meat, minced
10 g red chilies, seeded, finely diced
10 g green chilies, seeded, finely diced
2 g coriander powder
2 g cumin powder
80 ml cream (33% fat)
30 ml peanut oil

1   Spread the pigeons, skin side down, on a flat surface and rub lightly with salt. Set aside.
2   Process the chicken meat in a blender for 2-3 minutes until smooth. Remove from the blender and put in a cold bowl.
3   Add in the chilies, coriander and cumin powder. Slowly stir in the cream and season with salt. Combine this stuffing mixture well with a wooden spatula.
4   Preheat the oven to 180°C. Heat the oil in a roasting pan in the oven.
5   Spoon an even amount of the stuffing onto each pigeon.
6   Fold up the pigeons and shape them to their original form. Secure the opening with a toothpick.
7   Place the stuffed pigeons, breast side up, in the roasting pan and roast the pigeons in the oven for 35 minutes. Baste frequently to keep the meat moist. Remove the pigeons from the oven and keep them warm.

STEP 2: Garnish and Presentation
peanut oil for deep-frying
80 g sweet potatoes, cut into strips, blanched
salt
cinnamon powder
250 ml Spiced Soya Sauce, hot (see page 34)
10 g green chilies, sliced

1   Heat the peanut oil in a deep pan and deep-fry the sweet potato strips until golden. Drain off the oil, then sprinkle the salt and cinnamon powder over the sweet potato strips and keep them hot.
2   Spread some of the hot sauce on each plate.
3   Cut each pigeon in half, starting at the leg. Place the 2 halves on the sauce, one piece skin side down and the other, skin up.
4   Garnish with the fried sweet potato and chili slices.

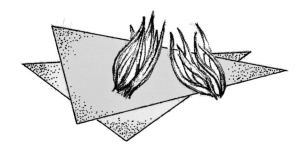

Ayam Saus Kacang Merah

CHICKEN WITH RED KIDNEY BEANS

STEP 1: Sautéed Chicken Breasts

4 x 150-160 g boneless chicken breasts
60 ml red chili juice (see page 23)
30 g brown sugar (gula Jawa)
10 g shallots (bawang merah), peeled, finely diced
5 g ginger, peeled, finely diced
salt
25 ml peanut oil

1   Place the chicken breasts in a small dish.
2   Pour the chili juice into a saucepan and bring to the boil. Mix in the brown sugar and simmer until the sugar has dissolved. Remove from the heat and let the liquid cool at room temperature.
3   When the sugared chili juice has cooled, make the marinade by adding the shallots, ginger and garlic to it.
4   Pour the marinade over the chicken breasts and refrigerate for 4 hours to allow the meat to absorb the flavour.
5   Remove the marinated chicken from the refrigerator and season with salt.
6   Heat the oil in a frying pan. Sauté the chicken on each side for approximately 3-4 minutes. Remove and keep warm.

STEP 2: Garnish and Presentation

20 ml peanut oil
80 g red kidney beans, soaked overnight, boiled until soft
8 long beans, blanched, tied in loops or braided
250 ml Red Kidney Bean Sauce, hot (see page 34)
2 red chilies, diced

1   Heat the oil in a pan and sauté the kidney beans and long beans for 1-2 minutes. Season with salt and withdraw the pan from the heat but keep the beans warm.
2   Cut each chicken breast lengthwise into 3-4 slices.
3   Pour the hot sauce onto individual plates. Arrange the chicken slices on the sauce.
4   Set the long beans on the plates and fill the loops with the sautéed kidney beans and the diced chilies.

Ayam Gulung Urap-urapan Saus Kemangi

CHICKEN WITH SPICY COCONUT STUFFING

Urap-urapan is a traditional boiled vegetable dish which is marinated with shredded coconut. Here it is used as a stuffing, thus resulting in a spicy dish on a mild, delicate sauce.

STEP 1: Spicy Coconut Stuffing

120 g grated coconut
80 g beansprouts, cleaned, blanched
60 ml red chili juice (see page 23)
20 g shallots (bawang merah), peeled, finely diced
10 g garlic, peeled, finely diced
10 g lesser galangal, peeled, finely diced
10 g lemon grass stalk, finely diced
½ egg, whisked
salt

1   Combine all the ingredients in a bowl and mix well with a wooden spatula.

NOTE: If fresh coconut is not available, use dried grated coconut soaked in warm water, then drained.

STEP 2: Steamed Chicken Breasts

4 x 100-140 g boneless chicken breasts, skinned
salt

1   Flatten each chicken breast with the flat side of a cleaver or chopper until the meat is 5 mm thick. Spread it out on a flat surface.
2   Season the chicken lightly with salt.
3   Spoon the stuffing made in Step 1 on the chicken breasts and spread it evenly with a spatula.
4   Roll each breast into a tight sausage shape and wrap each roll in kitchen plastic wrap. Tie the ends with twine or string.
5   Place the wrapped chicken rolls in a steamer and steam for 18-20 minutes.
6   Remove the rolls from the steamer and let them rest for 5 minutes before removing the plastic wrap. Set them aside and keep warm.

STEP 3: Garnish and Presentation

10 g yam bean, cut into wedges, blanched
250 ml Chili Basil Sauce, hot (see page 28)
4 sweet basil leaves (kemangi)

1   Pour a layer of the hot sauce onto each plate.
2   Slice each chicken roll into 4-6 and arrange the slices on the sauce.
3   Garnish with the sweet basil leaves and yam bean.

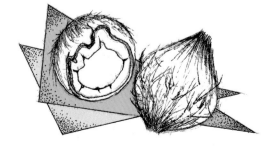

CHICKEN WITH SPICY COCONUT STUFFING

BABY CHICKEN BURA-HAY

CHICKEN WITH RED KIDNEY BEANS

Ayam Saus Kuning Bura-hay

BABY CHICKEN BURA-HAY

This chicken dish, stewed in coconut milk with spices, is deliciously sweet.

STEP 1: Stewed Baby Chickens

4 baby chickens or Cornish game hens, backbone removed
2 g anise powder
2 g coriander powder
2 g turmeric powder
salt
30 ml tamarind water (see page 23)
30 ml peanut oil
250 ml coconut milk (see page 22)

1   Flatten the baby chickens and lay them out like butterflies.
2   Season the baby chickens with the anise, coriander, turmeric and salt. Sprinkle the tamarind water over them and let them marinate in the refrigerator for approximately 8 hours.
3   Preheat the oven to 160°C, then take the chickens out of the fridge.
4   Heat the peanut oil in a stewing pan over high heat to approximately 200°C. Place the chickens in the hot pan and sear on each side for 2 minutes.
5   Pour in the coconut milk and cover the pan.
6   Place the stewing pan in the preheated oven and stew for approximately 15-18 minutes, stirring. Remove the chickens from the oven and keep warm.

STEP 2: Bura-hay Sauce (Saus Kuning Bura-hay)

15 ml peanut oil
30 g shallots (bawang merah), peeled, finely diced
15 g garlic, peeled, finely diced
5 g ginger, peeled, finely diced
5 g greater galangal, peeled, finely diced
1 lemon grass stalk, crushed
1 salam leaf
20 g candlenuts, ground
5 g turmeric root, finely diced
5 g anise powder
2 g coriander powder
30 ml tamarind water (see page 23)
375 ml coconut milk (see page 22)
salt

1   Heat the oil in a saucepan and sauté the shallots and garlic in the oil until light brown.
2   Add in the ginger, greater galangal and lemon grass, and continue to sauté for 2 minutes more.
3   Add the salam leaf and candlenuts, sprinkle in the turmeric root, anise and coriander, and sauté for an additional 2 minutes.
4   Pour in the tamarind water and coconut milk, and season with salt. Bring the mixture to the boil, reduce the heat and simmer for about 10 minutes.
5   Remove the pan from the heat and discard the lemon grass and salam leaf.
6   Pour the sauce into a blender and process until smooth. Serve hot. Yields 500 ml.

STEP 3: Garnish and Presentation

15 ml peanut oil
20 g red chilies, seeded, finely diced
160 g rice noodles, boiled for 4-6 minutes
40 g Javanese parkia
250 ml Bura-hay Sauce, hot

1   Heat the peanut oil in a frying pan. Sauté the chilies for 2-3 minutes, stirring constantly.
2   Stir in the noodles, season with salt and place a portion of this mixture on each plate.
3   Sauté the Javanese parkia for a minute, season with salt and put this aside.
4   Pour the hot Bura-hay Sauce on one side of the noodles.
5   Cut each chicken into pieces and place the pieces on the sauce. Garnish with the sautéed parkia.

Bebek Panggang Saus Bumbu Bajak

DUCK BREAST ON BAJAK SAUCE

2 x 300 g boneless duck breasts
1 g turmeric powder
1 tablespoon black peppercorns, crushed
salt
30 ml peanut oil
24 x 10 g pieces pumpkin, turned or carved, blanched
8 long beans, blanched, twisted into loops or cut into lengths
250 ml Spicy Bajak Sauce, hot (see page 27)
5 g red chilies, seeded, finely diced

1   Season the duck breasts with the turmeric, crushed black peppercorns and salt.
2   Preheat the oven to 220°C.
3   Pour half of the peanut oil into a roasting pan and place over very high heat until the oil reaches approximately 240°C.
4   Place the duck breasts in the pan and sear each side for 1 minute only.
5   Place the roasting pan in the preheated oven and roast for 10-12 minutes, basting constantly and turning the breasts over every 2 minutes. Remove from the oven and set aside.
6   Heat the remaining peanut oil in a frying pan. Add the blanched pumpkin pieces and long beans. Sauté for 2-3 minutes, stirring frequently, then season with salt. Remove the pan from the heat.
7   Pour some of the hot Spicy Bajak Sauce onto each plate.
8   Cut the duck breasts horizontally into thin slices and place the slices on the sauce. Sprinkle with the diced red chilies.
9   Arrange the sautéed vegetables next to the duck.

NOTE: If the duck breasts are smaller than suggested in this recipe, make sure to adjust the oven temperature and cooking time to get the same result — browned on the outside and medium inside.

Burung Dara Isi dan Nanas

CORIANDER PINEAPPLE PIGEON

STEP 1: Sautéed Stuffed Pigeon Breasts
30 ml vegetable oil
20 g shallots (bawang merah), peeled, finely diced
40 g leeks, finely diced
40 g carrot, peeled, finely diced
60 g pineapple, finely diced
salt
12 x 40-50 g pigeon breasts, boned except for the wing
pepper

1 Heat half the vegetable oil in a frying pan and sauté the shallots and leeks in the oil without browning.
2 Add the carrots and sauté for 2 minutes. Remove from the heat and let the mixture cool.
3 Stir the pineapple into the sautéed mixture and set this stuffing mixture aside.
4 Use a pointed knife to make a lengthwise incision in the thin side of each pigeon breast.
5 Fill the incision with the pineapple mixture.
6 Heat the remaining oil in a frying pan. Fry the pigeon breasts on each side for approximately 3 minutes. Remove from the heat and keep warm.

STEP 2: Coriander Pineapple Sauce
(Saus Ketumbar Nanas)
30 ml vegetable oil
40 g shallots (bawang merah), peeled, finely diced
5 g garlic, peeled, finely diced
15 g coriander leaves
60 g brown sugar (gula Jawa)
200 g pineapple, peeled, diced
60 ml chili juice (see page 23)
30 ml freshly squeezed lime juice
salt

1 Heat the peanut oil in a saucepan and sauté the shallots, garlic and coriander leaves for 3 minutes without browning.
2 Stir in the brown sugar and continue to sauté for another 2 minutes.
3 Add in the pineapple and sauté for 2 minutes more.
4 Pour in the chili and lime juices, season with salt and bring the mixture to the boil. Reduce the heat and simmer for approximately 5-8 minutes, stirring from time to time.
5 Remove the pan from the heat and pour the sauce into a blender. Process until fine and smooth. Remove and keep warm. Yields 250 ml.

STEP 3: Garnish and Presentation
160 ml Coriander Pineapple Sauce, hot
80 g pineapple, peeled, diced
60 g water apples, diced
16 coriander leaves

1 Spread a layer of the sauce on each plate.
2 Slice the pigeon breasts and place the pieces on the sauce.
3 Garnish with the fruits and coriander leaves.

Ayam Kaliurang

KALIURANG CHICKEN

This is a light, slightly sour dish.

STEP 1: Braised Spring Chickens
2 x 800 g spring chickens, backbone removed
30 ml peanut oil
salt
60 g shallots (bawang merah), peeled, finely diced
10 g greater galangal, peeled, finely diced
100 g sour finger carambolas, peeled, diced
1 lemon grass stalk, finely diced
2 kaffir lime leaves
10 g red chilies, seeded, finely diced
500 ml coconut milk (see page 22)
160 ml chicken stock, hot (see page 24), or water

1 Flatten the chickens and lay them out like butterflies on a flat surface.
2 Heat the peanut oil in a deep frying pan which is large enough to hold both chickens next to each other.
3 Season the chickens with salt and put them in the pan, skin side down. Brown quickly over high heat for 2-3 minutes on each side.
4 Reduce the heat, then add the next 6 ingredients to the pan. Sauté for another 2-3 minutes.
5 Pour in the coconut milk and let the chickens simmer for approximately 15-20 minutes. Add the chicken stock or water a little at a time to thin the coconut milk sauce when it gets too thick during the simmering process.
6 Remove the chickens from the sauce and keep them warm in a separate pan.
7 Discard the lime leaves, then pour the sauce into a blender and purée for 2-3 minutes until smooth.
8 Pour the sauce back over the chickens and keep both hot.

STEP 2: Garnish and Presentation
60 g ripe papaya, peeled, seeded, diced
2 kaffir lime leaves, finely cut into strips
5 ml freshly squeezed lime juice
4 x 30-40 g sour finger carambolas, finely sliced

1 Combine the papaya, lime leaves and lime juice in a bowl. Mix well and set aside.
2 Remove the chickens from the sauce, cut them into 8 pieces and arrange on individual plates.
3 Arrange the sour finger carambola slices next to the chicken pieces. Place the papaya garnish next to them.
4 Garnish with the sauce.

VEGETABLES AND PICKLES

VEGETABLES

Botok Kroket
RED BEAN CROQUETTES

80 g potatoes, boiled, peeled
5 ml peanut oil
5 g garlic, peeled, finely diced
2 g lesser galangal, peeled, finely diced
20 g shallots (bawang merah), peeled, finely diced
80 g red kidney beans, soaked overnight, boiled for 1 hour
     until soft, diced
salt
2 eggs

1 Mash the boiled potatoes until fine. Do not use any milk or butter when doing this.
2 In a frying pan, heat the peanut oil and add in the garlic, lesser galangal and shallots. Sauté for 2 minutes without browning. Remove from the pan and allow to cool.
3 Add the mashed potatoes and kidney beans to the sautéed ingredients. Season with salt. Add 1 egg to the mixture. Mix well with a wooden spatula.
4 Form the mixture into balls, squares, half-moons or any other shape you like.
5 Break the other egg and separate the white from the yolk. Use the yolk to brush the top of the croquettes.
6 Cook the croquettes on a griddle over high heat until slightly brown.

Ubi Jalar Masak Santan Gula Merah
SWEET POTATO GRATIN

vegetable oil
320 g sweet potatoes, peeled, sliced
250 ml coconut milk (see page 22)
1 egg yolk
60 g brown sugar (gula Jawa)
6 dried cloves
1 g nutmeg powder
salt

1 Preheat the oven to 200°C.
2 Grease a large earthenware or ovenproof dish with vegetable oil and place the sliced potatoes, one layer deep, in the greased dish.
3 Mix the coconut milk, egg yolk, brown sugar, cloves, nutmeg powder and salt with a whisk. Pour the mixture over the potatoes.
4 Place the dish in the preheated oven and bake for approximately 15-20 minutes.

Cabe Merah Isi dengan Sapi Muda
RED CHILIES WITH VEAL STUFFING

100 g veal, minced or ground
20 g shallots (bawang merah), peeled, finely diced
2 g garlic, peeled, finely diced
5 g red chilies, finely diced
½ egg yolk
salt
ground white pepper
8 medium-sized red chilies, seeded, stems removed
250 ml chicken stock, hot (see page 24)

1 Place the minced veal in a bowl. Add in the shallots, garlic, diced chilies and egg yolk. Season with salt and pepper.
2 Mix well with a wooden spatula until smooth.
3 Put the veal mixture into a piping bag with a small-holed nozzle.
4 Pipe the stuffing into the chilies, but only until they are three-quarters-full so that there is room for the stuffing to expand during the poaching process.
5 Place the stuffed chilies in a shallow pan. Add in the hot chicken stock and poach gently at 80°C for approximately 5-7 minutes.
6 Remove the chilies from the hot stock. Use them as a garnish or as a vegetable to accompany veal dishes.

Perkedel Jagung
SWEETCORN PERKEDEL

120 g potatoes, boiled, peeled
100 g canned sweetcorn kernels, drained
20 g lemon grass stalk, finely diced
10 g red chilies, seeded, finely diced
1 egg
salt
ground white pepper
oil for shallow frying

1 Mash the potatoes until fine. Do not use any butter or milk when doing this. Then use a wooden spoon to mix in the other ingredients, seasoning with salt and pepper.
2 Shape the mixture into 8 round or square patties (perkedel).
3 Sauté these perkedel quickly in hot vegetable oil on each side for 2 minutes. Serve with hot meat dishes.

Perkedel Ayam
CHICKEN PERKEDEL

200 g potatoes, boiled, peeled
15 ml vegetable oil
5 g garlic, peeled, finely diced
20 g shallots (bawang merah), peeled, finely diced
20 g leeks, finely diced
100 g chicken meat, minced or diced finely
salt
ground white pepper
nutmeg powder
2 eggs
oil for shallow frying

1 Mash the potatoes until fine. Do not use any butter or milk when doing this.
2 Heat the vegetable oil in a frying pan and sauté the garlic, shallots and leeks over medium heat for 2 minutes without browning. Stir constantly.
3 Add in the chicken and continue to sauté for 5 minutes more. Withdraw the pan from the heat.
4 In a bowl, combine the sautéed mixture with the hot mashed potatoes. Season with salt, pepper and nutmeg.
5 Break 1 egg and drop it in the mixture. Mix well with a wooden spoon.
6 Shape the mixture into patties (perkedel) of 40 g.
7 Beat the other egg with a whisk in another bowl. Dip each patty in the beaten egg before frying it for 2 minutes on each side in hot oil.

NOTE: Minced lamb or beef may be used instead of chicken.

Tauco Minang
GREEN BEANS MINANG

15 ml peanut oil
20 g shallots (bawang merah), peeled, finely diced
10 g garlic, peeled, finely diced
10 g greater galangal, peeled, finely diced
5 g shrimp paste
50 g green chilies, seeded, sliced
100 g long beans or stringbeans, cut in lengths
180 ml fermented black soya beans
375 ml coconut milk (see page 22)

1 Heat the peanut oil in a saucepan. Add in the shallots, garlic and greater galangal and sauté over high heat until light brown.
2 Reduce the heat and add in the shrimp paste, chilies and beans; continue to sauté over medium heat for 3 minutes more. Stir constantly.
3 Add in the fermented soya beans and coconut milk. Let the mixture simmer for approximately 3-5 minutes. Serve hot.

Kol Isi Rebung
BAMBOO SHOOTS IN CABBAGE LEAVES

15 ml peanut oil
20 g shallots (bawang merah), peeled, finely diced
1 red chili, seeded, finely diced
5 g garlic, peeled, finely diced
20 g leeks, finely diced
150 g bamboo shoots, diced
1 egg white, whisked
salt
white pepper
8 white cabbage leaves about 10-12 cm in size, blanched

1 Heat the peanut oil in a frying pan. Add in the shallots, chili and garlic and sauté over medium heat for 2 minutes, stirring constantly.
2 Add in the leeks and bamboo shoots and continue to sauté for 2 minutes more.
3 Withdraw the pan from the heat and let the mixture cool before mixing in the egg white with a wooden spoon. Season with salt and pepper.
4 Preheat the oven to 240°C.
5 Spoon a little of the bamboo shoot mixture onto each cabbage leaf. Fold the leaf over into a ball or a roll.
6 Place the folded cabbage leaves on an oiled baking sheet and cook in the preheated oven for approximately 10-15 minutes. Serve hot.

Sawi Hijau Isi Tauge
STUFFED MUSTARD GREEN LEAVES

15 ml peanut oil
20 g shallots (bawang merah), peeled, finely diced
5 g garlic, peeled, finely diced
1 red chili, seeded, finely diced
120 g beansprouts
salt
4 mustard green leaves, blanched

1 Heat the peanut oil in a frying pan. Sauté the shallots, garlic and chili for 1-2 minutes until light brown.
2 Add in the beansprouts and continue to sauté for 1 minute, until the beansprouts begin to turn slightly soft. Season with salt. Then remove the pan from the heat.
3 Flatten the mustard green leaves with the flat side of a cleaver or chopper and spread them out on the table top.
4 Divide the beansprout mixture into 4 batches. Place a portion of the mixture in the middle of each leaf.
5 Fold the leaf over the mixture and wrap it into a small tight ball. Tie with a piece of lemon grass or twine into a small bundle.
6 Steam for 1-2 minutes before serving.

BAMBOO SHOOTS IN CABBAGE LEAVES

GREEN BEANS MINANG

STUFFED MUSTARD GREEN LEAVES

COCONUT VEGETABLES

Urap Sayuran

COCONUT VEGETABLES

The Indonesian word *urap* means a vegetable dish with fresh or dried grated coconut.

    80 g grated coconut
    5 g shrimp paste
    10 g lesser galangal, finely diced
    10 g white sugar
    80 g long beans, cut into thin lengths, blanched
    80 g white cabbage, sliced finely, blanched
    80 g spinach leaves, sliced, blanched
    80 g beansprouts, cleaned, blanched
    salt
    sliced cucumber (optional)

1 Dry-fry the grated coconut in a pan, without oil, until the coconut becomes light brown, approximately 4-5 minutes. Stir constantly. During this process, the coconut oil is extracted, thus there is no need for oil.

2 Add in the shrimp paste and lesser galangal. Then mix in the sugar and continue sautéing over medium heat for 5 minutes more.

3 Withdraw the pan from the heat. Put the mixture in a bowl and let it cool at room temperature.

4 When cooled, add in the vegetables and season with salt. Toss well. Serve with sliced cucumbers if desired.

NOTE: If this is served as a main dish, it is enough for 4-6 persons; if served as an accompaniment, it is sufficient for 8-10 persons.

Urap Tauge Kedele
COCONUT-MARINATED BEANSPROUTS

80 g beansprouts, cleaned
5 g lesser galangal, peeled, finely diced
15 g brown sugar (gula Jawa)
3 g shrimp paste
salt
80 g coconut meat, cut into strips
10 g red chilies, seeded, cut into strips
5 g lemon grass stalk, finely diced
20 g grated coconut

1 Blanch the beansprouts in boiling water for 1 minute and plunge immediately in iced water to cool.
2 Pound together the lesser galangal, brown sugar, shrimp paste and a little salt with a pestle in a stone mortar until the mixture becomes a fine paste.
3 Combine the beansprouts, coconut meat, red chilies and lemon grass in a bowl. Add in the pounded paste and grated coconut. Mix well.
4 Let the mixture sit in a refrigerator for 2 hours to allow the flavours to be absorbed before serving.

Kukus Pare Sindang Laya
STUFFED BITTER GOURD

4 x 250 g bitter gourds
15 ml peanut oil
20 g shallots (bawang merah), peeled, finely diced
5 g garlic, peeled, finely diced
10 g red chilies, seeded, finely diced
220 g grated coconut
15 g brown sugar (gula Jawa)
10 g tamarind pulp
salt
2 eggs, whisked

1 Cut each bitter gourd lengthwise and scrape out the seeds and soft flesh. Discard the seeds, but retain the flesh.
2 Heat the peanut oil in a saucepan. Add in the shallots, garlic and red chilies. Sauté for 2 minutes without browning.
3 Stir in the young coconut, bitter gourd flesh, brown sugar and tamarind pulp. Season with salt. Sauté for 3 minutes more. Then remove the pan from the heat and let the mixture cool.
4 When cool, stir in the eggs and stuff the hollowed bitter gourd halves with the mixture.
5 Put the halves together and tie with kitchen string.
6 Steam the stuffed bitter gourds for 20 minutes.
7 Remove from the steamer and untie the string. Serve warm.

Tumis Bayam
STIR-FRIED SPINACH

The local variety of spinach has roundish leaves and comes in 2 colours, green or dark reddish-purple.

30 ml peanut oil
20 g onions, peeled, finely diced
10 g garlic, peeled, finely diced
20 g red chilies, seeded, cut into strips
250 g red spinach leaves
250 g green spinach leaves
salt
pepper

1 Heat the peanut oil in a frying pan. Sauté the onions, garlic and chilies in the oil for 1 minute over medium heat without browning the ingredients.
2 Add in the spinach and continue to sauté for 2-3 minutes. Season with salt and pepper. Serve.

Sayur Bumbu Jawa
VEGETABLES IN SPICED COCONUT MILK

30 ml peanut oil
10 g garlic, peeled, finely diced
30 g shallots (bawang merah), peeled, finely diced
10 g ginger, peeled, finely diced
5 g greater galangal, peeled, finely diced
5 g turmeric root, peeled, finely diced
50 g candlenuts, ground
500 ml coconut milk (see page 22)
180 g long beans, cut into short lengths, blanched for 2 minutes
20 g red chilies, seeded, cut into strips, blanched for 2 minutes
20 g green chilies, seeded, cut into strips, blanched for 2 minutes
30 ml white vinegar
10 g white sugar
salt
pepper

1 Heat the peanut oil in a shallow saucepan and sauté the garlic, shallots, ginger, greater galangal and turmeric root over medium heat for 2 minutes without colouring.
2 Add the candlenuts and continue to sauté for 2 minutes more.
3 Pour in the coconut milk and bring to the boil. Reduce the heat to simmering point.
4 Add the blanched beans and chilies, and simmer for 5-7 minutes.
5 Finally add in the vinegar and sugar, and season with salt and pepper. Simmer for 1 minute more, then serve immediately.

NOTE: If the sauce becomes too thick during the simmering process, add some water to thin it down.

Sayur Asam

SOUR VEGETABLES

15 ml peanut oil
30 g shallots (bawang merah), peeled, finely diced
5 g shrimp paste
15 g brown sugar (gula Jawa)
20 g tamarind paste
1 litre chicken stock (see page 24), or water
60 g young jackfruit sections
60 g young chayote, peeled, sliced
60 g baby corns, sliced
60 g long beans, sliced into lengths
60 g peanuts, shelled
10 g melinjo leaves
40 g melinjo nuts
salt
pepper

1 Heat the peanut oil in a shallow wide saucepan. Add the shallots and shrimp paste, and sauté over low heat for 2-3 minutes.
2 Add the brown sugar and tamarind paste, and continue to sauté for 1-2 minutes.
3 Pour in the chicken stock or water and bring to the boil. Let it boil for 5 minutes.
4 Turn down the heat and add in the remaining ingredients. Simmer for 5-8 minutes.
5 Remove from the heat and serve the vegetables in the stock.

NOTE: If either melinjo nuts or melinjo leaves are not available, drop them from the recipe as there is no substitute.

Sayur Masak Kari

CURRIED VEGETABLES

15 ml vegetable oil
10 g garlic, peeled, finely diced
45 g onions, peeled, finely diced
5 g fresh turmeric root, peeled, finely diced
30 g candlenuts, ground
250 ml coconut milk (see page 22)
60 g carrot, peeled, cubed
60 g cauliflower, cleaned, cubed
60 g stringbeans, sliced
20 g red chilies, seeded, sliced
water
15 ml vinegar
salt

1 Heat the vegetable oil in a frying pan and sauté the garlic, onions and turmeric in the hot oil for 1 minute without browning.
2 Add in the candlenuts and continue to sauté for 1 minute more without letting the ingredients colour.
3 Pour in the coconut milk and bring the mixture to the boil.
4 Add in the carrots and cauliflower, turn down the heat and let the mixture simmer until the vegetables are still crunchy, approximately 6-8 minutes.
5 Add the stringbeans and chilies and simmer for another 4 minutes. Use the water to thin the coconut milk mixture when it gets too thick during the simmering process.
6 Finally add the vinegar and season with salt. Serve hot.

Kentang dan Kunyit

TURMERIC POTATOES

This is a basic recipe and the amounts can be increased or decreased proportionately. It can be used for all kinds of potatoes, either carved, cubed, whole, etc. The idea is to use the turmeric to give a bright yellow colour to the potatoes.

500 ml water
5 g turmeric powder
2 g turmeric root, sliced
salt
1 kg potatoes

1 Combine the first 4 ingredients in a pot and bring the liquid to the boil.
2 Add in the potatoes and cook as long as you would when using plain water to boil potatoes.

Manisan Mangga

CANDIED MANGO

This *manisan* (candied fruit or sweetmeat) can be served cold as a relish or side dish, or hot, sautéed and added to main course dishes as a garnish.

120 g green young mango flesh, cut into fine strips
50 g white sugar
375 ml water
10 g red chilies, seeded, cut into fine strips
salt

1 Mix the mango strips together with the sugar in a bowl.
2 Boil the water and pour the hot water over the sugared mangoes.
3 Let the mangoes cool at room temperature before placing the bowl in a refrigerator to marinate overnight.
4 Drain off the liquid, add the strips of chili and season with salt. Mix well.

PICKLED GREEN MANGOES

PULASARI PICKLES

PICKLED PALM HEARTS

YELLOW PICKLES

MIXED PICKLES

CABBAGE AND BEANSPROUT PICKLES

PICKLES

The word *acar* literally means "pickle" or "pickled". Essential to the pickling process are ingredients such as vinegar, sugar, salt and water. There are many kinds of *acars*, and they are usually served as side dishes to accompany the meal.

Acar Rujak Poh
PICKLED GREEN MANGOES

> 240 *g young green mango flesh, cut into strips*
> 20 *g red chilies, seeded, cut into strips*
> 20 *g green chilies, seeded, cut into strips*
> 375 *ml water*
> 2 *pandanus leaves*
> 60 *ml white vinegar*
> 40 *g white sugar*
> 10 *g salt*
> 1 *cinnamon stick*

1   Put the mangoes and chilies in a bowl.
2   In a saucepan, combine the water, pandanus leaves, vinegar, sugar and salt. Boil for 5 minutes.
3   Remove from the heat and discard the pandanus leaves. Add in the cinnamon stick.
4   Pour the liquid over the mangoes and chilies and let them soak for a minimum of 2 hours. Drain off the liquid prior to serving this as a garnish.

Acar Pulasari
PULASARI PICKLES

> 50 *g carrot, carved into balls*
> 80 *g yam bean, peeled, scooped out with a melon baller*
> 80 *g kedongdong flesh, scooped out with a melon baller*
> 30 *g shallots (bawang merah), peeled*
> 20 *g red chilies, seeded, sliced into rounds*
> 20 *g green chilies, seeded, sliced into rounds*
> 60 *ml white vinegar*
> 60 *g white sugar*
> 5 *g salt*

1   Combine all the ingredients in a bowl and mix well with a wooden spoon.
2   Let the vegetables soak for a minimum of 2 hours and drain off the liquid if using as a garnish.

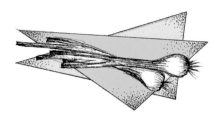

Acar Pondoh
PICKLED PALM HEARTS

> 200 *g palm hearts, cut into diamonds*
> 30 *g red chilies, seeded, finely diced*
> 30 *g green chilies, seeded, sliced into fine strips*
> 30 *g small shallots (bawang merah), peeled, diced*
> 300 *ml water*
> 2 *lemon grass stalks, crushed*
> 30 *ml white vinegar*
> 30 *g white sugar*
> 10 *g salt*

1   Place the palm hearts, chilies and shallots in a bowl.
2   Combine the rest of the ingredients in a saucepan and boil the mixture for 10 minutes.
3   Remove the lemon grass and pour the hot liquid over the vegetable mixture.
4   Let the vegetables soak for a minimum of 2 hours, and drain off the liquid if using as a garnish.

Acar Kuning
YELLOW PICKLES

> 30 *ml peanut oil*
> 20 *g shallots (bawang merah), peeled, finely diced*
> 5 *g garlic, peeled, finely diced*
> 10 *g greater galangal, peeled, finely diced*
> 15 *g red chilies, seeded, sliced into strips*
> 20 *g candlenuts, ground*
> 5 *g turmeric powder*
> 5 *g brown sugar (gula Jawa)*
> 1 *lemon grass stalk, bruised*
> 2 *salam leaves*
> 5 *ml white vinegar*
> 250 *ml coconut milk (see page 22)*
> 40 *g carrots, peeled, cut into strips, blanched for 4 minutes*
> 40 *g cauliflower florets, blanched for 2 minutes*
> 40 *g stringbeans, cut into strips, blanched for 2 minutes*
> 40 *g cucumber, seeded, cut into strips*
> *salt*

1   Heat the oil in a flat frying pan and sauté the shallots, garlic, greater galangal and chilies for 2 minutes without browning.
2   Stir in the candlenuts, turmeric powder and brown sugar, and continue to sauté for another 2 minutes without burning.
3   Add the lemon grass, salam leaves, vinegar and coconut milk. Bring to the boil.
4   Then mix in the carrots, cauliflower florets and stringbeans. Cook in the mixture until the vegetables are semi-soft, approximately 2 minutes.
5   Finally add in the cucumber, season with salt and cook for 1 minute more. Remove from the heat, let the pickles cool, then store in the refrigerator.

Acar Campur-campur
MIXED PICKLES

250 *ml water*
30 *ml white vinegar*
30 *g white sugar*
5 *g salt*
20 *g bird's eye chilies, stems removed*
20 *g red chilies, seeded, sliced into fine strips*
20 *g green chilies, seeded*
180 *g cucumber, skin on, seeded, cut into shapes*
40 *g carrot, peeled, cut into shapes*
20 *g onion, peeled, sliced into strips*

1 Pour the water into a saucepan, add the vinegar, sugar and salt, and bring to a rapid boil.
2 Add in the remaining ingredients and boil for 1-2 minutes. Then remove from the heat and let the vegetables cool in the liquid.
3 When cool, refrigerate the pickles. The liquid could be drained off if the pickles are to be used as a garnish.

Acar Kol dengan Tauge
CABBAGE AND BEANSPROUT PICKLES

500 *ml water*
30 *g white sugar*
5 *g salt*
30 *ml white vinegar*
1 *lemon grass stalk, crushed*
2 *pandanus leaves, or ¼ teaspoon pandan essence*
120 *g white cabbage, shredded*
120 *g beansprouts, cleaned*
60 *g carrot, peeled, cut into fine strips*
20 *g red chilies, seeded, finely diced*

1 Pour the water into a saucepan. Add the sugar, salt, vinegar, lemon grass and pandanus leaves and bring to the boil. Let it boil until the liquid is reduced by half.
2 Remove from the heat and strain the liquid into another saucepan. Discard the lemon grass and pandanus leaf.
3 Bring the strained liquid back to the boil and add in the remaining ingredients. Let them boil for 1-2 minutes.
4 Remove the pan from the heat and let the vegetables cool in the liquid.
5 When cool, refrigerate the pickles. The liquid could be drained off if the pickles are to be used as a garnish.

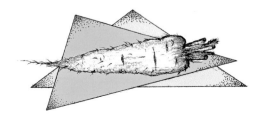

Dabu-dabu Lilang
CHILI TOMATO PICKLES

This is a very fiery garnish for meat dishes.

100 *g ripe tomatoes, peeled, seeded, diced*
40 *g red chilies, sliced*
20 *g bird's eye chilies, sliced*
40 *g shallots, peeled, sliced*
5 *ml white vinegar*
10 *ml freshly squeezed lime juice*

1 Combine all the ingredients in a bowl and mix well.
2 Let the vegetables marinate for at least 20 minutes before using.

NOTE: This garnish is particularly fierce as it uses unseeded chilies. If you want it to be milder, remove the seeds before slicing the chilies.

Acar Bawang Merah
PICKLED SHALLOTS

300 *g shallots (bawang merah), peeled*
375 *ml water*
60 *ml white vinegar*
15 *g salt*

1 Place the whole shallots in a bowl.
2 In a saucepan, combine the water, vinegar and salt. Boil for 5 minutes, then pour the boiling liquid over the shallots.
3 Let the mixture cool before putting it in a refrigerator. The shallots should be allowed to soak in the liquid for a minimum of 2 hours. Drain off the liquid if using as a garnish.

Acar Belimbing Wuluh
PICKLED SOUR FINGER CARAMBOLAS

140 *g sour finger carambolas, sliced*
30 *g red chilies, seeded, cut into strips*
30 *g shallots (bawang merah), peeled, cut into strips*
10 *g dill*
375 *ml water*
45 *ml white vinegar*
15 *g salt*
30 *g white sugar*

1 Put the sour finger carambolas, chilies, shallots and dill in a bowl.
2 In a saucepan, combine the water, vinegar, salt and sugar. Bring the mixture to the boil and let it boil for 5 minutes, then pour over the vegetables.
3 Let the vegetables soak in the liquid for at least 2 hours. Then drain off the liquid and serve the vegetables as a garnish.

DESSERTS, SHERBETS AND SYRUPS

DESSERTS

Martabak Manis dan Kacang Merah

PANCAKE WITH RED KIDNEY BEANS

This is a very popular dessert throughout Indonesia.

> 300 g flour
> 300 ml water
> 75 g white sugar
> 10 g baking soda
> 10 g yeast powder
> salt
> 3 egg whites, whisked until stiff
> 30 ml peanut oil
> 50 g unsalted peanuts, fried, ground
> 20 g chocolate vermicelli or finely chopped dark chocolate
> 60 ml condensed milk
> 250 ml Avocado Syrup (see page 143)
> 100 g red kidney beans, soaked overnight, boiled until soft —
>   about 1 hour
> 2 avocados, cut into sections

1 Combine the flour, water, 25 g of the sugar, baking soda, yeast and salt in a bowl. Stir vigorously with a whisk until a smooth batter results.
2 Strain this pancake batter through a fine sieve into another bowl.
3 Use a whisk to mix in the stiffly beaten egg whites, then let the mixture rest for 25 minutes.
4 Grease a cast-iron pan or heavy omelette pan, preferably teflon, about 30 cm in diameter and 3-4 cm in depth with the peanut oil, and heat it.
5 Pour half of the batter into the hot pan, cover with a lid and cook for approximately 15 minutes over low heat.
6 Take off the lid and sprinkle half the ground peanuts, chocolate vermicelli, condensed milk and half the remaining sugar on top of the pancake. Then loosen the edges with a spatula and fold the pancake in half.
7 Remove this 'D' shaped pancake from the pan, put it on a cutting board and cut it into triangles.
8 Arrange 2 triangles on each plate. Serve hot with the Avocado Syrup and sprinkle with the kidney beans, avocado sections and chopped peanuts.
9 Repeat this process with the other half of the batter.

NOTE: If you do not have a pan of the recommended size, just make more pancakes, but be sure to pour the batter 1 cm thick into the pan since it has to be baked very slowly. Also, if your pan is made of aluminium or a very thin material, decrease the temperature more.

Es Kopi dengan Jambu Biji

COFFEE PARFAIT WITH GUAVA COMPOTE

STEP 1: Coffee Parfait
> 4 egg yolks
> 100 g white sugar
> 15 g Java coffee powder
> 125 ml boiling water
> 90 ml liquid whipping cream
> 250 ml whipping cream, whipped until stiff

1 Cream the egg yolks with the sugar in a mixing bowl.
2 In a smaller bowl, dissolve the coffee powder in the boiling water. Pour this into the bowl with the creamed egg yolks, and stir in the liquid whipping cream. Mix well.
3 Pour this mixture into a saucepan and slowly bring to the boil over low heat for 2-3 minutes, stirring constantly with a whisk.
4 Dip a wooden spoon into the hot mixture and pull it out. If the mixture coats the wooden spoon lightly, it is cooked enough. Remove immediately from the heat.
5 Strain the mixture through a fine sieve into a bowl. Let it cool completely.
6 Carefully fold in the stiffly whipped cream with a whisk or wooden spoon. Then pour this mixture into a 750-1000 ml mould or 4 individual moulds. Freeze until solid.

NOTE: If Java coffee is not available, use any other strong coffee.

STEP 2: Guava Compote
> 500 ml water
> 250 g white sugar
> 30 ml freshly squeezed lime juice
> 1 x 5 g stick cinnamon
> 250 g ripe guavas, peeled, seeded, cut into 8-10 sections

1 Pour the water into a stockpot and bring it to the boil. Add in the sugar, lime juice and cinnamon. Boil for 5 minutes.
2 Add the guava pieces and reduce the heat. Simmer for 5-8 minutes.
3 Remove the pot from the heat and let the guavas cool in the syrup.
4 Pour the mixture into a bowl and refrigerate.

STEP 3: Presentation
> roasted coffee beans
> mint sprigs
> mango pieces
> 1 guava, quartered

1 Remove the parfait from the mould.
2 Garnish with the coffee beans, mint sprigs, mango and guava, and serve with the guava compote made in Step 2.

Srikaya Palembang

PALEMBANG COCONUT MOUSSE

6 eggs
50 g white sugar
100 g coconut cream
400 ml warm water
50 g brown sugar (gula Jawa)
180 ml Coconut Syrup (see page 142)
watermelon
4 pandanus leaves

1 Break the eggs into a bowl, add in the white sugar and stir vigorously with a whisk until the mixture becomes creamy but not foamy. Set this aside.
2 Prepare the coconut milk by whisking the coconut cream with the warm water in a bowl.
3 Pour the coconut milk into a saucepan and add in the brown sugar. Heat this for approximately 2-3 minutes, but do not let it boil or bubble.
4 Remove the pan from the heat and strain the coconut milk through a fine sieve into a bowl. Blend in the egg and sugar mixture with a whisk. Stir well.
5 Preheat the oven to 150°C.
6 Pour the mixture into small coffee cups or individual soufflé moulds. Set the cups in a shallow pan, pour hot water into the pan to reach half-way up the cups.
7 Place the pan in the preheated oven and poach gently for 40-50 minutes. Check occasionally that the water in the pan does not boil. If the water starts boiling, reduce the heat immediately and add some cold water to stop the bubbling.
8 Remove the cups or moulds from the pan and let them cool before removing the mousse.
9 Decorate with the Coconut Syrup, watermelon and pandanus leaves.

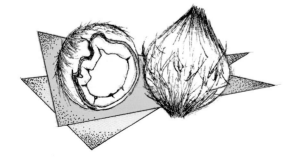

Lapis Pepe Buah Segar

RICE FLOUR LAYERS WITH FRUITS

Steamed rice flour cakes or rice cakes are popular in many parts of Indonesia. This particular layer cake will go well with any of the tropical fruit syrups given in this chapter.

125 g coconut cream
450 ml warm water
150 g rice flour
150 g white sugar
60 g brown sugar (gula Jawa)
½ teaspoon pandanus leaf juice or pandan essence
250 ml Soursop Syrup (see page 143)
120 g ripe papaya flesh, cubed or sliced
120 g ripe mango flesh, cubed or sliced
120 g mangosteen sections
8 pandanus leaves

1 Prepare the coconut milk by whisking together the coconut cream with the warm water.
2 In another bowl, combine the rice flour, coconut milk and white sugar. Stir vigorously with a whisk until it becomes a smooth mixture.
3 Divide this mixture into 3 even parts and place each portion in a bowl of its own.
4 Use a wooden spoon to mix the brown sugar into 1 portion of the mixture. Colour the second portion green with the pandanus juice. Leave the third portion uncoloured.
5 Pour the plain (uncoloured) mixture into a 800-ml rectangular or round cake mould.
6 Set the mould in a steamer or rice cooker and steam the mixture for approximately 5 minutes. Remove the mould from the steamer and let it cool for 2-3 minutes.
7 Pour the green-coloured mixture on top of the uncoloured one and return the mould to the steamer. Steam this for about 5 minutes, then let it cool.
8 Now pour the brown mixture on top and steam the cake for 25-30 minutes. Remove the mould from the steamer.
9 Let the cake cool completely, then put it in the refrigerator for at least 2 hours.
10 Remove the cake from the mould and cut it into portions.
11 Pour the Soursop Syrup next to the cake and decorate with the fruits and pandanus leaves.

NOTE: If pandanus leaf juice is not available, use any other green colouring agent. To make cakes with 6 thinner layers, cook the first 5 layers for 5 minutes each, then the last layer need only be cooked for 15 minutes.

PANCAKE WITH RED KIDNEY BEANS

COFFEE PARFAIT WITH GUAVA COMPOTE

PALEMBANG COCONUT MOUSSE

PAPAYA COCONUT PUDDING

RICE FLOUR LAYERS WITH FRUITS

BLACK AND WHITE CAKE

Kue Hitam Manis

BLACK AND WHITE CAKE

Grapes are grown in Indonesia in the northern part of Bali, around the city of Singaraja. This recipe combines a coconut pudding with a grape topping.

STEP 1: Coconut Pudding

150 g coconut cream
500 ml warm water
25 g cornflour
100 g white sugar
60 g grated coconut

1   Prepare the coconut milk by whisking together the coconut cream with the warm water. Put this in the fridge to cool.
2   Mix 60 ml of the cold coconut milk with the cornflour. Set this aside.
3   Pour the remaining coconut milk into a saucepan and add the sugar. Bring this to the boil.
4   Add in the grated coconut, reduce the heat and let the mixture simmer for approximately 5 minutes. Stir constantly with a whisk.
5   Gradually stir in the coconut-cornflour mixture, and continue simmering until the mixture starts to bind and get thick. Then remove the pan from the heat.
6   Line a tray with a piece of waxed or parchment paper and set a cake ring of about 14 cm in diameter and 4 cm in depth on top.
7   Pour the coconut mixture into the ring and let it cool at room temperature while making the topping for the cake.

STEP 2: Cake Topping and Presentation

100 ml water
15 g white sugar
150 g black grapes, peeled, seeded
15 g gelatine powder
180 ml Coconut Syrup or Kolak Sauce (see page 142, 143)
120 g grapes, peeled, quartered

1   Pour the water into a saucepan and bring to the boil. Add in the sugar and black grapes and boil for 2-3 minutes. Then pour this mixture into a blender and purée for 1-2 minutes.
2   Remove the grape purée from the blender and strain through a fine sieve or cheesecloth into a bowl.
3   Stir the gelatine powder into the strained liquid with a whisk and leave it to cool.
4   As soon as the liquid starts to thicken, pour it on top of the cake and spread it evenly over the cake's surface. Place the cake in the fridge for approximately 2 hours.
5   When set, remove the cake from the fridge and take off the cake ring.
6   Slice up the cake evenly and arrange the slices on serving plates.
7   Decorate with the Coconut Syrup or Kolak Sauce and grape quarters.

Poding Kelapa Lapis Pepaya

PAPAYA COCONUT PUDDING

STEP 1: Papaya Coconut Pudding

150 g coconut cream
500 ml warm water
200 g ripe papaya, peeled, seeded, sliced paper thin
30 g cornflour
60 g white sugar
50 g grated coconut

1   In a bowl, prepare the coconut milk by whisking the coconut cream with the warm water. Cool it in the refrigerator.
2   Line a rectangular 500-ml mould with the papaya slices so that the ends of the slices hang over the rim of the mould by 2-3 cm on each side.
3   Mix the cornflour with 100 ml of the cold coconut milk and set aside.
4   Pour the remaining coconut milk into a saucepan and bring it to the boil. Add in the sugar and grated coconut. Reduce the heat and let the mixture simmer for approximately 5 minutes, stirring constantly with a wooden spoon.
5   Add the coconut-cornflour mixture to the saucepan and continue to simmer for another 2 minutes.
6   Remove the pan from the heat and let the mixture cool for 2-3 minutes before pouring it into the papaya-lined mould.
7   Fold the overhanging papaya slices over the mixture and let it cool completely before placing the mould in a refrigerator for approximately 4 hours.
8   When set, remove the pudding from the mould and slice evenly.

STEP 2: Presentation

180 ml Pineapple Syrup (see page 142)
100 g ripe papaya flesh, scooped out with a melon baller
100 g young coconut meat, cut into strips

1   Pour some of the syrup on each plate.
2   Set 2-4 slices of the pudding on the syrup.
3   Garnish with the papaya and the fresh coconut strips rolled into balls.

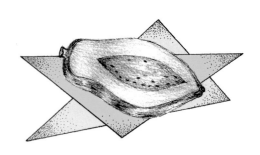

Cendole dengan Es Krim Nangka
JACKFRUIT CENDOLE

Avocado, Banana, Coconut Syrup or Kolak Sauce can be used to accompany this dessert as alternatives to the Jackfruit Syrup suggested, and the jackfruit in the batter can be replaced by young coconut or pineapple.

>   80 *g coconut cream*
>   250 *ml warm water*
>   100 *g flour*
>   90 *ml milk*
>   120 *g brown sugar (gula Jawa)*
>   1 *egg*
>   120 *g jackfruit flesh, diced*
>   *peanut oil for frying*
>   500 *ml Jackfruit Sherbet (see page 138)*
>   180 *ml Jackfruit Syrup (see page 142)*

1   Prepare the coconut milk by whisking together the coconut cream and warm water.
2   Combine this coconut milk with the flour, milk and brown sugar in a bowl. Blend in the egg and stir the mixture vigorously to form a smooth batter.
3   Strain the batter through a fine sieve.
4   Use a wooden spoon to mix in the diced jackfruit.
5   Grease a small teflon or omelette pan (approximately 10-12 cm in diameter) with a little peanut oil. Heat it.
6   Fry pancakes, using 60 ml of the batter at one time, for approximately 1-2 minutes on each side. The mixture will make around 8-9 pancakes.
7   Remove the pancakes from the pan and let them cool.
8   Place 2-3 pancakes on each plate. Spoon on some Jackfruit Sherbet and decorate with the syrup and pieces of fruit.

Sri Rasa Ketan
RICE CAKE

>   250 *g glutinous white rice*
>   80 *g coconut cream*
>   250 *ml warm water*
>   50 *g white sugar*
>   250 *ml water*
>   50 *ml pandanus leaf juice or 15 ml pandan essence*
>   180 *ml Banana Syrup (see page 143)*
>   4 *small sweet bananas, peeled*
>   8 *pandanus leaves*
>   *watermelon pieces*

1   Soak the glutinous white rice for 4 hours in plenty of cold water. Drain off the water and wash the rice with fresh cold water 2-3 times, until the water becomes clear. Drain off all excess water.
2   Prepare the coconut milk by whisking together the coconut cream and warm water.

3   Combine the washed rice, sugar, coconut milk, water and pandanus leaf juice in a saucepan. Bring this mixture to the boil, constantly stirring with a wooden spoon; then reduce the heat and simmer for approximately 30 minutes.
4   Place a cake ring approximately 14 cm in diameter in a rice steamer. Pour half of the rice mixture into the ring, cover the steamer with a lid and steam for 25-30 minutes.
5   Remove the rice cake from the ring, set it aside on a plate and repeat the steaming procedure for the remaining half of the mixture.
6   After the steamed rice cakes have cooled, cut them into wedges. Place pieces on each plate and decorate with the Banana Syrup, bananas, pandanus leaves and watermelon.

Apel Malang
POACHED APPLE ON SAPODILLA SYRUP

>   1.5 *litres water*
>   250 *g sugar*
>   2 x 5 *g sticks cinnamon*
>   10 *cloves*
>   45 *ml freshly squeezed lime juice*
>   4 *medium-sized apples, washed*
>   250 *ml Sapodilla Syrup (see page 142)*
>   *lime leaves*
>   4 *sapodillas, peeled, seeded, cut into sections*

1   Pour the water into a stockpot. Add in the sugar, cinnamon sticks, cloves and lime juice. Bring to the boil.
2   Add apples and reduce the heat. Let the apples simmer in the mixture for 8-10 minutes.
3   Remove the pot from the heat and pour the contents into a bowl. Let the apples cool completely in the syrup.
4   When cool, remove the apples from the syrup and, using a sharp, pointed knife, make 12 downward incisions from the top in the skin of each apple. Peel alternate sections of the skin from top to bottom, but leave a part of the skin on when you reach the bottom. (See picture.)
5   Spread a layer of the Sapodilla Syrup on each plate.
6   Place the poached apple in the middle of the sauce and garnish with the lime leaves and sapodilla.

NOTE: If time permits, leave the apples in the syrup overnight in a refrigerator. This will allow the apples to absorb fully the syrup.

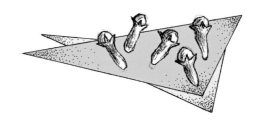

POACHED APPLE ON SAPODILLA SYRUP

JACKFRUIT CENDOLE

RICE CAKE

STARFRUIT SHERBET WITH CINNAMON

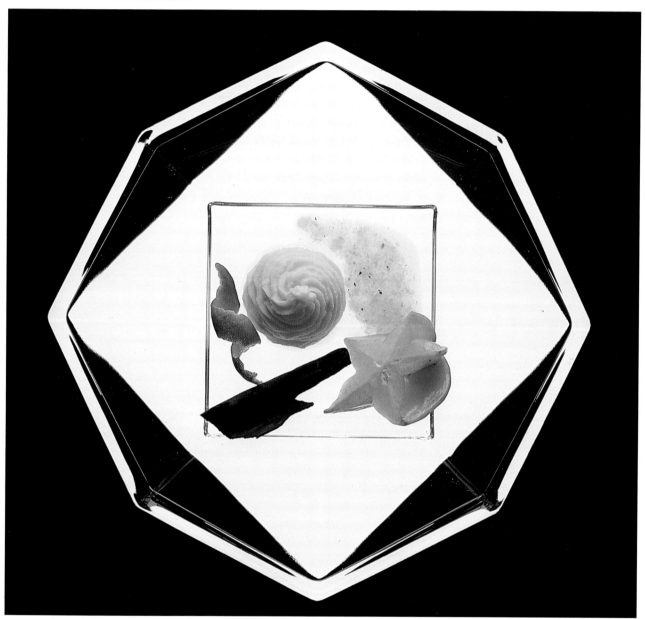

JACKFRUIT SHERBET

TAMARIND SHERBET

SHERBETS

If you do not have an electric ice cream machine to freeze your sherbets, follow the procedure below:

1. Place the mixture in a large bowl and put it in a freezer.
2. After 30-40 minutes, a layer of ice will form. Using a balloon whisk or an electric hand-mixer, whisk the mixture vigorously. Return the mixture to the freezer.
3. Repeat this process until the sherbet is frozen into a smooth mass. (The more you whisk, the smoother your sherbet will become.)

Obviously this process will take a longer time than if you have an electric ice cream machine handy. The results will also depend on how low (degrees below 0°C) the temperature of your freezer is set.

It should be noted that the freezing time given in these recipes are in accordance with our own electric ice cream machine. Depending on the make of the machine, the freezing time can range from 10-50 minutes, using the same quantity stated in the recipe. Therefore, you will have to make adjustments according to your own machine.

Es Krim Belimbing Manis
STARFRUIT SHERBET WITH CINNAMON

350 ml water
300 g starfruits, diced
75 g white sugar
1 x 5 g stick cinnamon
200 ml sugar syrup (see page 23)
30 ml freshly squeezed lime juice
½ egg white, lightly whisked

1. Bring the water to the boil in a saucepan.
2. Add in the next 3 ingredients and boil for 8-10 minutes.
3. Drain off all the liquid and discard the cinnamon stick.
4. Purée the starfruit in a blender for 2-3 minutes. Remove from the blender and strain this through a fine sieve into a bowl. Leave it to cool. This gives 300 g of starfruit purée.
5. Combine the starfruit purée, sugar syrup and lime juice in a bowl. Stir in the egg white with a whisk.
6. Put the mixture in an electric ice cream machine and freeze for approximately 20-25 minutes.

Es Krim Nangka
JACKFRUIT SHERBET

250 ml water
250 g jackfruit flesh, diced
150 g white sugar
15 ml freshly squeezed lime juice
1 pandanus leaf
½ egg white, lightly whisked

1. Bring the water to the boil in a saucepan.
2. Add in the jackfruit, sugar, lime juice and pandanus leaf. Reduce the heat and let the mixture simmer for 8-10 minutes.
3. Remove the pan from the heat and discard the pandanus leaf.
4. Pour the mixture into a blender and purée for 3-4 minutes. Then pour the mixture into a bowl to cool.
5. Mix in the egg white with a whisk.
6. Put the mixture in an electric ice cream machine and freeze for 15-20 minutes.

Es Krim Asam Jawa
TAMARIND SHERBET

This sherbet may be served between courses as a palate refresher, but decrease the amount of white sugar by half and serve only 30-40 ml per person.

550 ml water
300 g tamarind pulp
160 g white sugar
80 g brown sugar (gula Jawa)
½ egg white, lightly whisked

1. Prepare the tamarind juice by boiling 300 ml of the water with the tamarind pulp for about 10 minutes. Strain this through a fine sieve.
2. Combine the resulting tamarind juice with the remaining water in a saucepan. Add the sugar and boil for 5 minutes.
3. Remove from the heat and let the mixture cool.
4. When cool use a whisk to mix in the egg white.
5. Put this mixture in an electric ice cream machine and freeze for approximately 20 minutes.

Es Krim Kelapa Muda
YOUNG COCONUT SHERBET

300 g young coconut meat, diced
200 ml coconut milk (see page 22)
150 g white sugar
½ egg white, lightly whisked

1. Combine the coconut meat, coconut milk and sugar in a blender. Purée for 2-3 minutes, then pour the mixture into a bowl.
2. Mix in the egg white with a whisk.
3. Put the mixture in an electric ice cream machine and freeze for 20-25 minutes.

Es Krim Ketan Hitam

BLACK RICE SHERBET

A Coconut Syrup or Kolak Sauce will go well with this sherbet.

> *70 g black glutinous rice*
> *475 ml water*
> *60 ml rice wine*
> *50 g white sugar*
> *1 egg white, lightly whisked*

1 Wash the black rice several times in plenty of cold water until the water becomes clear. Then soak the rice in fresh cold water for 12 hours.
2 Drain off all liquid from the rice, then bring 325 ml of water to the boil in a saucepan.
3 Add in the drained, washed rice and cook for approximately 20-25 minutes. Remove from the heat and let the rice cool in its liquid.
4 In another saucepan, bring the remaining 150 ml of water to the boil.
5 Add the rice wine and sugar, and let this syrup boil for approximately 5 minutes. Remove the pan from the heat and let it cool.
6 Pour the cooled syrup into a blender and add in the cooked black rice together with its liquid. Purée this for 2-3 minutes.
7 Remove the mixture from the blender and strain through a sieve into a bowl.
8 Mix in the egg white with a whisk.
9 Put the mixture in an electric ice cream machine and freeze for 15-20 minutes.

NOTE: Any rice wine may be used in making this sherbet but, if possible, choose a brown-coloured one.

Es Krim Brem Bali dengan Cengkeh

BALINESE RICE WINE SHERBET

> *125 ml water*
> *150 g white sugar*
> *325 ml rice wine*
> *15 ml freshly squeezed lime juice*
> *5 g whole cloves*
> *½ egg white, lightly whisked*

1 Bring the water to the boil in a saucepan.
2 Add in the sugar, rice wine, lime juice and cloves. Reduce the heat and simmer for approximately 8-10 minutes.
3 Remove the pan from the heat, discard the cloves and let the mixture cool.
4 When cool mix in the egg white with a whisk
5 Put the mixture in an electric ice cream machine and freeze for 15-20 minutes.

Es Krim Lada Hijau

GREEN PEPPERCORN SHERBET

This sherbet may also be served as a palate refresher between courses, but the quantity of sugar used in making the syrup must be decreased — only 250 g sugar to 500 ml water.

> *250 ml water*
> *45 ml freshly squeezed lime juice*
> *50 g whole green peppercorns*
> *salt*
> *600 ml sugar syrup (see page 23)*
> *½ egg white, lightly whisked*

1 Bring the water to the boil in a saucepan.
2 Add in 15 ml of the lime juice, all the peppercorns and the salt. Reduce the heat and simmer the mixture for 5 minutes.
3 Drain off all the liquid from the saucepan and set aside 15 g of the boiled green peppercorns.
4 In a blender, combine the remaining peppercorns, sugar syrup and the rest of the lime juice. Purée for 2-3 minutes.
5 Pour the mixture into a bowl and mix in the egg white with a whisk. Stir in the whole peppercorns.
6 Put the mixture in an electric ice cream machine and freeze for approximately 15-20 minutes.

Es Krim Durian

DURIAN SHERBET

> *375 ml water*
> *200 g white sugar*
> *280 ml coconut cream*
> *1 pandanus leaf*
> *400 g durian flesh*
> *1 egg white, lightly whisked*

1 Bring the water to the boil in a saucepan.
2 Add in the sugar, coconut cream, pandanus leaf and durian flesh. Reduce the heat and let this mixture simmer for approximately 10 minutes.
3 Remove the pan from the heat and discard the pandanus leaf.
4 Pour the mixture into a blender and purée at high speed for 2-3 minutes.
5 Remove from the blender and pour the mixture into a bowl to cool.
6 When cool, mix in the egg white with a whisk.
7 Put the mixture in an electric ice cream machine and freeze for approximately 15-20 minutes.

GUAVA SHERBET

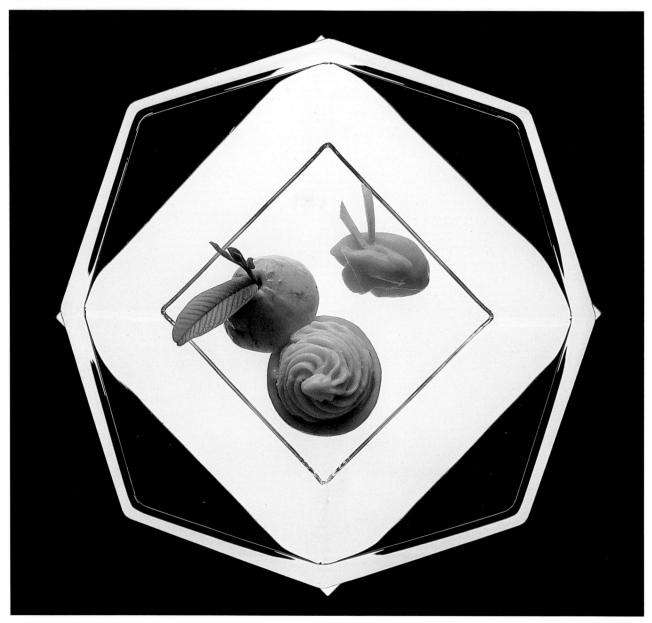

DURIAN SHERBET

Es Krim Jambu Biji

GUAVA SHERBET

150 ml water
150 g white sugar
15 ml freshly squeezed lime juice
250 g guava, peeled, seeded, diced
½ egg white, lightly whisked

1   Bring the water to the boil in a saucepan.
2   Add in the sugar, lime juice and guava, and boil for 12-15 minutes.
3   Pour the mixture into a blender and purée for 3-4 minutes. Then remove from the blender and pour into a bowl to cool.
4   When cool mix in the egg white with a whisk.
5   Put the mixture in an electric ice cream machine and freeze for approximately 20-25 minutes.

SOURSOP SHERBET

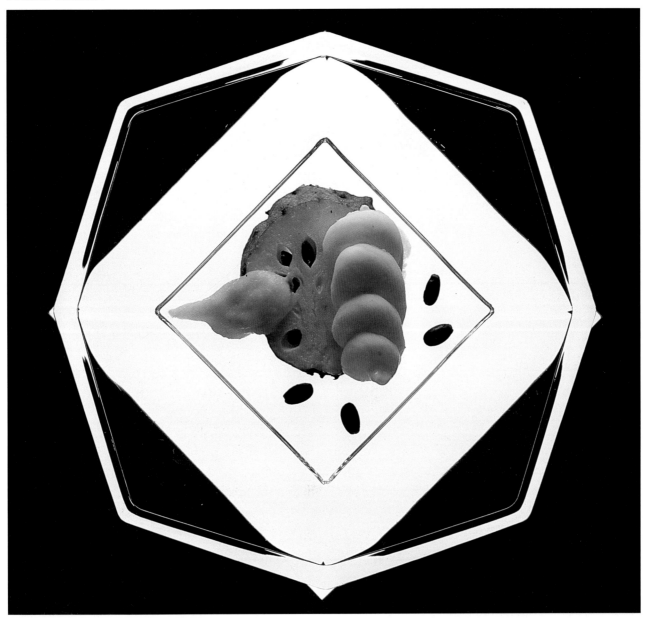

Es Krim Sirsak

SOURSOP SHERBET

400 g soursop, peeled, seeded
250 ml sugar syrup (see page 23)
15 ml freshly squeezed lime juice
½ egg white, lightly whisked

1 Combine the soursop, sugar syrup and lime juice in a blender, and purée for 2-3 minutes. Then pour the mixture into a bowl.
2 Mix in the egg white with a whisk.
3 Put the mixture in an electric ice cream machine and freeze for approximately 20 minutes.

SAPODILLA SHERBET

Es Krim Sawo

SAPODILLA SHERBET

400 g sapodilla, peeled, seeded, diced
300 ml sugar syrup (see page 23)
30 ml freshly squeezed lime juice
½ egg white, lightly whisked

1 Combine the sapodilla, sugar syrup and lime juice in a blender, and purée for 2-3 minutes. Then pour the mixture into a bowl.
2 Mix in the egg white with a whisk.
3 Put the mixture in an electric ice cream machine and freeze for approximately 20-25 minutes.

Es Krim Teh Parahiyangan

BLACK TEA SHERBET

This sherbet is also good when served between courses as a palate refresher. However, decrease the quantity of sugar to 80 g only and serve a small amount of sherbet per person.

500 ml water
10 g black Java tea leaves
150 g brown sugar (gula Jawa)
½ egg white, lightly whisked

1 Bring the water to the boil in a saucepan.
2 Add in the tea leaves and brown sugar. Boil rapidly for 3-5 minutes.
3 Remove from the heat, then strain the liquid through a fine sieve into a bowl and discard the tea leaves. Let the liquid cool.
4 Mix the egg white into the cooled liquid with a whisk.
5 Put the mixture in an electric ice cream machine and freeze for 20-25 minutes.

Es Krim Klengkeng

LYCHEE SHERBET

500 ml water
150 g white sugar
300 g lychees, peeled, seeded, diced
½ egg white, lightly whisked

1 Combine the water and sugar in a saucepan and boil for 5 minutes. Remove the pan from the heat and let the syrup cool.
2 Combine the syrup and lychees in a blender. Purée for 2-3 minutes, then pour this into a bowl.
3 Mix in the egg white with a whisk.
4 Put the mixture in an electric ice cream machine and freeze for 10-15 minutes.

SYRUPS

Sirop Nanas

PINEAPPLE SYRUP

250 ml water
100 g white sugar
200 g ripe pineapple, peeled, diced
1 x 5 g stick cinnamon
10 medium-sized cloves
15 ml freshly squeezed lime juice

1 Bring the water to the boil in a saucepan.
2 Add in the other ingredients, then reduce the heat and let the mixture simmer for 10-12 minutes.
3 Remove from the heat and discard the cinnamon stick and cloves.
4 Pour the mixture into a blender and purée at high speed for 2-3 minutes. Let the syrup cool completely before using. Yields 375 ml.

Sirop Sawo

SAPODILLA SYRUP

250 g sapodilla, peeled, seeded, diced
60 ml sugar syrup (see page 23)
30 ml freshly squeezed lime juice
120 ml water

1 Combine all the ingredients in a blender.
2 Purée at high speed for 2-3 minutes. Remove from the blender and serve. Yields 400 ml.

Sirop Kelapa

COCONUT SYRUP

200 g fresh young coconut meat
100 ml sugar syrup (see page 23)

1 Combine the ingredients in a blender.
2 Purée at high speed for 2-3 minutes until velvety. Remove fom the blender and serve. Yields 250 ml.

Sirop Nangka

JACKFRUIT SYRUP

375 ml water
150 g jackfruit flesh, peeled, segments diced
1 x 5 g stick cinnamon
50 g white sugar

1 Bring the water to the boil in a saucepan.
2 Stir in the other ingredients, then reduce the heat and let the mixture simmer for 8-10 minutes.
3 Remove from the heat and discard the cinnamon.
4 Pour the mixture into a blender and purée at high speed for 2-3 minutes. Remove from the blender and serve. Yields 500 ml.

Saus Kayu Manis

CINNAMON SABAYON

This should be used either as a topping or a glaze.

 5 egg yolks
 140 g white sugar
 3 g cinnamon powder
 3 g ginger, finely diced
 30 ml rice wine

1 Combine all the ingredients in a heat-resistant bowl.
2 Place the bowl in a hot water bath, making sure the water does not boil. Then beat the mixture in the bowl vigorously with a balloon whisk until it becomes creamy, approximately 2-3 minutes.
3 Remove from the hot water bath and continue stirring with the whisk until the mixture is cool, another 2-3 minutes. Use immediately. Yields 375 ml.

Sirop Pisang

BANANA SYRUP

It is best to prepare this syrup just before using it as bananas discolour very easily.

 250 g ripe bananas, peeled, diced
 60 ml sugar syrup (see page 23)
 15 ml freshly squeezed lime juice

1 Combine all the ingredients in a blender.
2 Purée at high speed for 2-3 minutes. Remove from the blender and serve. Yields 250 ml.

Saus Kolak

KOLAK SAUCE

This is a very versatile sauce that can be served with many different hot or cold desserts, particularly those which contain bananas.

 375 ml water
 150 g brown sugar (gula Jawa)
 15 g ginger, finely diced
 5 g cornflour, dissolved in 15 ml cold water

1 Pour the water into a saucepan and bring it to the boil.
2 Add in all the other ingredients, reduce the heat and let the mixture simmer for approximately 8-10 minutes.
3 Remove the pan from the heat and strain the sauce through a fine sieve. Use hot or cold as desired. Yields 375 ml.

Sirop Sirsak

SOURSOP SYRUP

 250 g soursop, peeled, seeded, diced
 150 ml sugar syrup (see page 23)
 15 ml freshly squeezed lime juice
 60 ml water

1 Combine all the ingredients in a blender.
2 Purée the mixture at high speed for 2-3 minutes. Remove and serve. Yields 375 ml.

Sirop Apokat

AVOCADO SYRUP

This syrup should only be prepared shortly before serving since the avocado flesh turns brown very fast.

 250 g avocado flesh, peeled, seeded, diced
 90 ml sugar syrup (see page 23)
 60 ml condensed milk
 15 ml freshly squeezed lime juice
 185 ml water

1 Combine all the ingredients in a blender and purée, at high speed, for 2-3 minutes.
2 Remove from the blender and serve. Yields 400 ml.

Sirop Melon

GREEN MELON SYRUP

 250 g green melon flesh, peeled, seeded, diced
 100 g icing sugar

1 Combine the ingredients in a blender. Purée for 2-3 minutes.
2 Remove from the blender and serve. Yields 250 ml.

Sirop Jambu Biji

GUAVA SYRUP

 90 ml water
 200 g ripe guavas, peeled, seeded, diced
 100 g white sugar
 120 ml canned guava juice
 15 ml freshly squeezed lime juice

1 Bring the water to the boil in a saucepan.
2 Add the remaining ingredients, reduce the heat and allow to simmer for 10-12 minutes.
3 Remove the pan from the heat and pour the mixture into a blender. Purée at high speed for 2-3 minutes.
4 Remove the mixture from the blender and strain through a very fine sieve into a bowl. Let the syrup cool completely before using. Yields 400 ml.

GLOSSARY

GLOSSARY

In this section we have provided information on any ingredients used in the book which we feel might be unfamiliar to some readers. They are entered under their English name, followed by the Indonesian in brackets. In a few instances where there is no English translation, the entries are headed by the Indonesian word. The scientific name, where applicable, is given at the end of the entry.

ANISE (*jintan manis*). This aromatic seed may be used to flavour liquors and sweets. It is said that anise was known in Java before A.D. 1200 although it is not certain whether it was indigenous or had come from India. (*Pimpinella anisum*)

ASPARAGUS BEAN (*kecipir*). A winged bean with a very mild asparagus flavour, it is eaten raw when marinated or cooked as a vegetable. (*Psophocarpus tetragonolobus*)

AUBERGINE (*terung*). Also known as eggplant, this fruit vegetable is native to Southeast Asia. The larger variety has a shiny purple or white skin. The small, round variety, known as *terung engkol* in Indonesia, has a slightly bitter taste and is eaten either cooked or raw before it is ripe. When cooking aubergines, make sure that they are always firm and dry. (*Solanum melongena*)

BAMBOO SHOOT (*rebung*). The tender young ivory-white shoot of the bamboo. Crisp in texture and sweet in taste, it is mainly used in vegetable dishes and soups. Canned bamboo shoots are widely available. They should be boiled before use — 10 minutes if canned, 30 minutes if fresh. (*Bambusa*)

BASIL (*kemangi*) The local variety, *kemangi*, is milder in flavour than the basil found in Western countries. Another variety, *selasih*, grows wild in Indonesia and is more common elsewhere. Though it is used in salads, its flavour is inferior to that of *kemangi*, but whichever variety is available can be used. (*Ocimum americanum; O. basilicum*)

BEANCURD (*tahu*). Also known as *tofu*, this is made from soya bean milk and comes in soft, white blocks. It also can be compressed to make firmer white or yellow (coloured with turmeric) flat squares.

BEANSPROUT (*tauge*). The young sprouts of the green mung bean, these are used raw or cooked as a vegetable, in salads, in soups and in stuffings. They are easily available. (*Phaseolus aureus*)

BITTER GOURD (*peria* or *pare*). A dark green, bitter, cucumber-like vegetable with a wrinkled skin, it is usually pickled or cooked in curries when not quite ripe. Used as a vegetable, it can be cooked in the same ways as courgettes. (*Momordica charantia*)

BROWN SUGAR (*gula Jawa*). This very sweet, thick brown sugar is made from the sap of the flower of the coconut or Palmyra palm. A real home industry — every *kampung* (or village) makes *gula Jawa* — there is no large-scale commercial production, although it is sold at the markets in hard cakes. Any unrefined brown sugar may be used as a substitute.

CANDLENUT (*kemiri*). The hard nut of the candleberry tree. It has diverse uses — to this day, in remote villages, the nut is pounded with materials like cotton and copra to make candles, hence the common name "candlenut". *Kemiri* is roasted before it is used in cooking, then it is usually pounded and added as a binding agent to hot and cold sauces. When mixed with other spices and condiments, it may be eaten as a relish or used in curries. It is available in cans or sealed plastic packs in Asian food stores. The *kemiri* flavour is distinctive, but macadamia nuts or Brazil nuts may be used as substitutes if necessary. (*Aleurites moluccana*)

CARDAMOM (*kepulaga*). This grows wild in the lower hills of Java but is now widely cultivated throughout Indonesia. The oils obtained from the stems and leaves are used as flavourings, but it is the dried fruit which serves as a warm, aromatic spice. It can be purchased green, white or black — the colour depending on the drying method. Cardamom should always be used ground in order to release its oils. (*Amomum cardamomum*)

CASHEWNUT (*kacang mete* or *kacang monyet*). Native to the American tropics, the cashewnut plant was probably introduced to Southeast Asia by the Portuguese. The large, reddish cashew apple virtually hides the nut growing underneath. The ripe fruit and very young leaves are eaten raw and are much liked by the Javanese, who use the leaves as flavouring for rice. In the recipes in this book, we use the leaves cooked in vegetable dishes. (*Anacardium occidentale*)

CASSAVA (*ubi kayu*). A hardy, drought-resistant root plant seen along roadsides throughout Indonesia. The long brown tuber can be used as a vegetable, although several varieties are very bitter and are used only to make a type of flour. The young leaves resemble papaya leaves and are cooked as green vegetables. Tapioca is prepared from the starch. (*Manihot utilissima*)

CHAYOTE (*labu Siam*). A medium-sized, light green vegetable, slightly oval in shape and bearing a close resemblance to the cucumber in flavour. A soft squash may be used as a substitute. The young shoots of the plant are also eaten. (*Sechium edule*)

CHILI (*cabe*). Originally from Central America, this is now so basic to Indonesian cooking that virtually every household has several chili plants growing in the garden. Three types are commonly used: the long green chili, *cabe hijau*, which is the least hot; the long red chili, *cabe merah*, which is a bit hotter; and the bird's eye chili, or *cabe rawit*, a tiny dark green chili which is the hottest and most pungent of all. In all varieties, the seeds are the fieriest part of the chili. (*Capsicum*)

CINNAMON (*kayu manis*). The cinnamon tree is found in abundance in the mountains of Sumatra. The innermost layer of the bark is sold as thin, fragile quills used for flavouring meat, poultry and desserts. The spice is also available powdered, although the flavour and aroma disappears relatively quickly in this form. (*Cinnamomum cassia; C. zeylanicum*)

CLOVE (*cengkeh*). The clove tree is a native of the Maluku Islands, formerly the Moluccas or the Spice Islands. Cloves are actually the flower buds which are harvested and dried under the sun for days. The dried clove resembles a nail with a round tip and an elongated stem. Even in its powdered form, the clove retains its strong, aromatic flavour and is often used in soups and sauces. (*Eugenia aromatica*)

COCONUT (*kelapa*). One of the basics of Indonesian cooking. Coconuts at three stages of maturity are sold in Indonesian markets: *kelapa muda*, young coconut about 10 months old, has plenty of coconut water and transparent white flesh that can be scraped out with a spoon; *kelapa setengah tua* (literally middle-aged coconut) is about a year old and has firm flesh that is good for grating; and *kelapa tua*, the old nut in which most of the water has dried up and the flesh has become fibrous (this, unfortunately, is the age of most of the coconuts that reach cities in Western countries). Coconut milk, or *santan*, is made from grated coconut flesh (see page 22). When a recipe calls for grated coconut, dried grated coconut, soaked in water and then drained, may be a substitute. (*Cocos nucifera*)

CORIANDER (*ketumbar*). The seeds of this spice are used fresh, dried or powdered and one form should not be substituted for another. It is a strong spice and should be used sparingly. In Indonesia, fresh young coriander leaves are also used. (*Coriandrum sativum*)

CUMIN (*jintan putih*). The seeds are used as a spice, especially for seasoning curries, and are available both whole and in powdered form. They have a powerful aromatic flavour. Since different varieties range in strength and colour, it is wise to experiment to see which is most pleasing. (*Cuminum cuminum*)

CUP LEAF (*daun mangkok*). These leaves are traditionally used in Indonesia as platters in the same way as banana leaves. The leaves may also be boiled in vegetable dishes. (*Polyscias scutellerium*)

DILL (*adas manis*). The leaves of this herb are often used in flavouring pickles. The leaves (fresh or dried) as well as the seeds are also used in soups, fish and egg dishes and sauces. (*Anethum graveolens*)

DRIED SHRIMPS (*ebi*). Shelled, cleaned small prawns or shrimps that are subsequently steamed and sun-dried, they are widely used in soups, sauces, seafood and vegetable dishes and for making side dishes like *sambals* to accompany curries.

DURIAN. This nutritious, seasonal fruit is infamous for its strong smell. Fruits vary in size (from 20-35 cm), in texture and in flavour. All have a hard, dull greeny-yellow shell covered with sharp, pointed spines. This shell can be split open into 4-5 sections with 2-5 seeds encased in a soft, creamy pulp. The pulp is eaten raw, or used to make sherbets, ice creams, desserts, dessert sauces and candies. There are two durian seasons a year but the fruits are seldom seen in the West as they spoil easily. (*Durio zibethinus*)

FENNEL (*jintan*). This grows wild throughout the world and the leaves (fresh or dried), seeds and dried root are often used with fish. The seeds are sweet and have a licorice flavour. If not available, anise seeds make an acceptable substitute. (*Foeniculum vulgare*)

FERMENTED BEAN CAKE (*tempe*). This rather crunchy cake is made from boiled soya beans which have been pressed dry, then allowed to ferment. In Indonesian markets, *tempe* is usually available in rectangular slabs and may be fried as a snack. It is used in this book in salads and as a stuffing ingredient, as well as a garnish for soups. If *tempe* is not available, firm white beancurd is a possible substitute.

FERMENTED SOYA BEANS (*tauco*). A thick, strong, aromatic paste which is produced by fermenting either black or yellow whole soya beans. It is readily available, bottled or canned, in Asian food stores and may be labelled "Yellow Bean Sauce".

FERNTOP (*daun pakis* or *sayur paku*). The curled tip is cooked as a vegetable like fiddlehead or bracken fern, which makes a good substitute. (*Athyrium esculentum*)

GINGER (*halia*). This rhizome is native to Southeast Asia and it is available in root, powdered or pickled forms. The fresh root is used in most of the recipes in this book. (*Zingiber officinale*)

GREATER GALANGAL (*laos*). Less aromatic and pungent than lesser galangal (q.v.), it is always used fresh in Indonesia. The flowers can be used in salads. It also comes in powdered form. If not available, use ginger but double the amount. (*Languas galanga*)

GUAVA (*jambu biji*). This yellow-green fruit has a firm inner flesh filled with tiny seeds. There are many different types of guavas, but most common are the large fruits with rosy-pink or creamy-white flesh. Guavas are excellent for sherbets, ice creams and compotes. The juice has a delicate, sweet-sour taste and fragrant aroma. (*Psidium guajava*)

JACKFRUIT (*nangka*). Green in colour with thick, sharp spines, the young fruit is used mainly as a vegetable, but is eaten as a dessert when fully ripe. When ripe the pulp is yellow, with a waxy texture and very sweet taste. Its strong fragrance can overpower the scent of other ingredients. (*Artocarpus heterophyllus*)

JAVANESE PARKIA (*pete cina*). These flat pods are best eaten young as a vegetable either raw or cooked. Snowpeas may be served as a substitute. (*Leucaena glauca*)

KEDONGDONG. A small, oval-shaped green fruit with a slightly tart flavour and a fibrous round seed. The very young leaves can be eaten or cooked as a flavouring. (*Spondias cytherea*)

KENIKIR LEAF. This small leaf resembles a young carrot leaf. Kenikir has a sharp, bitter taste and is used in salads and sauces, or sometimes cooked as a vegetable. If necessary, chervil may be used as a substitute. (*Cosmos caudatus*)

ASPARAGUS BEAN

CASSAVA

AUBERGINE (TERUNG ENGKOL)

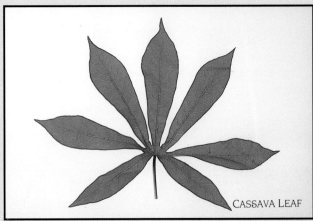

CASSAVA LEAF

BITTER GOURD

CUP LEAF

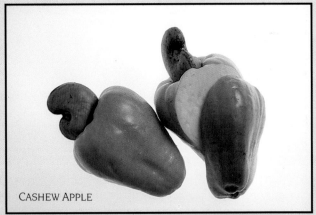

CASHEW APPLE

DURIAN

GINGER

MANGOSTEEN

GREATER GALANGAL

MACE

JACKFRUIT

MELINJO FRUIT

KEDONGDONG

MUSTARD GREEN

LEMON GRASS (*sereh*). This long, delightfully aromatic grass is a very popular flavouring for soups, fish, meats, sauces and curries. Fresh lemon grass stalks are now available in the United States and some countries in Europe. Although the powdered form is available, it should only be used as a substitute in the sauce recipes and the quantity should be reduced by two-thirds. (*Cymbopogon nardus*)

LESSER GALANGAL (*kencur*). This rhizome which originally came from India is used like greater galangal (q.v.), but more sparingly since it has a stronger, hotter flavour. Fresh *kencur* can be found in Asian food stores but, if it is not available fresh, the powdered form may be used instead. (*Kaempferia galanga*)

LIME. The two types of lime most commonly used in Indonesian cooking are the small, juicy lime (*jeruk nipis*) and the kaffir lime (*jeruk purut*). The latter has a dark green, wrinkled outer skin. The kaffir lime peel, which has a sharp bitter-sweet taste, is sometimes used in flavouring, and the highly acidic fruit, which does not have much juice, is used in *sambals*. The leaves are most commonly used in cooking. If no kaffir lime leaves are available, curry leaves may be used as a substitute.

LONG BEAN (*kacang panjang*). Sometimes called "the yard-long bean" because the thin pods can literally grow up to 1 metre in length. It is used extensively in these recipes either whole or cut in pieces. Stringbeans may be used as a substitute if necessary. (*Vigna sinensis* var. *sesquipedalis*)

MANGO (*mangga*). A pear-shaped tropical fruit with a smooth yellow or green skin. A ripe mango is sweet, its flesh creamy in texture. It is a popular dessert fruit and is also used in making sherbets, ice creams, compotes and sauces. The unripe mango is used in chutney, as well as salads; sliced and eaten raw with special sauces; or blended as a tart fruit juice. Unhappily, there is no substitute for fresh mango but it is widely available internationally nowadays. (*Mangifera indica*)

MANGOSTEEN (*manggis*). This round fruit has a smooth purple skin. It is extremely sweet with a delicate sweet-sour aftertaste when ripe. The snowy white flesh is segmented and has oval pits. Be careful when squeezing the fruit open because its thick rind contains mangostin, which stains. (*Garcinia mangostana*)

MELINJO. The small yellow or red-coloured fruit may be eaten raw, but it is not very tasty. The melinjo kernel is used to make *emping*, a flattened, thin cracker which is fried to a crisp and used as garnish for salads and soups. The leaves and young flowers are cooked and eaten like a vegetable. (*Gnetum gnemon*)

MUSHROOM. Although mushrooms grow wild on a number of the islands of Indonesia, they were not used in traditional cooking. Now there are three varieties being raised commercially in Java and Bali. They are the small, button-like straw mushroom, (*jamur*); the black Chinese mushroom (*jamur hitam*); and the oyster mushroom (*jamur tiram*).

MUSTARD GREEN (*sawi*). Popularly known by its Chinese name *caixin*, this pale green leafy plant is cooked as a vegetable. (*Brassica juncea*)

NOODLES. There are many types of Chinese noodles and they may be available either fresh or dried. Packaged dried noodles should be soaked in warm water before use to soften them. In the recipes in this book, noodles are used mainly for garnish.

Egg noodles are yellow as they are made from wheat flour and egg. Some varieties are available fresh, while others are only available dried.

Glass noodles are thin, brittle and semi-transparent. Sold dried in packets, they need not be soaked if they are to be deep-fried. When soaked they become almost transparent.

Rice noodles are thicker and whiter than glass noodles and they are the only type of noodle that is packaged wet.

NUTMEG (*pala*). The ripe fruit is oval, light yellow in colour and yields two aromatic spices: nutmeg, which is the seed inside the kernel and has a spicy sweet flavour; and mace, the red net which surrounds the kernel and has a stronger, more pungent flavour. Both are available dried or in powdered form. In Indonesia, the flesh of the fruit is traditionally candied, used in jams, cakes and tarts and as the syrup base for fruit drinks. The candied flesh may be available in packets in Asian food stores. (*Myristica fragrans*)

PALM HEART (*pondoh*). The centre of the palm tree obtained by cutting down the tree and splitting it near the base of the leaves. This is white, crunchy in texture and has a light, buttery-sweet flavour. It can be eaten raw or cooked and is used in salads and soups, as a vegetable, for garnish and as a filling for spring rolls. Available precooked in cans.

PALM NUT (*siwalan*). The sweetish, transparent, gelatinous substance extracted from the fruit of the Palmyra palm (*Borrassus flabellifer*). It is used mainly for desserts and sometimes in soups. Palm nuts can be bought in tins or jars.

PALM WINE. This is a fermented wine produced from the sap of the bruised young flower spikes of the Palmyra palm. It can be quite a potent brew and has a sweet, acid taste. A young white wine with a sweet, acid taste can be used as a substitute.

PANDANUS LEAF (*daun pandan*). This plant with long narrow leaves is commonly grown in Indonesian gardens. The leaves are used for fragrance, while the juice may be used for colouring. In Java, the leaves are sometimes used in preparing beancurd. A drop of vanilla can be used as a substitute in desserts if pandan essence is not available; in hot dishes, there is no substitute for the leaf. (*Pandanus amaryllifolius*)

PAPAYA (*pepaya*). A large, orange-fleshed fruit commonly eaten as a dessert. The green young papaya is cooked as a vegetable or pickled. (*Carica papaya*)

PEANUTS (*kacang tanah*). A highly nutritious underground legume. Vendors selling the roasted nuts are found in almost every Indonesian city and town. Peanuts are used extensively in Indonesian cooking, especially in sauces. *Oncom*, a fermented paste, is prepared from the ground nuts, and is usually eaten fried. (*Arachis hypogaea*)

PUMPKIN (*labu merah*). The local variety of the pumpkin has red flesh and a slightly rougher skin than the one found in the West. The leaves are also eaten in Indonesia. (*Cucurbita moschata*)

RAMBUTAN. A round, reddish fruit covered with soft spiny growth quite like hair (*rambut* in Indonesian), this is a seasonal dessert fruit. Its sweet, translucent white flesh bears a slight resemblance to the lychee in texture. (*Nephelium lappaceum*)

RED KIDNEY BEAN (*kacang merah*). This may vary from pink to maroon in colour. It is usually associated with another spicy cuisine as the basic ingredient of the Mexican dish, chili con carne. It has a floury texture and is fairly sweet in flavour. (*Phaseolus vulgaris*)

RICE WINE (*brem* Bali). Made from fermented boiled glutinous rice. A not-too-sweet Japanese *saki* or Chinese rice wine is an acceptable substitute.

SALAM LEAF. This tough, aromatic leaf, similar in shape and size to the bay leaf, is used to flavour soups, meat and fish dishes, as well as sauces. Bay leaf can be used as a substitute, but halve the quantity and expect a slightly different flavour. (*Eugenia polyantha*)

SAMBAL. This is usually a fragrant thick sauce or paste made with pounded chilies and other ingredients like shrimp paste, shallots and lime juice. It may be cooked or uncooked. (See page 26 for some recipes.)

SAPODILLA (*sawo* or *chiku*). A sweet, plum-sized fruit with smooth brown skin and a firm brown inner flesh. It is also known as chicle, and the sap is used as the base for making chewing gum. (*Manilkara achras*)

SHALLOT (*bawang merah*). An essential ingredient of Indonesian cooking. The local form is milder than the varieties generally found in the West. Although *bawang merah* is the ideal type to use, it can be replaced by any variety available.

SHRIMP PASTE (*terasi*). This strongly pungent paste is made from pounding shrimp heads to a pulp and then drying it in the sun. The dark, brownish-red paste is sold in round cakes or thick flat slabs in markets. It is used as a flavouring for soups, sauces, fish dishes, vegetables and *sambals*. It should be used sparingly and can last for a very long time if sealed and kept in the refrigerator or a cool dry place. *Terasi* or *belacan*, its Malay equivalent, can be bought from Asian food stores in small 20-50 g blocks.

SNAKEFRUIT (*salak*). This smallish, pear-shaped fruit of a squat, thorny palm has a brown, rough outer skin which is similar to snakeskin. The flesh is firm, starchy and rather crunchy with a sharp taste. Usually there are several segments with large brown pits. The sweetest and best *salak* are said to grow in Bali. (*Zalacca edulis*)

SOUR FINGER CARAMBOLA (*belimbing wuluh*). This light green, finger-like fruit is very sour and acid. It is used primarily in cooking soups, making sauces, as a pickle or garnish and may also be used as a vegetable. If not available, peeled and seeded gooseberries may be used as a substitute. (*Averrhoa belimbi*)

SOURSOP (*sirsak* or *durian belanda*). The long, heart-shaped fruit of a small tree. The skin is dark green with soft short spines. It usually weighs about 1 kg or more and its fragrant, white flesh is soft and juicy with tear-shaped black seeds in it. The flesh is eaten raw or can be used to make delicious drinks, sherbets, ice creams and fruit sauces. (*Annona muricata*)

SOYA BEAN (*kacang kedele*). This small yellow or black bean is an essential ingredient in several items basic to Indonesian cooking. The black bean is the basis for *kecap manis* (dark sweet soya sauce) and *kecap asin* (salty soya sauce). Soya bean milk is used to make *tahu* (beancurd). *Tauco* (fermented soya beans) is a paste made either from yellow or black soya beans, while *tempe* (fermented bean cake) is a cake made from fermented soya beans. (*Glycine soja*)

SOYA SAUCE (*kecap*). The Indonesian soya bean-based *kecap* comes in two varieties: the dark sweet *kecap manis* and the saltier *kecap asin*. The sweet *kecap manis* is used more often in this book, but both types may be found in Asian food stores. *Kecap manis* may be replaced by a sweet, dark Japanese or Chinese soya sauce, though the taste is not exactly the same. If no sweet variety is available, add a little brown sugar to the saltier soya sauce. *Kecap manis* keeps well without refrigeration.

SPINACH (*bayam*). *Bayam* is the tropical version of spinach and is widely cultivated. It has roundish, medium-sized green leaves which are cooked and eaten just like spinach. Another less common variety with reddish purple leaves is known as *bayam merah* or red spinach. Any spinach may be used as a substitute. (*Celosia argentea*)

STARFRUIT (*belimbing manis*). A sweet, yellow fruit which in cross-section looks like a five-pointed star, it is often eaten raw as a dessert and may be candied. (*Averrhoa carambola*)

SWEET POTATO (*ubi jalar* or *ubi manis*). A tuber with red, white or purple skin and white, red, orange or yellow flesh. It is eaten as a vegetable and sometimes cooked in sauces. The young leaves are also used in salads. (*Ipomoea batatas*)

TAMARIND (*asam*). The sour fruit of a large tree originally brought to Indonesia from India, it looks like the broad bean in shape but the skin is brown and very brittle. The flesh, which has tough fibres running through it, is green and very sour when immature. When ripe, the fruit turns brown and soft, but maintains its tart flavour. In Java, the pulp of the fruit is extracted and mixed with salt or sugar. The salted pulp is formed into blocks or balls and is called *asam kawak*. (*Tamarindus indica*)

TARO (*talas*). A staple food of Asia — the starchy tubers are boiled or fried, like potatoes. The huge, heart-shaped leaves must be boiled before eating. (*Colocasia esculentum*)

TORCH GINGER (*kecombrang* or *honje*). An exceptionally tall, aromatic native ginger widely cultivated for its reddish young flower shoots, which are either used raw in salads or cooked as a vegetable. (*Nicolaia elatior*)

TURMERIC (*kunyit*). A knobbly rhizome which looks rather like ginger but is bright orange beneath the rind. It is used fresh, dried or in powdered form to give a yellow colour to food. Always try to use the fresh root as the powdered form produces a slightly grainy texture. If only the powdered form is available, use half the quantity called for in the recipe. The broad, shiny, leaves are also used for flavouring. (*Curcuma domestica*)

WATER APPLE (*jambu air*). This pretty, bell-shaped rosy-white fruit is very juicy and only slightly scented. It is normally eaten raw and used in salads and desserts. The similar rose apple is a slightly larger, oblong-shaped fruit with red-and-white striped skin. It is tastier than the water apple but more delicate. (*Eugenia aquea; E. malaccensis*)

WATER CHESTNUT. The dark-skinned corm of a wild sage, it should be peeled before being eaten, either raw or in soups. The flesh is crisp, white and slightly sweet. Available ready-peeled in cans. (*Eleocharis dulcis*)

WATER CONVOLVULUS (*kangkung*). A leafy vegetable with dark green, heart-shaped leaves and hollow stems, it grows wild or in cultivation in swampy areas of Asia. It is more delicate in flavour than the spinach of the West and is sometimes called swamp spinach. Extremely cheap, it is usually stir-fried or used raw in salads. (*Ipomoea aquatica*)

WHITE RADISH (*lobak*). There are two varieties: the white radish is preferable to the red for its milder taste. The radish and its green leaves may be used raw in salads or cooked as a vegetable, (*Raphanus sativus*)

WOOD FUNGUS (*jamur kuping*). This type of mushroom is sometimes called cloud ear fungus because it swells to a curled shape when soaked in water. Wood fungus is now extensively used in Indonesian cooking, especially in soups and vegetable dishes. It is sold in dried form and is normally greyish black in colour, but becomes brown and translucent when soaked in water. (*Auricularia polytricha*)

YAM BEAN (*bengkuang*). A sweet, starchy tuber which can be served raw in salads, but is more often cooked as a vegetable in this book. The brown outer skin should be peeled off before use; it keeps well if stored in a cool dry place. (*Pachyrrhizus bulbosus*)

PALM NUT

PANDANUS LEAF

RED SPINACH (BAYAM MERAH)

SALAM LEAF

SNAKEFRUIT

TORCH GINGER

SOUR FINGER CARAMBOLA

WATER APPLE

STARFRUIT

WATER CONVOLVULUS

TARO ROOT

YAM BEAN

CONVERSION TABLES

Cooks in Indonesia do not normally weigh or measure ingredients because the practised cook goes very much by taste, sight and feeling when cooking. But for the benefit of those unfamiliar with Indonesian food and cuisine, all recipes in this book have been tested and their ingredients carefully weighed and measured. However, this does not mean that they cannot be changed; in fact, it is always a good idea to experiment, either increasing or decreasing the quantities in order to reach the desired flavour or spiciness. Tasting the food constantly during the cooking process is also most important. This book uses the metric system of measurement because it is the most accurate, but conversion charts are provided below for your reference.

GRAMS TO OUNCES

g	oz
1	0353
10	.353
28	1
100	3.5
200	7
500	17.5
1000 or 1 kg	35.3 or 2.205 lb

To convert, multiply the number of grams by .0353 to get the number of ounces. Alternatively divide the gram figure by 31. The second method is easier but it will not be as accurate as the first method.

CENTIMETRES TO INCHES

cm	inch
1	½
2.5	1
5	2
7.5	3
10	4
13	5
15	6
18	7
20	8
23	9
25	10
28	11
30	12

OUNCES TO GRAMS

oz/lb	Approx. g to nearest whole figure	Conversion to most convenient unit of 25 g
1 oz	28 g	25 g
2 oz	57 g	50 g
3 oz	85 g	75 g
4 oz	113 g	125 g
5 oz	142 g	150 g
6 oz	170 g	175 g
7 oz	199 g	200 g
8 oz	226 g	250 g
9 oz	254 g	275 g
10 oz	283 g	300 g
11 oz	311 g	325 g
12 oz	340 g	350 g
13 oz	368 g	375 g
14 oz	396 g	400 g
15 oz	425 g	425 g
1 lb	453 g	500 g
1½ lb	679 g	750 g
2 lb	905 g	1 kg

LIQUID AND VOLUME MEASURES

Metric	Imperial	American
2.5 ml	½ teaspoon	½ teaspoon
5 ml	1 teaspoon	1 teaspoon
15 ml	1 tablespoon	1 tablespoon
30 ml	2 tablespoons	2 tablespoons
45 ml	3 tablespoons	3 tablespoons
60 ml	4 tablespoons	¼ cup
75 ml	5 tablespoons	⅓ cup
90 ml	6 tablespoons	6 tablespoons
105 ml	7 tablespoons	7 tablespoons
125 ml	4 fl oz	½ cup
150 ml	¼ pint	⅔ cup
175 ml	6 fl oz	¾ cup
200 ml	⅓ pint	⅞ cup
250 ml	8 fl oz	1 cup
300 ml	½ pint	1¼ cups
350 ml	12 fl oz	1½ cups
400 ml	14 fl oz	1¾ cups
450 ml	¾ pint	2 cups
500 ml	18 fl oz	2¼ cups
600 ml	1 pint	2½ cups
750 ml	1¼ pints	3 cups
900 ml	1½ pints	3¾ cups
1 litre	1¾ pints	4¼ cups

DRY VOLUME MEASURES

In many American kitchens ingredients are measured in cups rather than by weight. The following chart is a useful reference for converting the metric measurement of dry ingredients into cups. It is based on all-purpose flour but, in fact, every dry ingredient has its own weight which is not necessarily the same as an equal volume of flour. This chart, therefore, shows only an approximation for any other dry ingredient.

All-purpose Flour

1 teaspoon	3 g
1 tablespoon	9 g
¼ cup	36 g
⅓ cup	46 g
½ cup	72 g
¾ cup	108 g
1 cup	144 g

Examples of volume (cup) conversions for other commonly used ingredients are as follows:-

Basil leaves, loosely packed, no stems	5 g	½ cup
Candlenut, ground	20 g	2 tablespoons
Chili, julienne	10 g	⅓ cup
Chili, diced	5 g	1 tablespoon
Coriander powder	2 g	½ tablespoon
	3 g	1 tablespoon
	5 g	1½ tablespoons
Coriander leaves, loosely packed	4 g	½ cup
Ginger, diced	5 g	1 tablespoon
Lemon grass, diced	5 g	1 tablespoon
Lime or lemon leaves	10 g	½ cup
Mace, dried	2 g	1 flake
Onions, diced	5 g	½ tablespoon
Peppercorns	30 g	1 tablespoon
Salam leaves, loosely packed	10 g	1 cup
Shallots, chopped	5 g	½ tablespoon
Tomato purée	10 g	1 tablespoon
Turmeric powder	2 g	½ tablespoon
	5 g	1 tablespoon

AMERICAN TERMINOLOGY

Listed below are the American equivalents for certain words used in this book.

UK/American
fillet/ tenderloin
prawn/ shrimp
courgette/ zucchini
spring onion/ scallion
aubergine/ eggplant
peanut/ groundnut
grill/ broil
tomato purée/ tomato paste

OVEN TEMPERATURE GUIDE

	Electricity		Gas Mark
	°C	°F	
Very cool	110	225	¼
	120	250	½
Cool	140	275	1
	150	300	2
Moderate	160	325	3
	180	350	4
Moderately hot	190	375	5
	200	400	6
Hot	220	425	7
	230	450	8
Very hot	240	475	9

TEMPERATURE CONVERSION

°C	°F	°C	°F	°C	°F
-40	-40	60	140	160	320
-34	-30	66	150	166	330
-29	-20	71	160	171	340
-23	-10	77	170	177	350
-18	0	82	180	182	360
-12	10	88	190	188	370
-6	20	93	200	193	380
-1	30	99	210	199	390
0	32	100	212	204	400
4	40	104	220	210	410
10	50	110	230	216	420
16	60	116	240	221	430
21	70	121	250	227	440
27	80	127	260	232	450
32	90	132	270	238	460
38	100	137	280	243	470
43	110	143	290	249	480
49	120	149	300	254	490
54	130	154	310	260	500

SPOON MEASURES: All spoon measures given in this book are level.

PINTS: The British and Australian pint is 20 fluid ounces as opposed to the American pint which is 16 fluid ounces.

NOTES FOR AUSTRALIAN USERS: In Australia the American 8-oz measuring cup is used in conjunction with the imperial pint of 20 fluid ounces. It is important to remember that the Australian tablespoon differs from both the British and American tablespoons. The British standard tablespoon holds 17.7 millilitres, the American 14.2 millilitres, and the Australian 20 millilitres. A teaspoon holds approximately 5 millilitres in all three countries.

SERVINGS: All these recipes serve 4 unless otherwise stated.

INDEX

INDEX

NOTE: All entries with asterisks are sub-recipes.

ACKNOWLEDGEMENTS

The authors and editor would like to thank the *keluarga besar* of the Jakarta Hilton International Hotel, especially Michael Schuetzendorf, general manager, for backing the project and making this book possible; Clive Scott, food and beverage manager, for his encouragement and support; and Jane Kandou, secretary to the executive chef, for coping admirably with the additional workload this project imposed. Many thanks also to all the cooks of the kitchen brigade, and in particular to the following chefs whose knowledge, creativity and hard work helped the authors immeasurably: S. Johan Darussalam; Arief Susanto; Anton Panji; Bob Leonard; Endin Junaedi; Iwan Setiawan; Rudi Syafruddin; Toto Sunarto; Budiono; Boyke Permadi; Roychan Thaif; Ibnu Santoso; Harito Gentur Respati; Garry Salmons; Gerard Zysset.

Special thanks to: Yayasan Nusantara Jaya, its board members and staff, for promoting this new Indonesian cuisine, particularly Dr. Mochtar Kusuma-Atmadja, Judi Achjadi and also Anne Saxon, who first introduced the authors; the Directorate General of Tourism, under the direction of Joop Ave and Cri Murthi Adi, especially Luther Barrung in Jakarta, who ensured that we were warmly welcomed throughout the archipelago, and the offices in Ambon, Lampung, Manado and Ujung Pandang; Garuda Indonesia and Merpati Airlines; Iwan Tirta, for the use of his collection of *ikat* and *batik*; A.S. Wolfel of Hutschenreuther A.G. for the use of porcelain dinnerware; Mrs. Djuadi of Gracia in Jakarta for several dishes; and Clive Williams for his assistance at the cattle ranch.

Our thanks also to the many other people who gave their time and expertise, including: Des Alwi; Amiruddin Saharuna; Nuzwar Anwar; Dinas Perkebunan; Gina and Caesar Atienza; Rudy Badil; Nahrong Chivangkur; Gregory Churchill; Cokorda Isteri Manik; Dr. Darmawan Masud; Janet and Paul Drok; Arifin and Djohan Effendi; Elzhivago T.; I.G.N. Exawirya, Office of the Agricultural Counsellor, U.S. Embassy, Jakarta; Ramze Hasiboan, Association of Indonesian Pepper Exporters; Hanafi T. and Lie Doe Sen; H.M. Hasan; Locky Herlambang; Baktiawan Honandar; Doc Jarden; Jeffrey Kirana; John McGlynn; Kristina J. Melcher; Timothy Moley; Ny. Mariana; Bob Sadino; H. Sanuar; Mohd Samadikun Hardjodarsono; Dewi Soeprapto Onzko; Sumeleh; Charles Sutjiawan, Asosiasi Pala Indonesia; I. Gusti Made Sumung; Johny Sundah; Edwin Thebez; Andy Toth; C.H. Tulong; Timothy Watts; Jantje A. Worotitjan.

To Tina Miraflores Skrobanek, our deepest gratitude not only for all her excellent research and the seemingly endless typing of recipes, but also for her unfailing good humour and encouragement throughout the project, as well as a cheerful willingness to go anywhere — or just about anywhere — for a story. Finally, our appreciation to Angelina Phillips, the assistant editor, and to Woon Mee Lan, the designer, for their long hours of hard work pouring over recipes and layouts to put this book together.

Most of the photographs in this book are by Gerald Gay,
but pages 12, 15 (bottom) and 16 (top) are by
Suzanne Charlé, and pages 2-3, 8, 9, 10, 13, 14, 15 (top) and 17
are by Lawrence Lim.